the AMAZING SPIDER-MAN

AMERICAN SON

Writer: **JOE KELLY**

Pencilers: **PHIL JIMENEZ, PAULO SIQUEIRA, MARCO CHECCHETTO & STEPHEN SEGOVIA**

Inkers: **ANDY LANNING, AMILTON SANTOS, MARCO CHECCHETTO & PAULO SIQUEIRA**

Colorists: **CHRIS CHUCKRY & JEROMY COX**

Letterers: **VC'S JOE CARAMAGNA & CHRIS ELIOPOULOS**

"NICE THINGS"

Writer: **JOE KELLY**

Art: **DALE EAGLESHAM**

Colorist: **RAIN BEREDO**

Letterer: **RUSS WOOTON**

Assistant Editor: **TOM BRENNAN**

Editor: **STEPHEN WACKER**

Executive Editor: **TOM BREVOORT**

Spidey's Web-Heads: **BOB GALE, MARC GUGGENHEIM, JOE KELLY, DAN SLOTT, FRED VAN LENTE, MARK WAID & ZEB WELLS**

Collection Editor: **JENNIFER GRÜNWALD** • Assistant Editors: **ALEX STARBUCK** & **JOHN DENNING**

Editor, Special Projects: **MARK D. BEAZLEY** • Senior Editor, Special Projects: **JEFF YOUNGQUIST**

Senior Vice President of Sales: **DAVID GABRIEL** • Production: **JEFF POWELL**

Editor in Chief: **JOE QUESADA** • Publisher: **DAN BUCKLEY** • Executive Producer: **ALAN FINE**

PREVIOUSLY: How did J. Jonah Jameson become Mayor? Heck if I know, I was out of the dimension for 2 months with the Fantastic Four. But in that time he made it happen, and now he's out to get me. Why not, right? So I decided to get him back and go on duty 24 hours a day, 7 days a week. Really rub it in his eyes — till I met this new Vulture, who spits some sort of acid. He decided to rub that in my eyes. Wonderful.

I took the new Vulchy out, but not without accidentally ruining a Yankee game. End result? Ol' Flat Top's back on the top of the polls and everyone outside of the bleachers hates me. Balance restored.

Meanwhile, my civilian life is getting worse by the minute. My roommate Vin may be awaiting his court date, but his sister took over the room. And she's not particularly nice. 'Course, the first impression wasn't my best — take a look! Speaking of awkward naked situations, Aunt May's in love — with Jonah's estranged dad. Groovy.

Ultimately, there's only one thing REALLY wrong — somehow Norman Osborn is the most powerful man in the world. Defeat one little alien invasion and they hand you the keys to the kingdom?! C'mon! Well I won't stand for it — it's time to take this guy down. And I know just the friends to help…

SPIDER-MAN: AMERICAN SON. Contains material originally published in magazine form as AMAZING SPIDER-MAN #595-599 and AMAZING SPI... 3870-9. Softcover ISBN# 978-0-7851-4083-2. Published by MARVEL PUBLISHING, INC., a subsidiary of MARVEL ENTERTAINMENT, INC. OFFICE ... Marvel Characters, Inc. All rights reserved. Hardcover: $19.99 per copy in the U.S. (GST #R127032852). Softcover: $16.99 per copy in the U... featured in this issue and the distinctive names and likenesses thereof, and all related indicia are trademarks of Marvel Characters, Inc. No sim... this magazine with those of any living or dead person or institution is intended, and any such similarity which may exist is purely coincidental. P... Entertainment, Inc. & CMO Marvel Characters B.V.; DAN BUCKLEY, Chief Executive Officer and Publisher - Print, Animation & Digital Media; JIM... Sales & Circulation; DAVID BOGART, SVP of Business Affairs & Talent Management; MICHAEL PASCIULLO, VP Merchandising & Communications; JIM O'KEEFE, VP of Operations... of Publishing Technology; JUSTIN F. GABRIE, Director of Publishing & Editorial Operations; SUSAN CRESPI, Editorial Operations Manager; ALEX MORALES, Publishing Operations Manager; STAN LEE, Chairman Emeritus. For information regarding advertising in Marvel Comics or on Marvel.com, please contact Mitch Dane, Advertising Director, at mdane@marvel.com. For Marvel subscription inquiries, please call 800-217-9158. **Manufactured** between 9/14/09 (hardcover) and 9/14/09 and 2/17/10 (softcover) by R.R. DONNELLEY INC., SALEM, VA, USA.

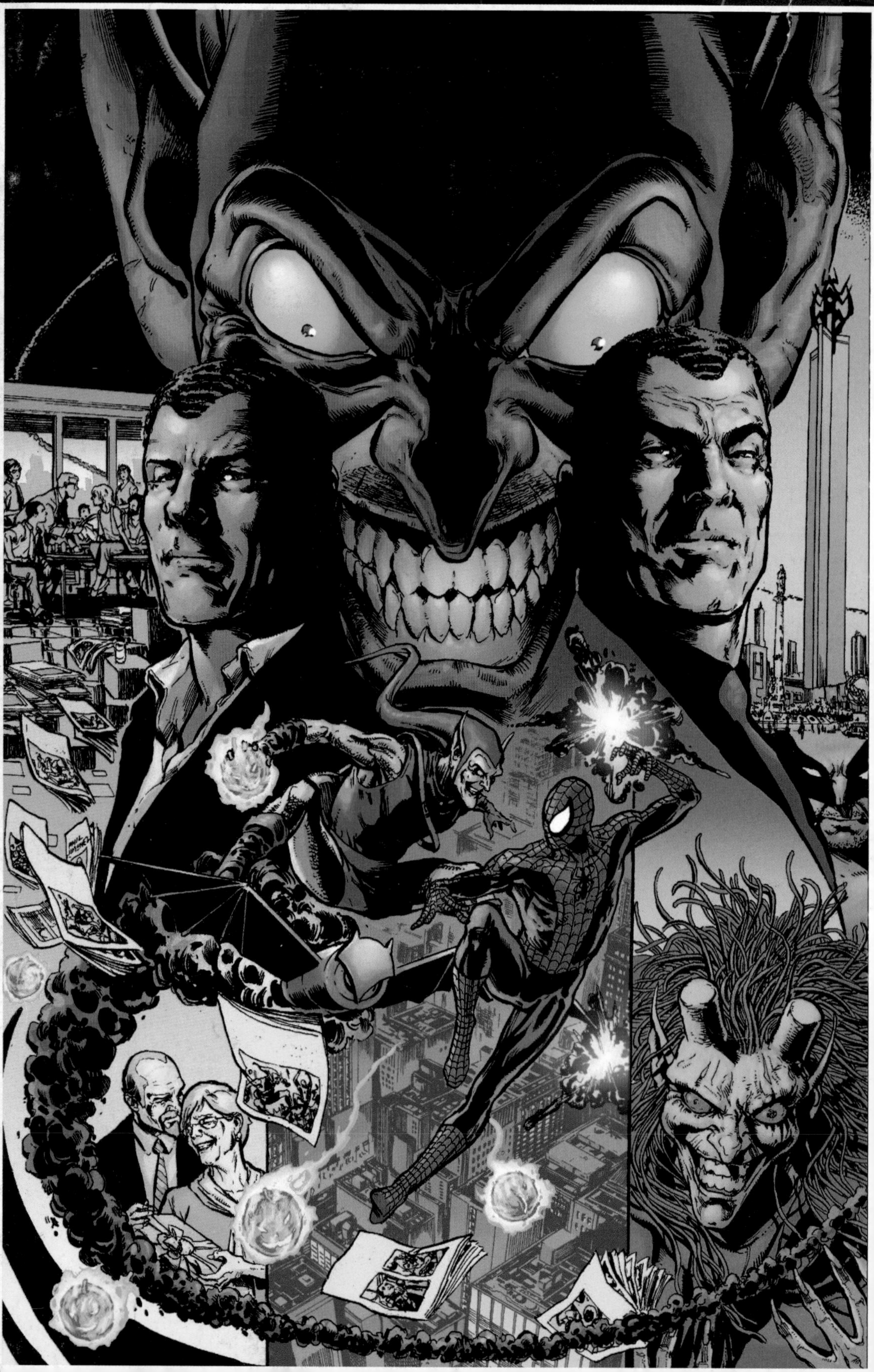

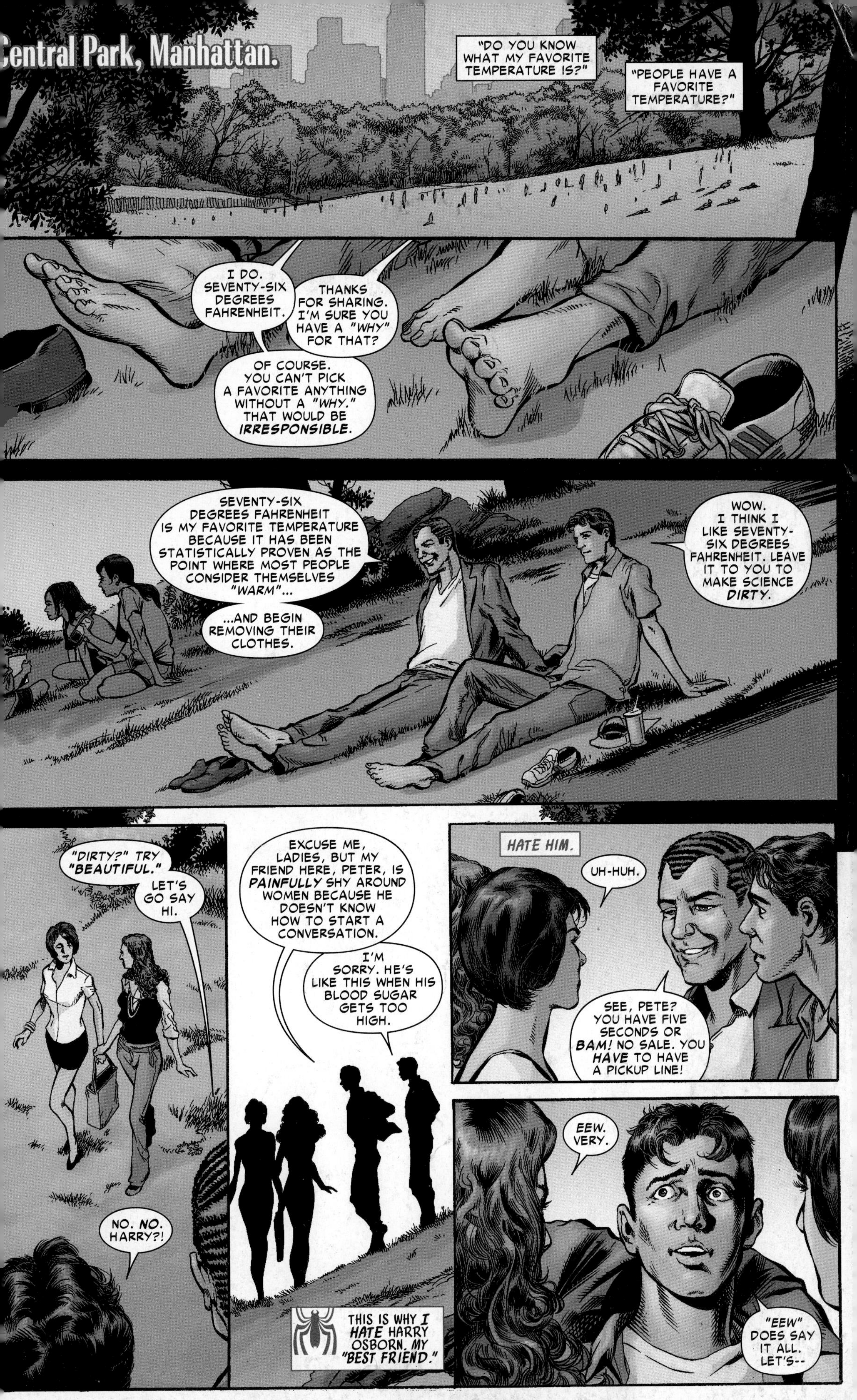
Central Park, Manhattan.
"DO YOU KNOW WHAT MY FAVORITE TEMPERATURE IS?"
"PEOPLE HAVE A FAVORITE TEMPERATURE?"
I DO. SEVENTY-SIX DEGREES FAHRENHEIT.
THANKS FOR SHARING. I'M SURE YOU HAVE A "WHY" FOR THAT?
OF COURSE. YOU CAN'T PICK A FAVORITE ANYTHING WITHOUT A "WHY." THAT WOULD BE IRRESPONSIBLE.
SEVENTY-SIX DEGREES FAHRENHEIT IS MY FAVORITE TEMPERATURE BECAUSE IT HAS BEEN STATISTICALLY PROVEN AS THE POINT WHERE MOST PEOPLE CONSIDER THEMSELVES "WARM"...
...AND BEGIN REMOVING THEIR CLOTHES.
WOW. I THINK I LIKE SEVENTY-SIX DEGREES FAHRENHEIT. LEAVE IT TO YOU TO MAKE SCIENCE DIRTY.
"DIRTY?" TRY "BEAUTIFUL."
LET'S GO SAY HI.
NO. NO. HARRY?!
EXCUSE ME, LADIES, BUT MY FRIEND HERE, PETER, IS PAINFULLY SHY AROUND WOMEN BECAUSE HE DOESN'T KNOW HOW TO START A CONVERSATION.
I'M SORRY. HE'S LIKE THIS WHEN HIS BLOOD SUGAR GETS TOO HIGH.
THIS IS WHY I HATE HARRY OSBORN. MY "BEST FRIEND."
HATE HIM.
UH-HUH.
SEE, PETE? YOU HAVE FIVE SECONDS OR BAM! NO SALE. YOU HAVE TO HAVE A PICKUP LINE!
EEW. VERY.
"EEW" DOES SAY IT ALL. LET'S--

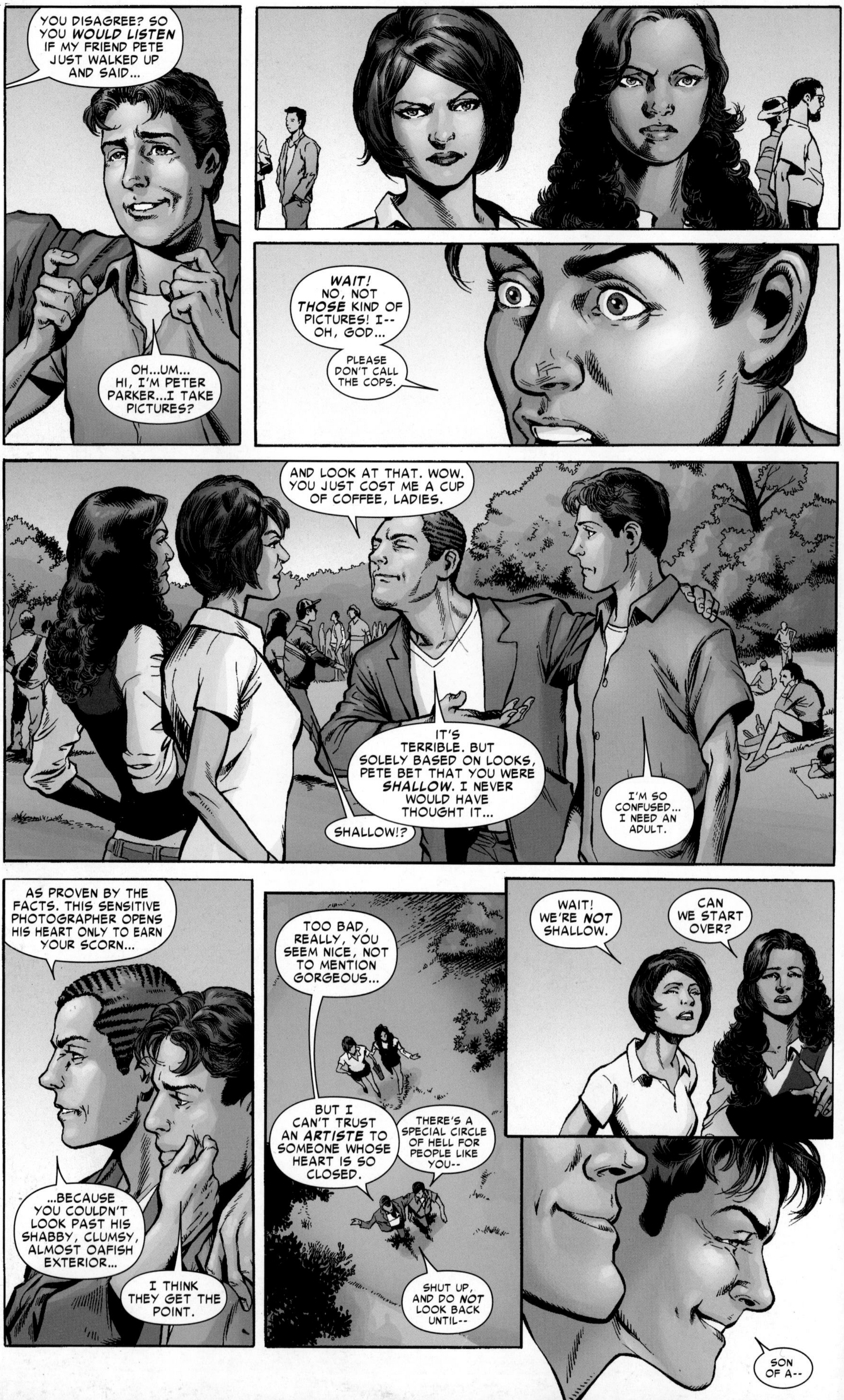
YOU DISAGREE? SO YOU WOULD LISTEN IF MY FRIEND PETE JUST WALKED UP AND SAID...
OH...UM... HI, I'M PETER PARKER...I TAKE PICTURES?
WAIT! NO, NOT THOSE KIND OF PICTURES! I-- OH, GOD...
PLEASE DON'T CALL THE COPS.
AND LOOK AT THAT. WOW. YOU JUST COST ME A CUP OF COFFEE, LADIES.
IT'S TERRIBLE. BUT SOLELY BASED ON LOOKS, PETE BET THAT YOU WERE SHALLOW. I NEVER WOULD HAVE THOUGHT IT...
SHALLOW!?
I'M SO CONFUSED... I NEED AN ADULT.
AS PROVEN BY THE FACTS. THIS SENSITIVE PHOTOGRAPHER OPENS HIS HEART ONLY TO EARN YOUR SCORN...
...BECAUSE YOU COULDN'T LOOK PAST HIS SHABBY, CLUMSY, ALMOST OAFISH EXTERIOR...
I THINK THEY GET THE POINT.
TOO BAD, REALLY, YOU SEEM NICE, NOT TO MENTION GORGEOUS...
BUT I CAN'T TRUST AN ARTISTE TO SOMEONE WHOSE HEART IS SO CLOSED.
THERE'S A SPECIAL CIRCLE OF HELL FOR PEOPLE LIKE YOU--
SHUT UP, AND DO NOT LOOK BACK UNTIL--
WAIT! WE'RE NOT SHALLOW.
CAN WE START OVER?
SON OF A--

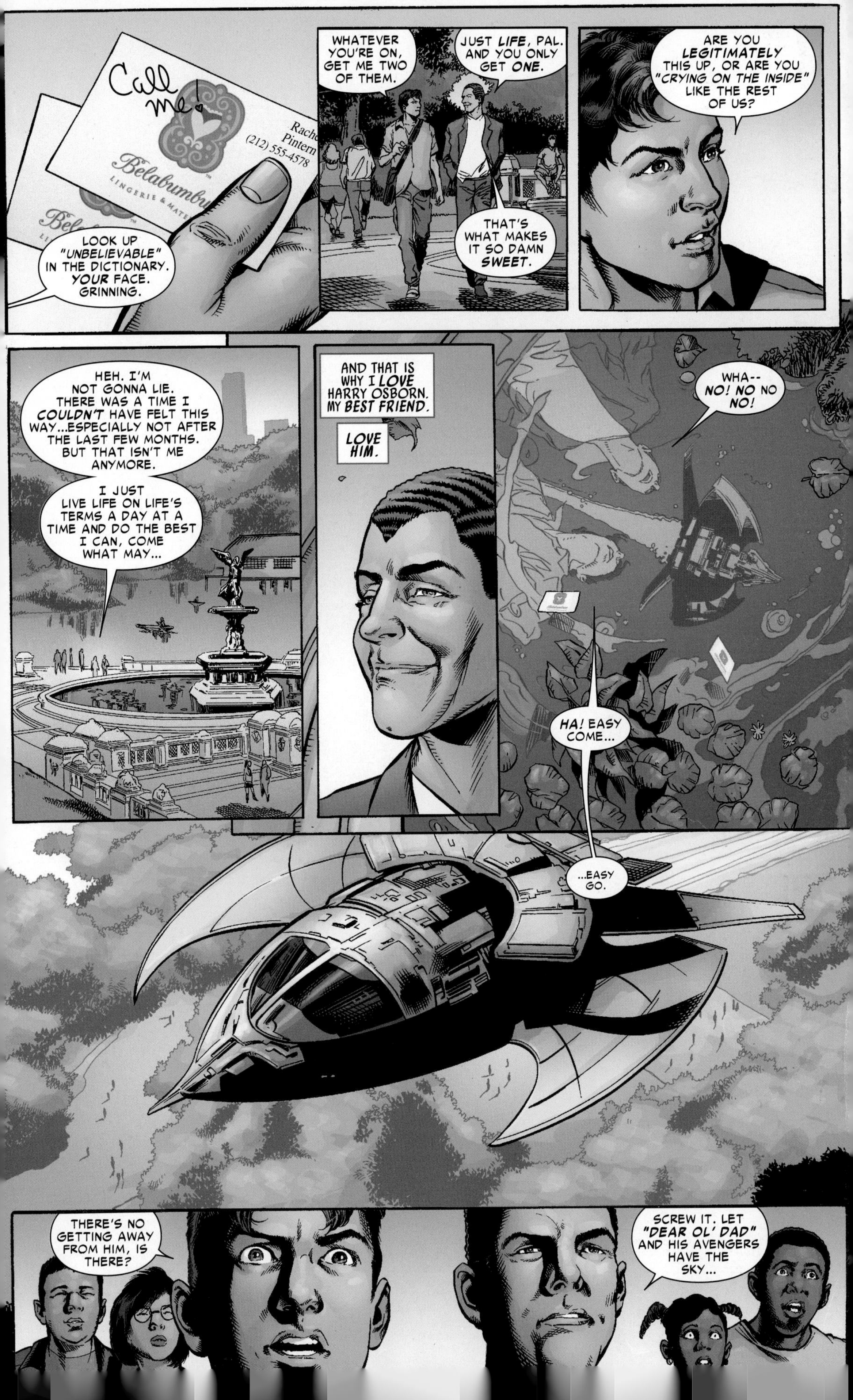
Call me!
Belabumbum
LINGERIE & MATE
Rache
Pintern
(212) 555-4578
LOOK UP "UNBELIEVABLE" IN THE DICTIONARY. YOUR FACE. GRINNING.
WHATEVER YOU'RE ON, GET ME TWO OF THEM.
JUST LIFE, PAL. AND YOU ONLY GET ONE.
THAT'S WHAT MAKES IT SO DAMN SWEET.
ARE YOU LEGITIMATELY THIS UP, OR ARE YOU "CRYING ON THE INSIDE" LIKE THE REST OF US?
HEH. I'M NOT GONNA LIE. THERE WAS A TIME I COULDN'T HAVE FELT THIS WAY...ESPECIALLY NOT AFTER THE LAST FEW MONTHS. BUT THAT ISN'T ME ANYMORE.
I JUST LIVE LIFE ON LIFE'S TERMS A DAY AT A TIME AND DO THE BEST I CAN, COME WHAT MAY...
AND THAT IS WHY I LOVE HARRY OSBORN. MY BEST FRIEND.
LOVE HIM.
WHA-- NO! NO NO NO!
HA! EASY COME...
...EASY GO.
THERE'S NO GETTING AWAY FROM HIM, IS THERE?
SCREW IT. LET "DEAR OL' DAD" AND HIS AVENGERS HAVE THE SKY...

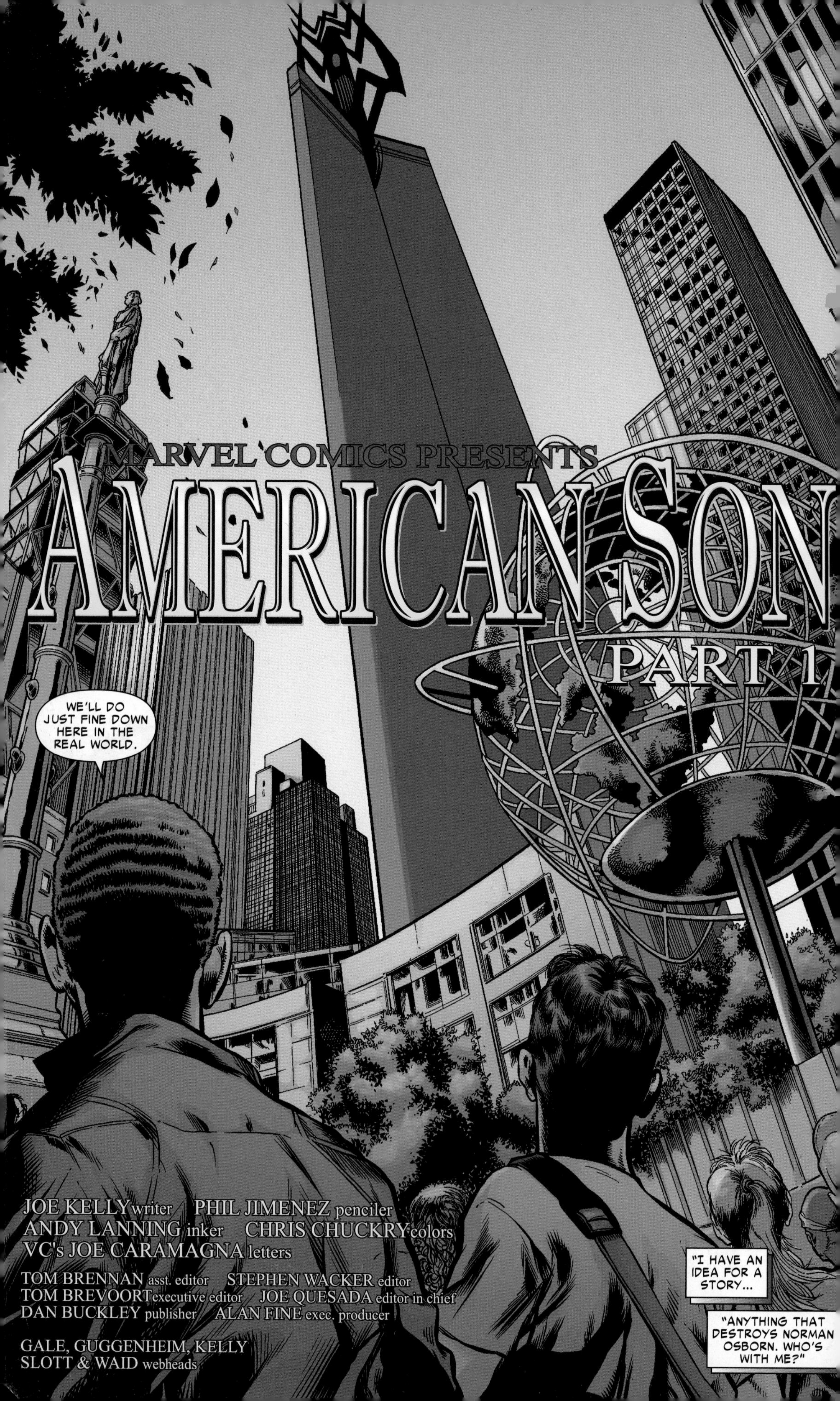
MARVEL COMICS PRESENTS
AMERICAN SON
PART 1
WE'LL DO JUST FINE DOWN HERE IN THE REAL WORLD.
JOE KELLY writer PHIL JIMENEZ penciler
ANDY LANNING inker CHRIS CHUCKRY colors
VC's JOE CARAMAGNA letters
TOM BRENNAN asst. editor STEPHEN WACKER editor
TOM BREVOORT executive editor JOE QUESADA editor in chief
DAN BUCKLEY publisher ALAN FINE exec. producer
GALE, GUGGENHEIM, KELLY
SLOTT & WAID webheads
"I HAVE AN IDEA FOR A STORY...
"ANYTHING THAT DESTROYS NORMAN OSBORN. WHO'S WITH ME?"

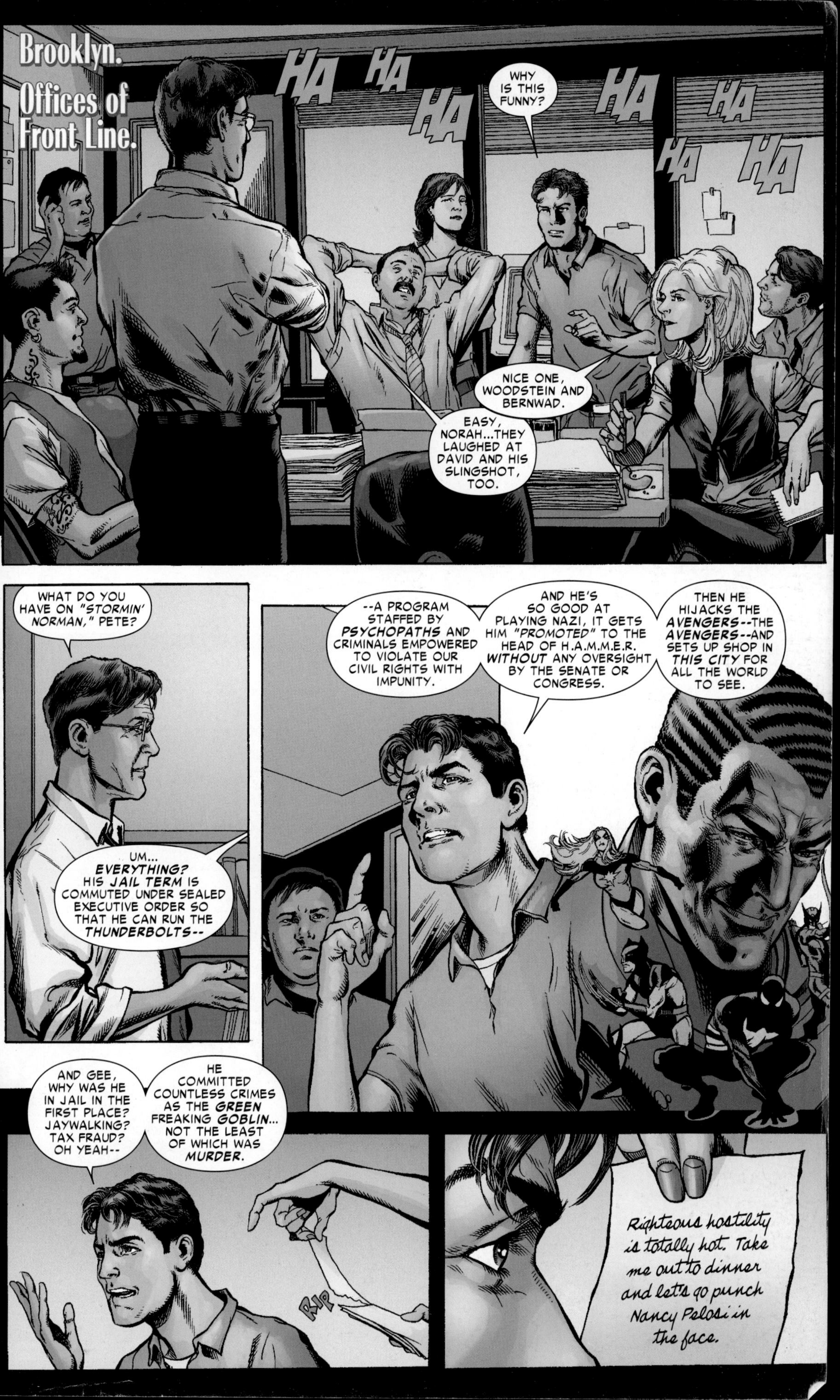
Brooklyn.
Offices of Front Line.
HA HA HA
WHY IS THIS FUNNY?
HA HA HA HA
NICE ONE, WOODSTEIN AND BERNWAD.
EASY, NORAH...THEY LAUGHED AT DAVID AND HIS SLINGSHOT, TOO.
WHAT DO YOU HAVE ON "STORMIN' NORMAN," PETE?
UM... EVERYTHING? HIS JAIL TERM IS COMMUTED UNDER SEALED EXECUTIVE ORDER SO THAT HE CAN RUN THE THUNDERBOLTS--
--A PROGRAM STAFFED BY PSYCHOPATHS AND CRIMINALS EMPOWERED TO VIOLATE OUR CIVIL RIGHTS WITH IMPUNITY.
AND HE'S SO GOOD AT PLAYING NAZI, IT GETS HIM "PROMOTED" TO THE HEAD OF H.A.M.M.E.R. WITHOUT ANY OVERSIGHT BY THE SENATE OR CONGRESS.
THEN HE HIJACKS THE AVENGERS--THE AVENGERS--AND SETS UP SHOP IN THIS CITY FOR ALL THE WORLD TO SEE.
AND GEE, WHY WAS HE IN JAIL IN THE FIRST PLACE? JAYWALKING? TAX FRAUD? OH YEAH--
HE COMMITTED COUNTLESS CRIMES AS THE GREEN FREAKING GOBLIN... NOT THE LEAST OF WHICH WAS MURDER.
RIP
Righteous hostility is totally hot. Take me out to dinner and let's go punch Nancy Pelosi in the face.

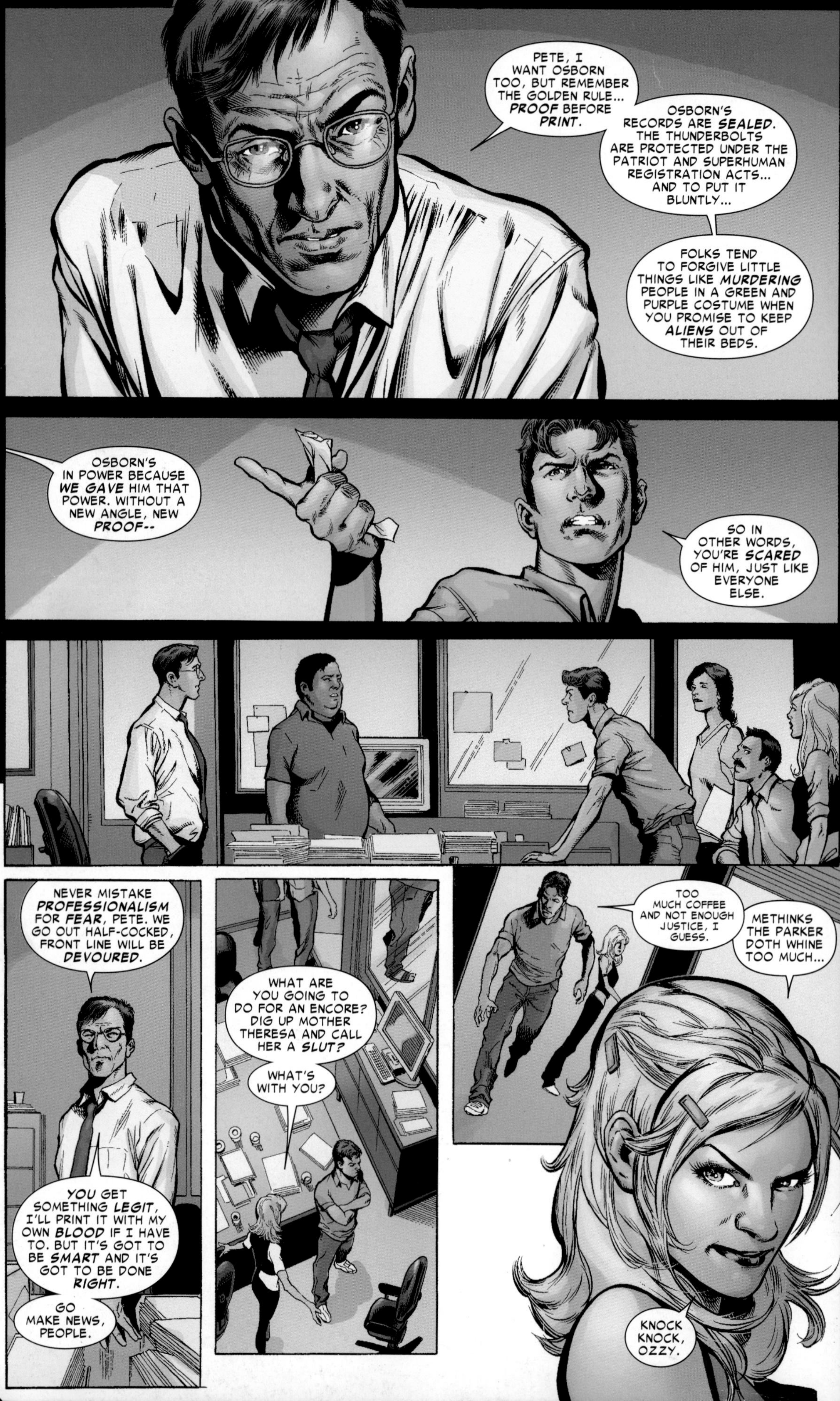
PETE, I WANT OSBORN TOO, BUT REMEMBER THE GOLDEN RULE... PROOF BEFORE PRINT.
OSBORN'S RECORDS ARE SEALED. THE THUNDERBOLTS ARE PROTECTED UNDER THE PATRIOT AND SUPERHUMAN REGISTRATION ACTS... AND TO PUT IT BLUNTLY...
FOLKS TEND TO FORGIVE LITTLE THINGS LIKE MURDERING PEOPLE IN A GREEN AND PURPLE COSTUME WHEN YOU PROMISE TO KEEP ALIENS OUT OF THEIR BEDS.
OSBORN'S IN POWER BECAUSE WE GAVE HIM THAT POWER. WITHOUT A NEW ANGLE, NEW PROOF--
SO IN OTHER WORDS, YOU'RE SCARED OF HIM, JUST LIKE EVERYONE ELSE.
NEVER MISTAKE PROFESSIONALISM FOR FEAR, PETE. WE GO OUT HALF-COCKED, FRONT LINE WILL BE DEVOURED.
YOU GET SOMETHING LEGIT, I'LL PRINT IT WITH MY OWN BLOOD IF I HAVE TO. BUT IT'S GOT TO BE SMART AND IT'S GOT TO BE DONE RIGHT.
GO MAKE NEWS, PEOPLE.
WHAT ARE YOU GOING TO DO FOR AN ENCORE? DIG UP MOTHER THERESA AND CALL HER A SLUT?
WHAT'S WITH YOU?
TOO MUCH COFFEE AND NOT ENOUGH JUSTICE, I GUESS.
METHINKS THE PARKER DOTH WHINE TOO MUCH...
KNOCK KNOCK, OZZY.

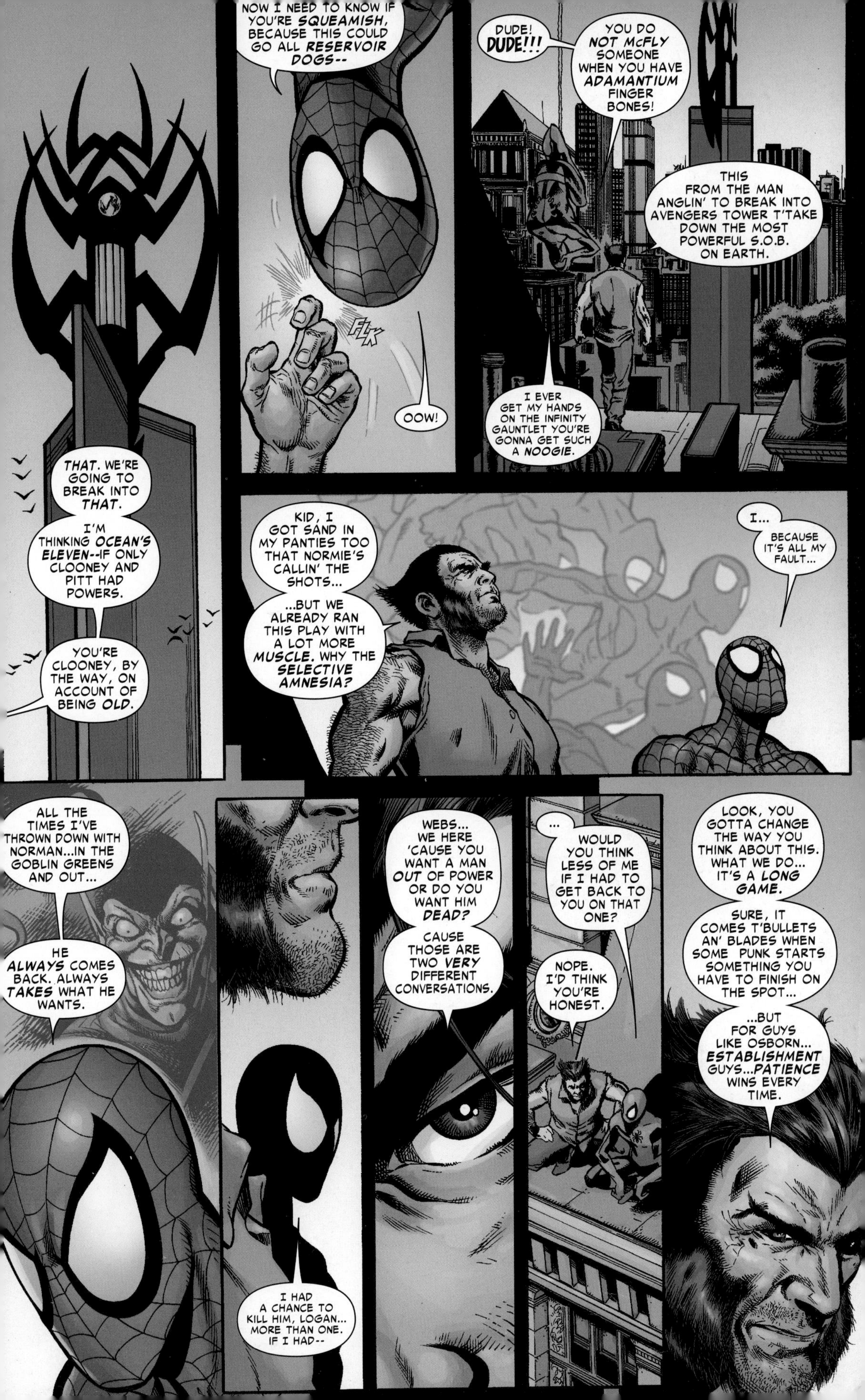
NOW I NEED TO KNOW IF YOU'RE SQUEAMISH, BECAUSE THIS COULD GO ALL RESERVOIR DOGS--
FLK
OOW!
DUDE! DUDE!!!
YOU DO NOT McFLY SOMEONE WHEN YOU HAVE ADAMANTIUM FINGER BONES!
I EVER GET MY HANDS ON THE INFINITY GAUNTLET YOU'RE GONNA GET SUCH A NOOGIE.
THIS FROM THE MAN ANGLIN' TO BREAK INTO AVENGERS TOWER T'TAKE DOWN THE MOST POWERFUL S.O.B. ON EARTH.
THAT. WE'RE GOING TO BREAK INTO THAT.
I'M THINKING OCEAN'S ELEVEN--IF ONLY CLOONEY AND PITT HAD POWERS.
YOU'RE CLOONEY, BY THE WAY, ON ACCOUNT OF BEING OLD.
KID, I GOT SAND IN MY PANTIES TOO THAT NORMIE'S CALLIN' THE SHOTS...
...BUT WE ALREADY RAN THIS PLAY WITH A LOT MORE MUSCLE. WHY THE SELECTIVE AMNESIA?
I...
BECAUSE IT'S ALL MY FAULT...
ALL THE TIMES I'VE THROWN DOWN WITH NORMAN...IN THE GOBLIN GREENS AND OUT...
HE ALWAYS COMES BACK. ALWAYS TAKES WHAT HE WANTS.
I HAD A CHANCE TO KILL HIM, LOGAN... MORE THAN ONE. IF I HAD--
WEBS... WE HERE 'CAUSE YOU WANT A MAN OUT OF POWER OR DO YOU WANT HIM DEAD?
CAUSE THOSE ARE TWO VERY DIFFERENT CONVERSATIONS.
...
WOULD YOU THINK LESS OF ME IF I HAD TO GET BACK TO YOU ON THAT ONE?
NOPE. I'D THINK YOU'RE HONEST.
LOOK, YOU GOTTA CHANGE THE WAY YOU THINK ABOUT THIS. WHAT WE DO... IT'S A LONG GAME.
SURE, IT COMES T'BULLETS AN' BLADES WHEN SOME PUNK STARTS SOMETHING YOU HAVE TO FINISH ON THE SPOT...
...BUT FOR GUYS LIKE OSBORN... ESTABLISHMENT GUYS...PATIENCE WINS EVERY TIME.

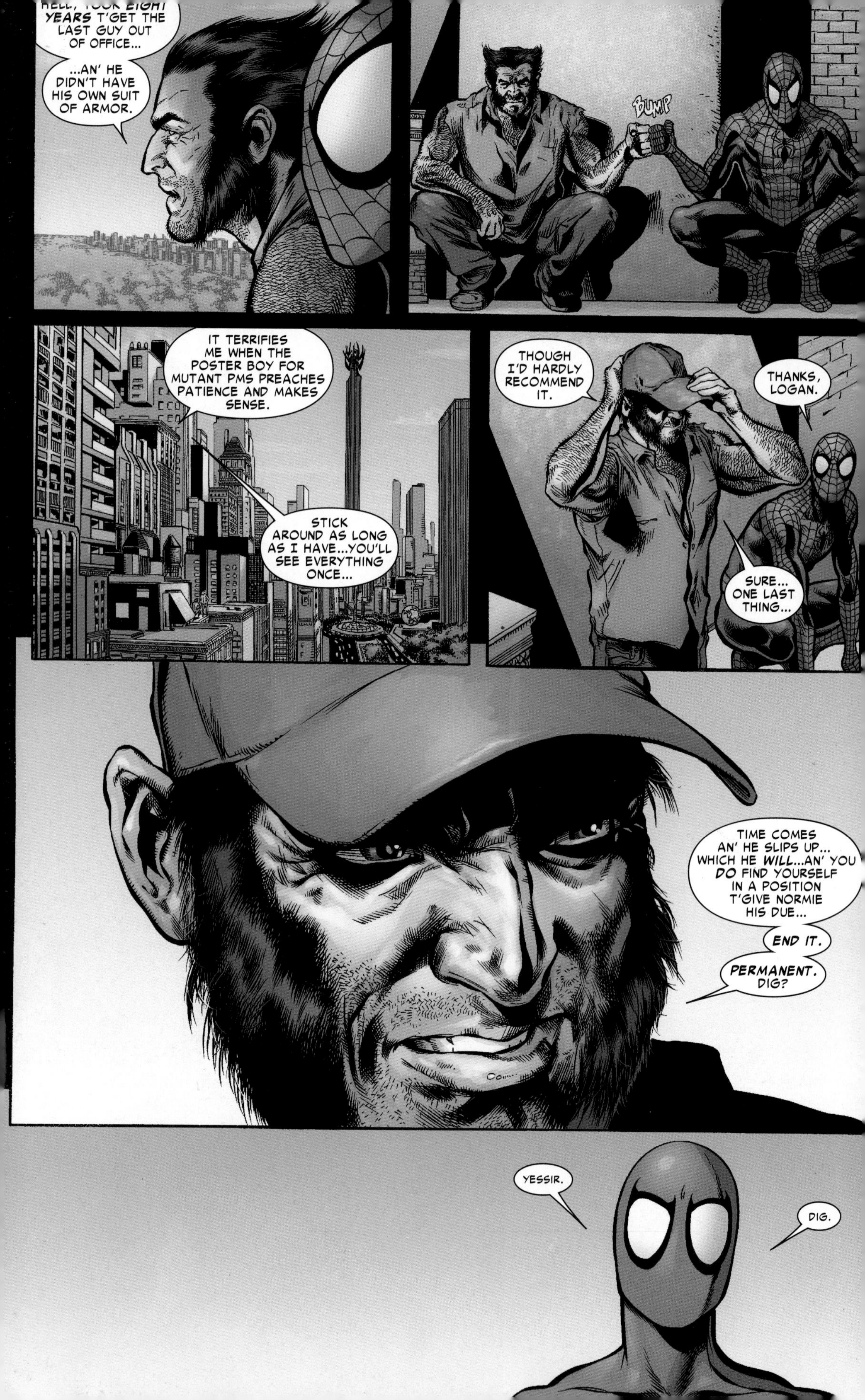
HELL, TOOK EIGHT YEARS T'GET THE LAST GUY OUT OF OFFICE...
...AN' HE DIDN'T HAVE HIS OWN SUIT OF ARMOR.
BUMP
IT TERRIFIES ME WHEN THE POSTER BOY FOR MUTANT PMS PREACHES PATIENCE AND MAKES SENSE.
STICK AROUND AS LONG AS I HAVE...YOU'LL SEE EVERYTHING ONCE...
THOUGH I'D HARDLY RECOMMEND IT.
THANKS, LOGAN.
SURE... ONE LAST THING...
TIME COMES AN' HE SLIPS UP... WHICH HE WILL...AN' YOU DO FIND YOURSELF IN A POSITION T'GIVE NORMIE HIS DUE...
END IT.
PERMANENT. DIG?
YESSIR.
DIG.

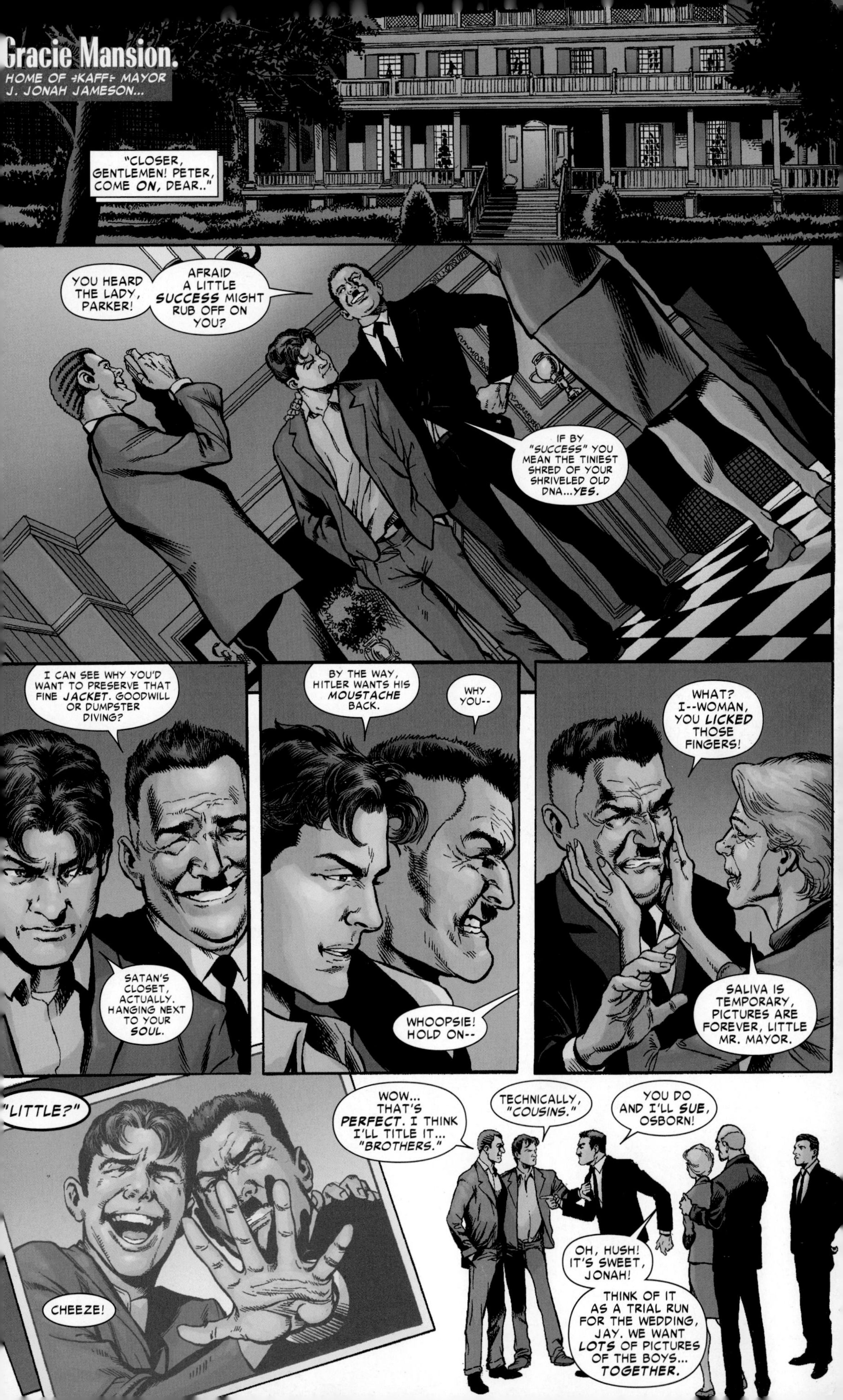
Gracie Mansion.
HOME OF ≠KAFF≠ MAYOR J. JONAH JAMESON...
"CLOSER, GENTLEMEN! PETER, COME ON, DEAR.."
YOU HEARD THE LADY, PARKER!
AFRAID A LITTLE SUCCESS MIGHT RUB OFF ON YOU?
IF BY "SUCCESS" YOU MEAN THE TINIEST SHRED OF YOUR SHRIVELED OLD DNA...YES.
I CAN SEE WHY YOU'D WANT TO PRESERVE THAT FINE JACKET. GOODWILL OR DUMPSTER DIVING?
SATAN'S CLOSET, ACTUALLY. HANGING NEXT TO YOUR SOUL.
BY THE WAY, HITLER WANTS HIS MOUSTACHE BACK.
WHY YOU--
WHOOPSIE! HOLD ON--
WHAT? I--WOMAN, YOU LICKED THOSE FINGERS!
SALIVA IS TEMPORARY, PICTURES ARE FOREVER, LITTLE MR. MAYOR.
"LITTLE?"
CHEEZE!
WOW... THAT'S PERFECT. I THINK I'LL TITLE IT... "BROTHERS."
TECHNICALLY, "COUSINS."
YOU DO AND I'LL SUE, OSBORN!
OH, HUSH! IT'S SWEET, JONAH!
THINK OF IT AS A TRIAL RUN FOR THE WEDDING, JAY. WE WANT LOTS OF PICTURES OF THE BOYS... TOGETHER.

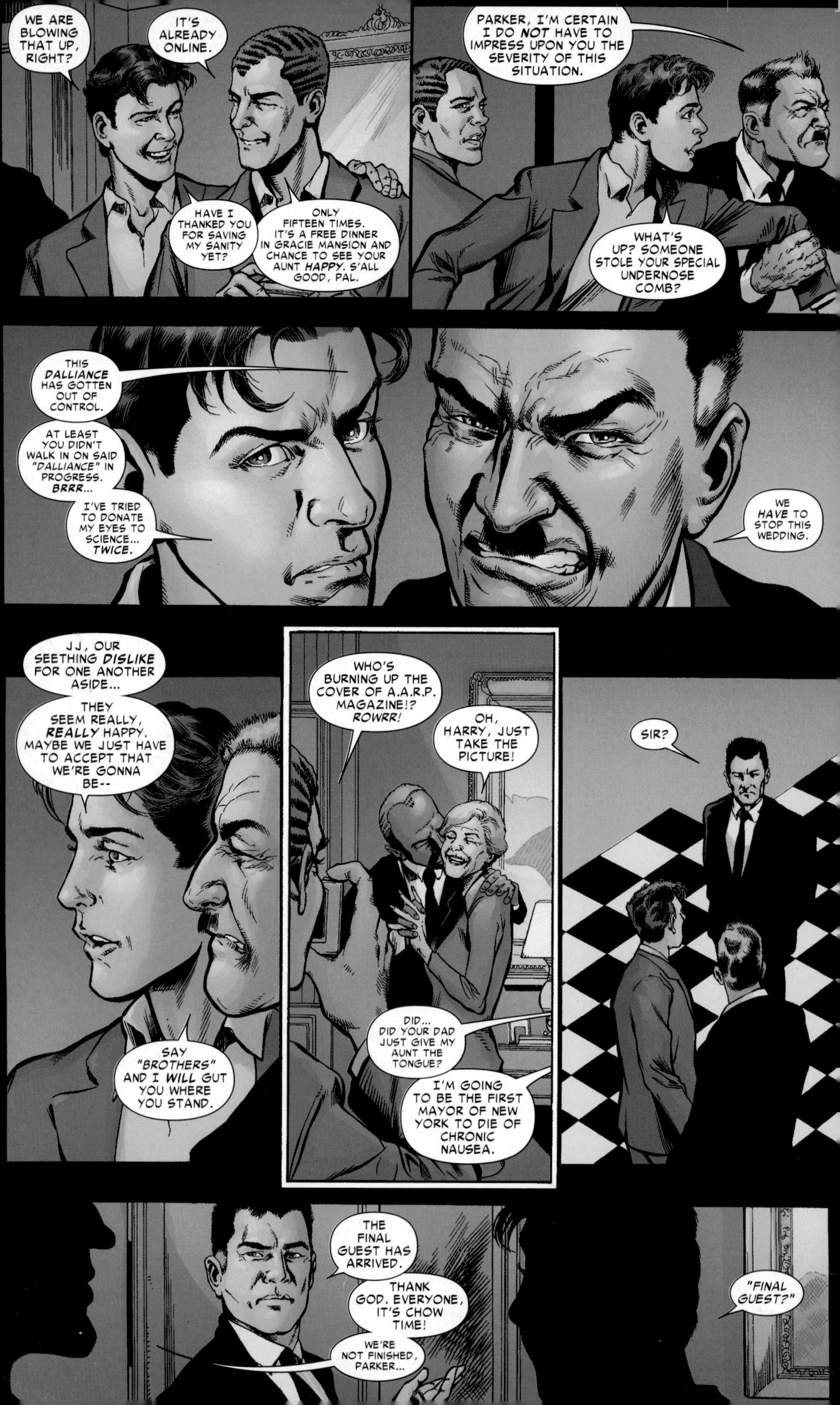
WE ARE BLOWING THAT UP, RIGHT?
IT'S ALREADY ONLINE.
HAVE I THANKED YOU FOR SAVING MY SANITY YET?
ONLY FIFTEEN TIMES. IT'S A FREE DINNER IN GRACIE MANSION AND CHANCE TO SEE YOUR AUNT HAPPY. S'ALL GOOD, PAL.
PARKER, I'M CERTAIN I DO NOT HAVE TO IMPRESS UPON YOU THE SEVERITY OF THIS SITUATION.
WHAT'S UP? SOMEONE STOLE YOUR SPECIAL UNDERNOSE COMB?
THIS DALLIANCE HAS GOTTEN OUT OF CONTROL.
AT LEAST YOU DIDN'T WALK IN ON SAID "DALLIANCE" IN PROGRESS. BRRR...
I'VE TRIED TO DONATE MY EYES TO SCIENCE... TWICE.
WE HAVE TO STOP THIS WEDDING.
JJ, OUR SEETHING DISLIKE FOR ONE ANOTHER ASIDE...
THEY SEEM REALLY, REALLY HAPPY. MAYBE WE JUST HAVE TO ACCEPT THAT WE'RE GONNA BE--
SAY "BROTHERS" AND I WILL GUT YOU WHERE YOU STAND.
WHO'S BURNING UP THE COVER OF A.A.R.P. MAGAZINE!? ROWRR!
OH, HARRY, JUST TAKE THE PICTURE!
DID... DID YOUR DAD JUST GIVE MY AUNT THE TONGUE?
I'M GOING TO BE THE FIRST MAYOR OF NEW YORK TO DIE OF CHRONIC NAUSEA.
SIR?
THE FINAL GUEST HAS ARRIVED.
THANK GOD. EVERYONE, IT'S CHOW TIME!
WE'RE NOT FINISHED, PARKER...
"FINAL GUEST?"

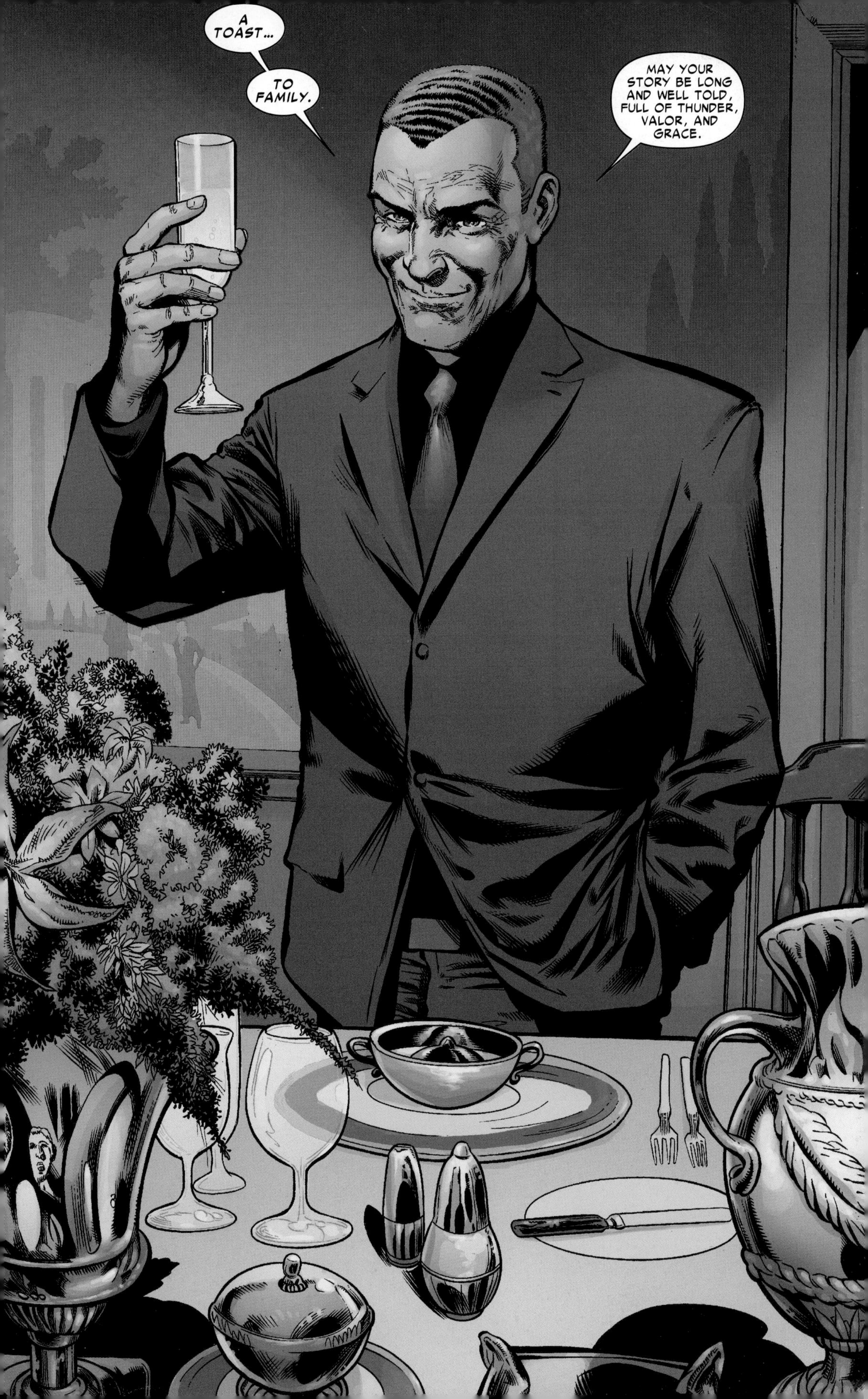
A TOAST...
TO FAMILY.
MAY YOUR STORY BE LONG AND WELL TOLD, FULL OF THUNDER, VALOR, AND GRACE.

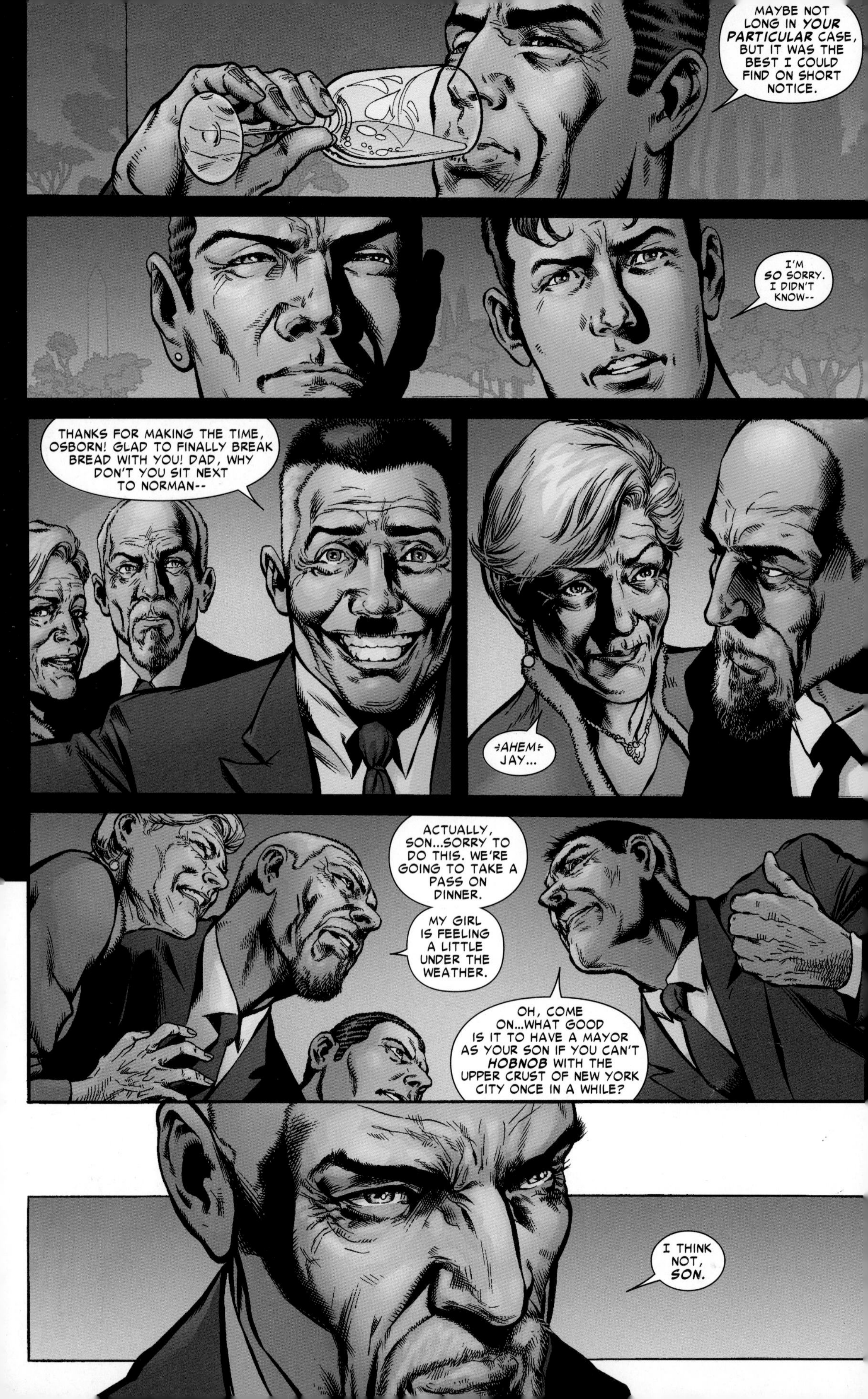
MAYBE NOT LONG IN YOUR PARTICULAR CASE, BUT IT WAS THE BEST I COULD FIND ON SHORT NOTICE.
I'M SO SORRY. I DIDN'T KNOW--
THANKS FOR MAKING THE TIME, OSBORN! GLAD TO FINALLY BREAK BREAD WITH YOU! DAD, WHY DON'T YOU SIT NEXT TO NORMAN--
AHEM JAY...
ACTUALLY, SON...SORRY TO DO THIS. WE'RE GOING TO TAKE A PASS ON DINNER.
MY GIRL IS FEELING A LITTLE UNDER THE WEATHER.
OH, COME ON...WHAT GOOD IS IT TO HAVE A MAYOR AS YOUR SON IF YOU CAN'T HOBNOB WITH THE UPPER CRUST OF NEW YORK CITY ONCE IN A WHILE?
I THINK NOT, SON.

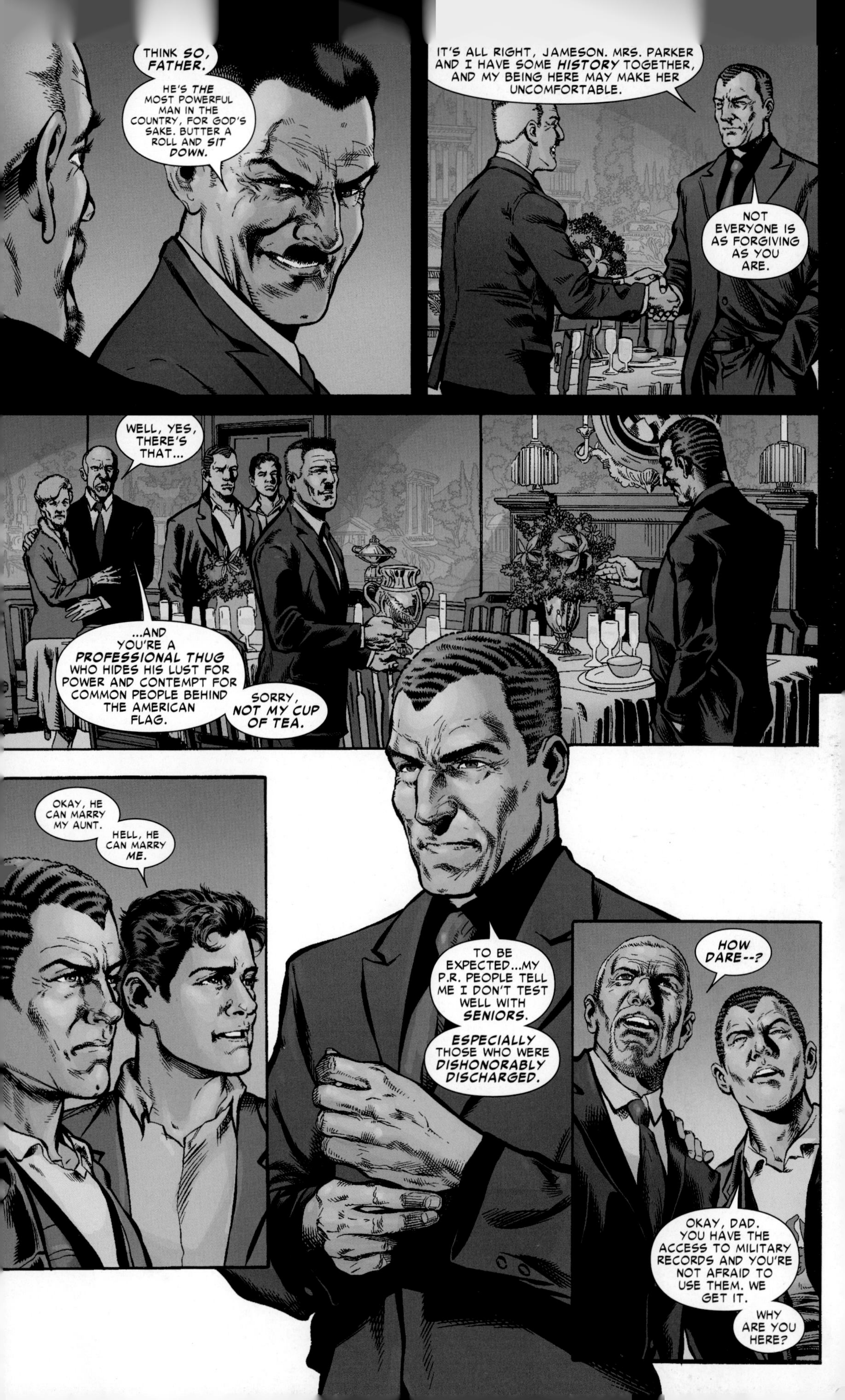
THINK SO, FATHER.
HE'S THE MOST POWERFUL MAN IN THE COUNTRY, FOR GOD'S SAKE. BUTTER A ROLL AND SIT DOWN.
IT'S ALL RIGHT, JAMESON. MRS. PARKER AND I HAVE SOME HISTORY TOGETHER, AND MY BEING HERE MAY MAKE HER UNCOMFORTABLE.
NOT EVERYONE IS AS FORGIVING AS YOU ARE.
WELL, YES, THERE'S THAT...
...AND YOU'RE A PROFESSIONAL THUG WHO HIDES HIS LUST FOR POWER AND CONTEMPT FOR COMMON PEOPLE BEHIND THE AMERICAN FLAG.
SORRY, NOT MY CUP OF TEA.
OKAY, HE CAN MARRY MY AUNT.
HELL, HE CAN MARRY ME.
TO BE EXPECTED...MY P.R. PEOPLE TELL ME I DON'T TEST WELL WITH SENIORS.
ESPECIALLY THOSE WHO WERE DISHONORABLY DISCHARGED.
HOW DARE--?
OKAY, DAD. YOU HAVE THE ACCESS TO MILITARY RECORDS AND YOU'RE NOT AFRAID TO USE THEM. WE GET IT.
WHY ARE YOU HERE?

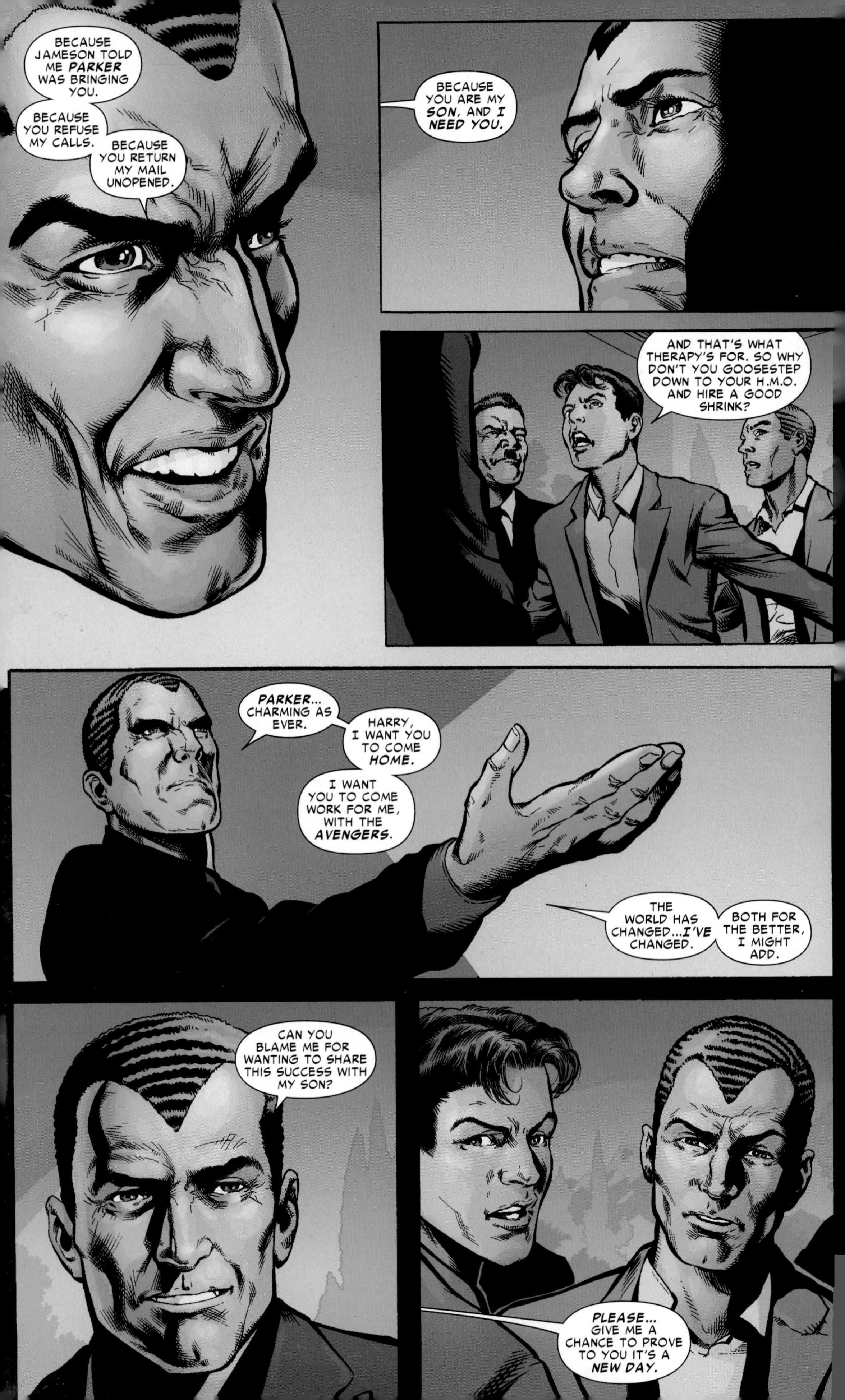
BECAUSE JAMESON TOLD ME PARKER WAS BRINGING YOU.
BECAUSE YOU REFUSE MY CALLS.
BECAUSE YOU RETURN MY MAIL UNOPENED.
BECAUSE YOU ARE MY SON, AND I NEED YOU.
AND THAT'S WHAT THERAPY'S FOR. SO WHY DON'T YOU GOOSESTEP DOWN TO YOUR H.M.O. AND HIRE A GOOD SHRINK?
PARKER... CHARMING AS EVER.
HARRY, I WANT YOU TO COME HOME.
I WANT YOU TO COME WORK FOR ME, WITH THE AVENGERS.
THE WORLD HAS CHANGED...I'VE CHANGED.
BOTH FOR THE BETTER, I MIGHT ADD.
CAN YOU BLAME ME FOR WANTING TO SHARE THIS SUCCESS WITH MY SON?
PLEASE... GIVE ME A CHANCE TO PROVE TO YOU IT'S A NEW DAY.

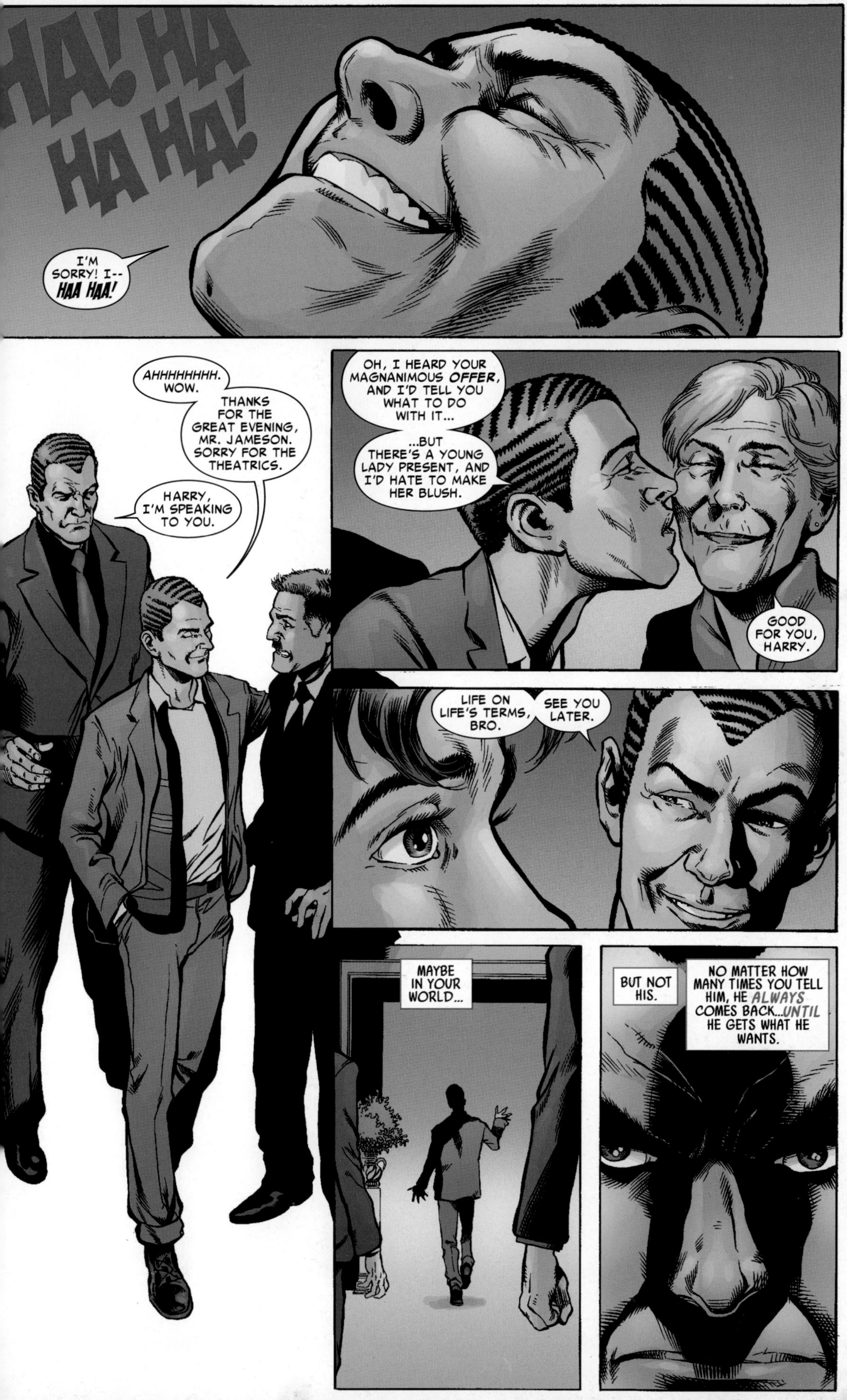
HA! HA HA HA HA!
I'M SORRY! I-- HAA HAA!
AHHHHHHHHH. WOW.
THANKS FOR THE GREAT EVENING, MR. JAMESON. SORRY FOR THE THEATRICS.
HARRY, I'M SPEAKING TO YOU.
OH, I HEARD YOUR MAGNANIMOUS OFFER, AND I'D TELL YOU WHAT TO DO WITH IT...
...BUT THERE'S A YOUNG LADY PRESENT, AND I'D HATE TO MAKE HER BLUSH.
GOOD FOR YOU, HARRY.
LIFE ON LIFE'S TERMS, BRO.
SEE YOU LATER.
MAYBE IN YOUR WORLD...
BUT NOT HIS.
NO MATTER HOW MANY TIMES YOU TELL HIM, HE ALWAYS COMES BACK...UNTIL HE GETS WHAT HE WANTS.

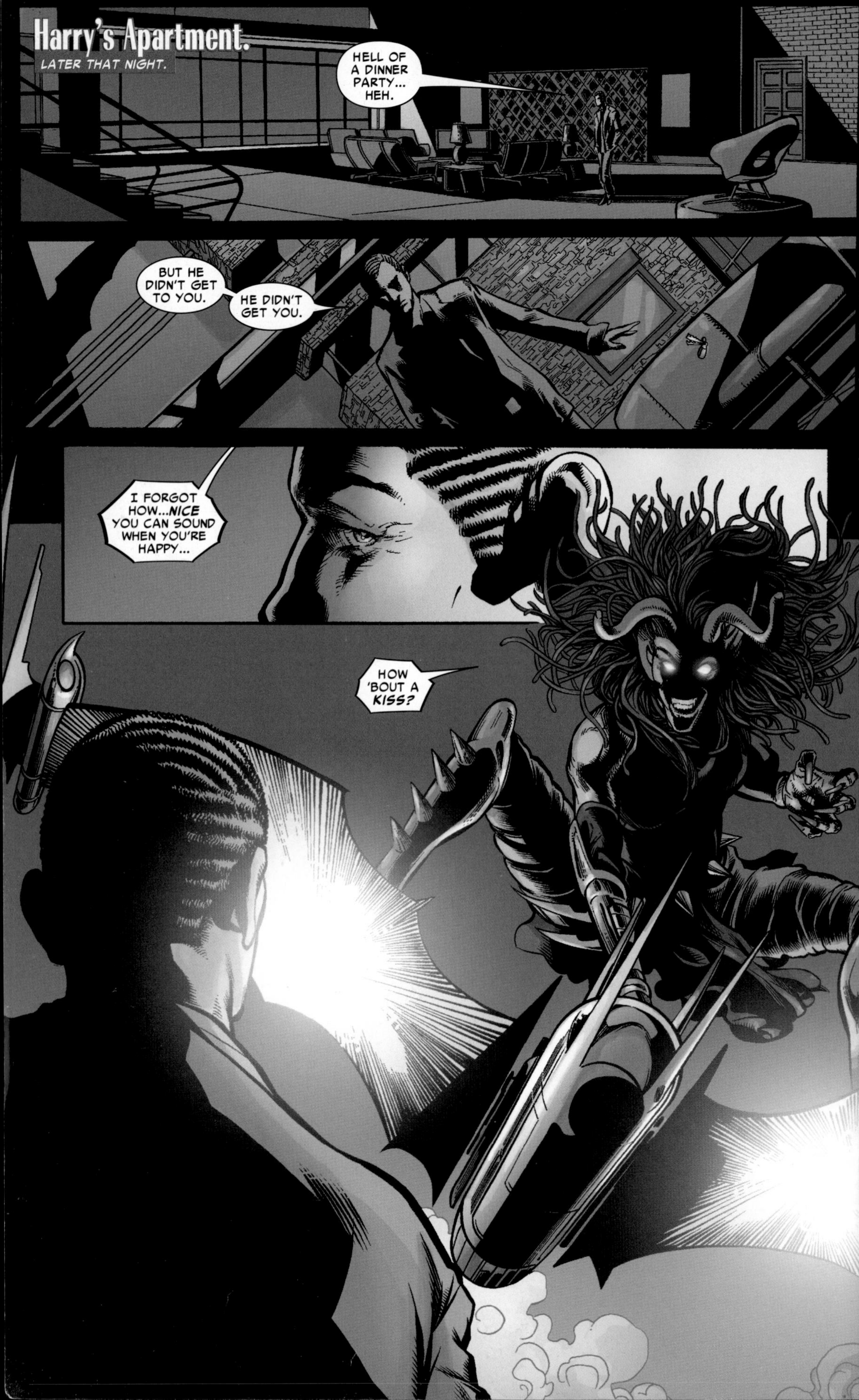
Harry's Apartment.
LATER THAT NIGHT.
HELL OF A DINNER PARTY... HEH.
BUT HE DIDN'T GET TO YOU.
HE DIDN'T GET YOU.
I FORGOT HOW...NICE YOU CAN SOUND WHEN YOU'RE HAPPY...
HOW 'BOUT A KISS?

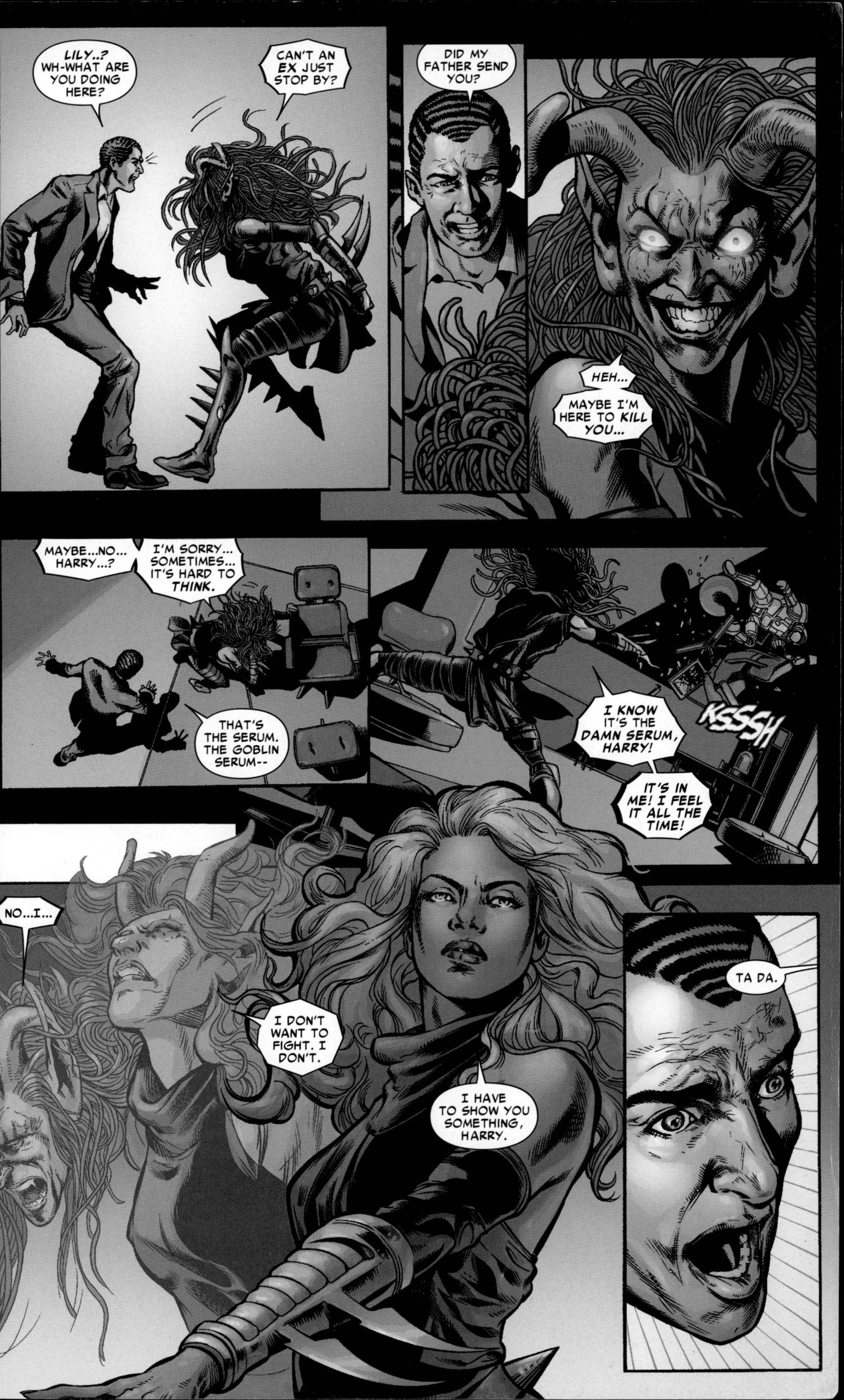
LILY..? WH-WHAT ARE YOU DOING HERE?
CAN'T AN EX JUST STOP BY?
DID MY FATHER SEND YOU?
HEH...
MAYBE I'M HERE TO KILL YOU...
MAYBE...NO... HARRY...?
I'M SORRY... SOMETIMES... IT'S HARD TO THINK.
THAT'S THE SERUM. THE GOBLIN SERUM--
I KNOW IT'S THE DAMN SERUM, HARRY!
KSSSH
IT'S IN ME! I FEEL IT ALL THE TIME!
NO...I...
I DON'T WANT TO FIGHT. I DON'T.
I HAVE TO SHOW YOU SOMETHING, HARRY.
TA DA.

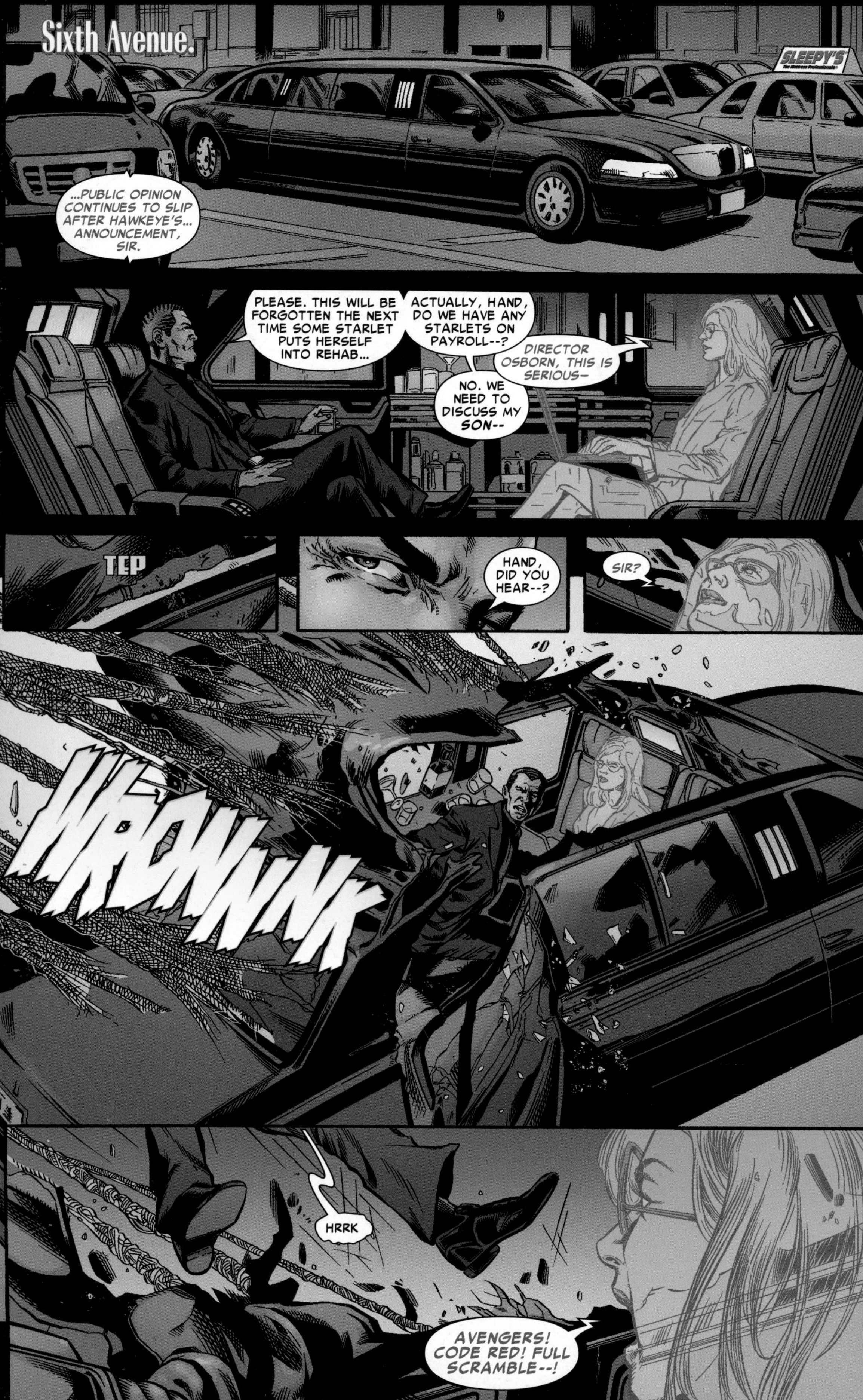
Sixth Avenue.
SLEEPY'S
...PUBLIC OPINION CONTINUES TO SLIP AFTER HAWKEYE'S... ANNOUNCEMENT, SIR.
PLEASE. THIS WILL BE FORGOTTEN THE NEXT TIME SOME STARLET PUTS HERSELF INTO REHAB...
ACTUALLY, HAND, DO WE HAVE ANY STARLETS ON PAYROLL--?
DIRECTOR OSBORN, THIS IS SERIOUS–
NO. WE NEED TO DISCUSS MY SON--
TEP
HAND, DID YOU HEAR--?
SIR?
WRONNNK
HRRK
AVENGERS! CODE RED! FULL SCRAMBLE--!

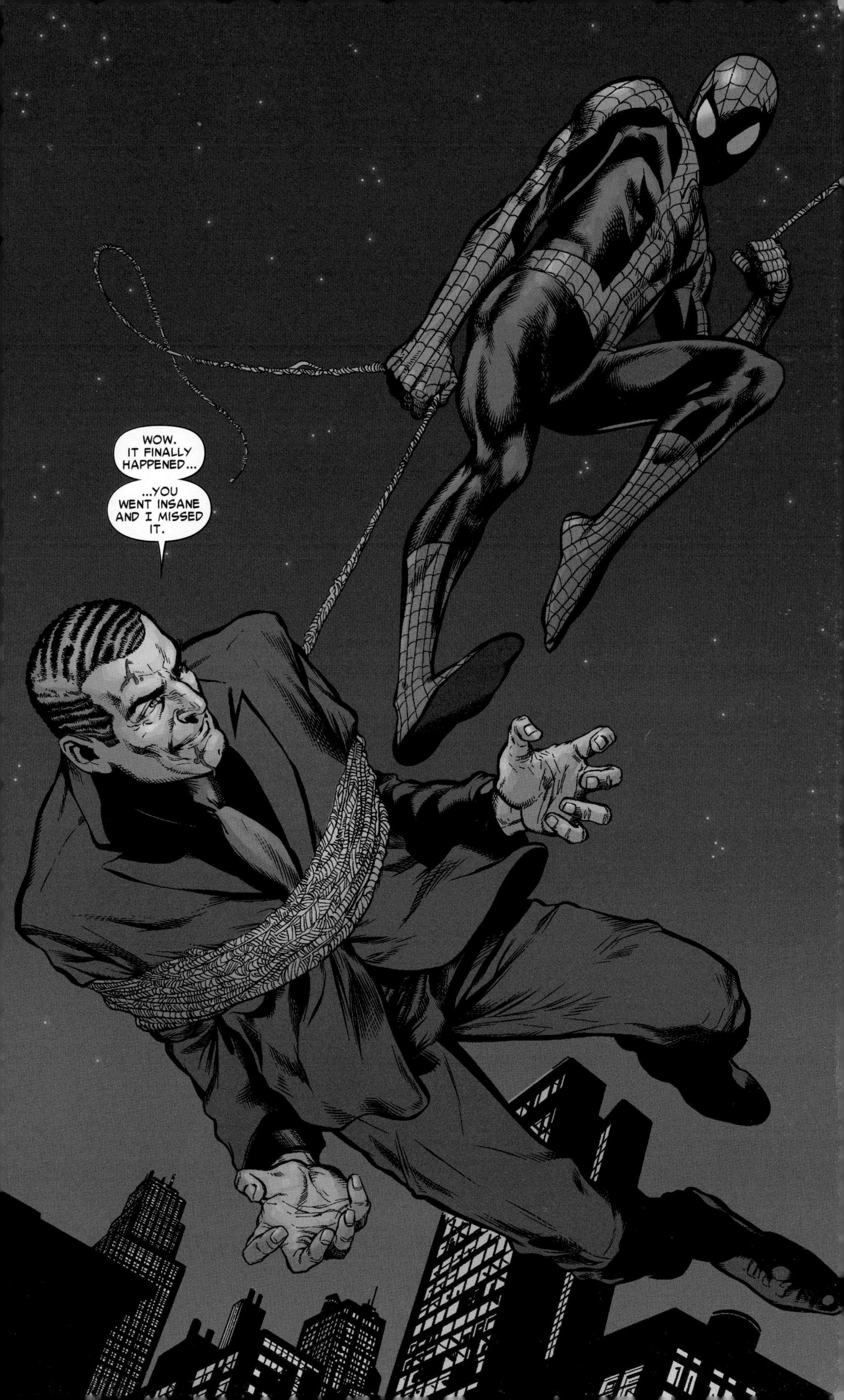
WOW. IT FINALLY HAPPENED...
...YOU WENT INSANE AND I MISSED IT.

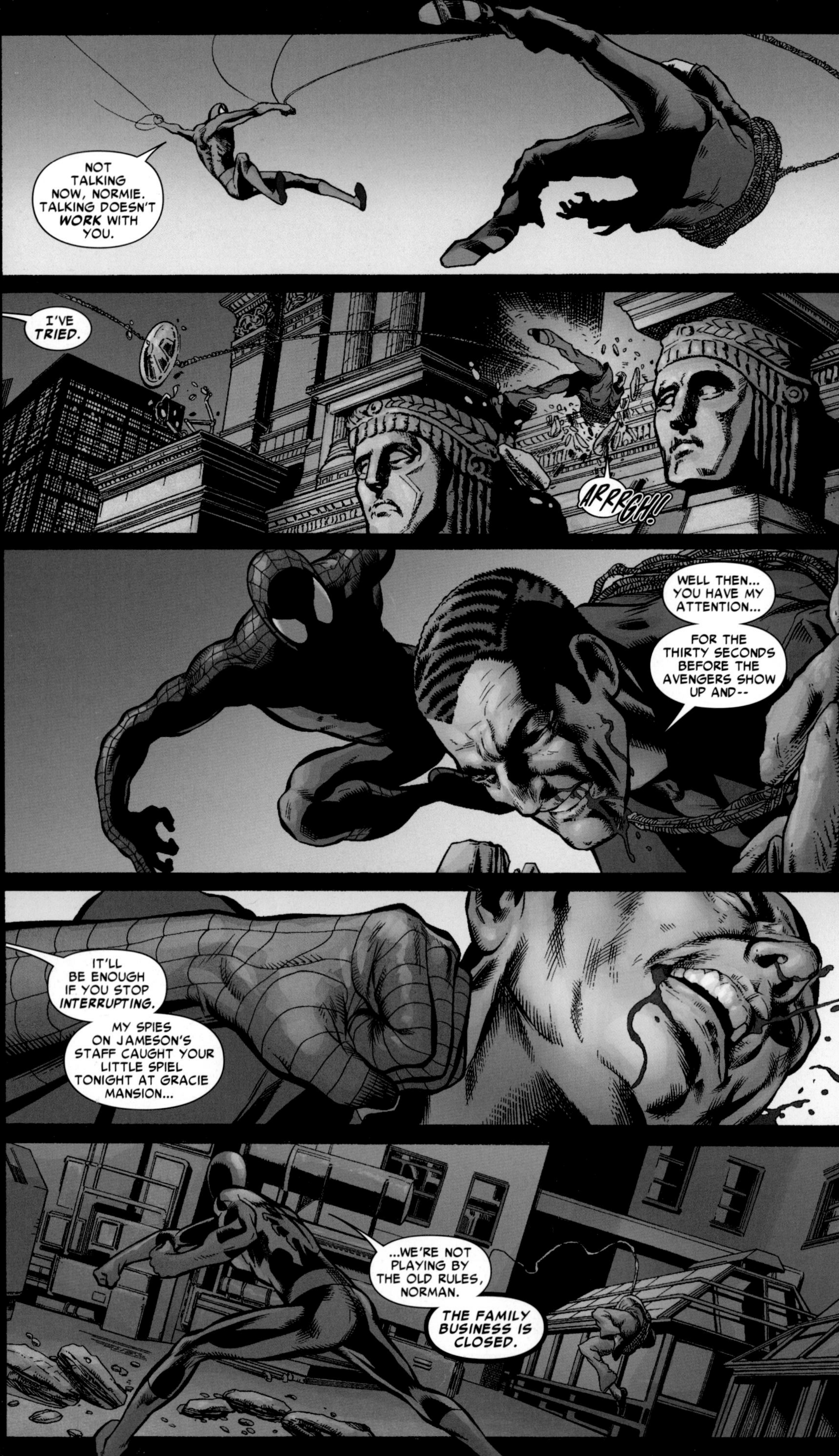
NOT TALKING NOW, NORMIE. TALKING DOESN'T WORK WITH YOU.
I'VE TRIED.
ARRRGH!
WELL THEN... YOU HAVE MY ATTENTION...
FOR THE THIRTY SECONDS BEFORE THE AVENGERS SHOW UP AND--
IT'LL BE ENOUGH IF YOU STOP INTERRUPTING.
MY SPIES ON JAMESON'S STAFF CAUGHT YOUR LITTLE SPIEL TONIGHT AT GRACIE MANSION...
...WE'RE NOT PLAYING BY THE OLD RULES, NORMAN.
THE FAMILY BUSINESS IS CLOSED.

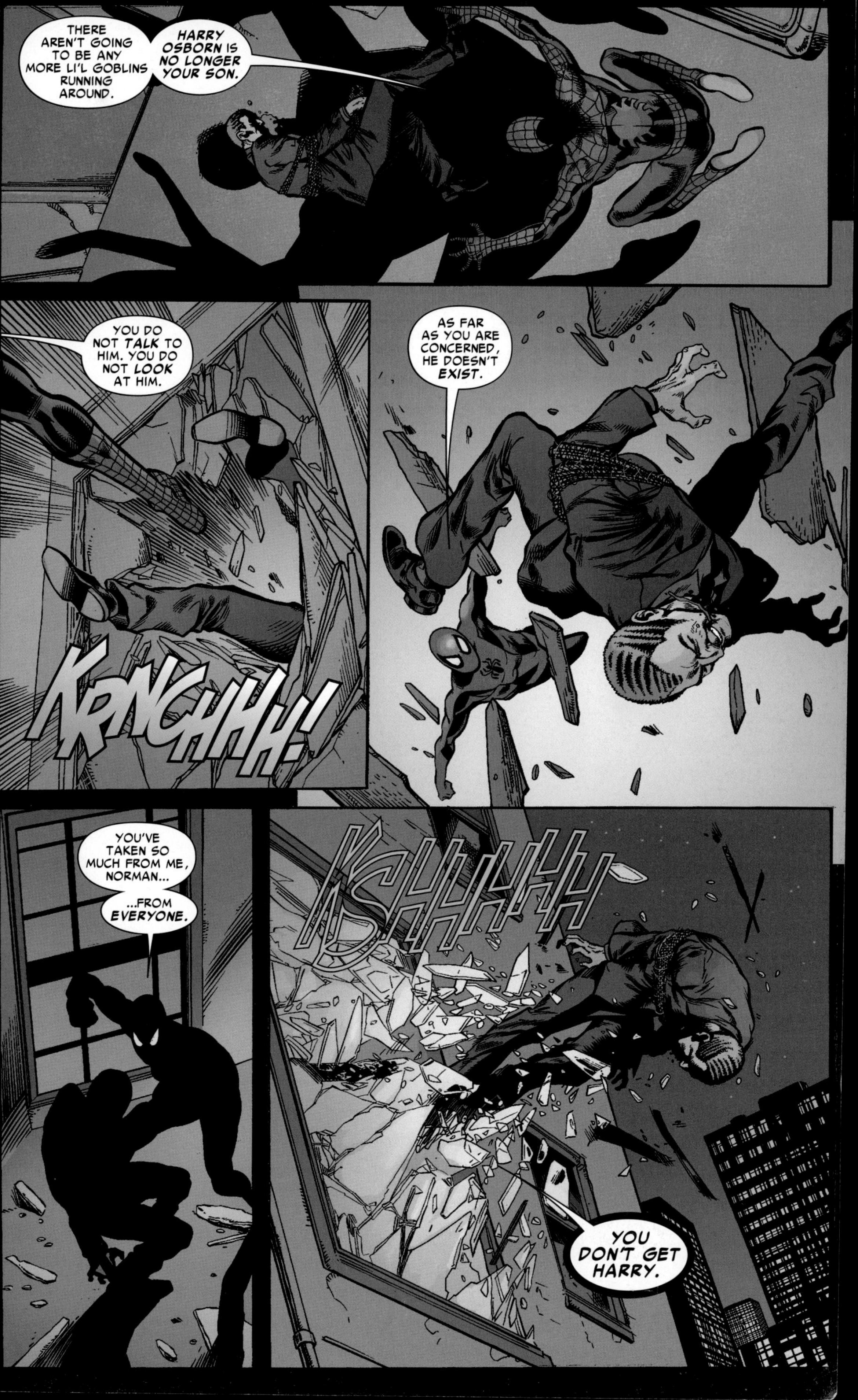
THERE AREN'T GOING TO BE ANY MORE LI'L GOBLINS RUNNING AROUND.
HARRY OSBORN IS NO LONGER YOUR SON.
YOU DO NOT TALK TO HIM. YOU DO NOT LOOK AT HIM.
KRNCHHH!
AS FAR AS YOU ARE CONCERNED, HE DOESN'T EXIST.
YOU'VE TAKEN SO MUCH FROM ME, NORMAN...
...FROM EVERYONE.
KSHHHHH
YOU DON'T GET HARRY.

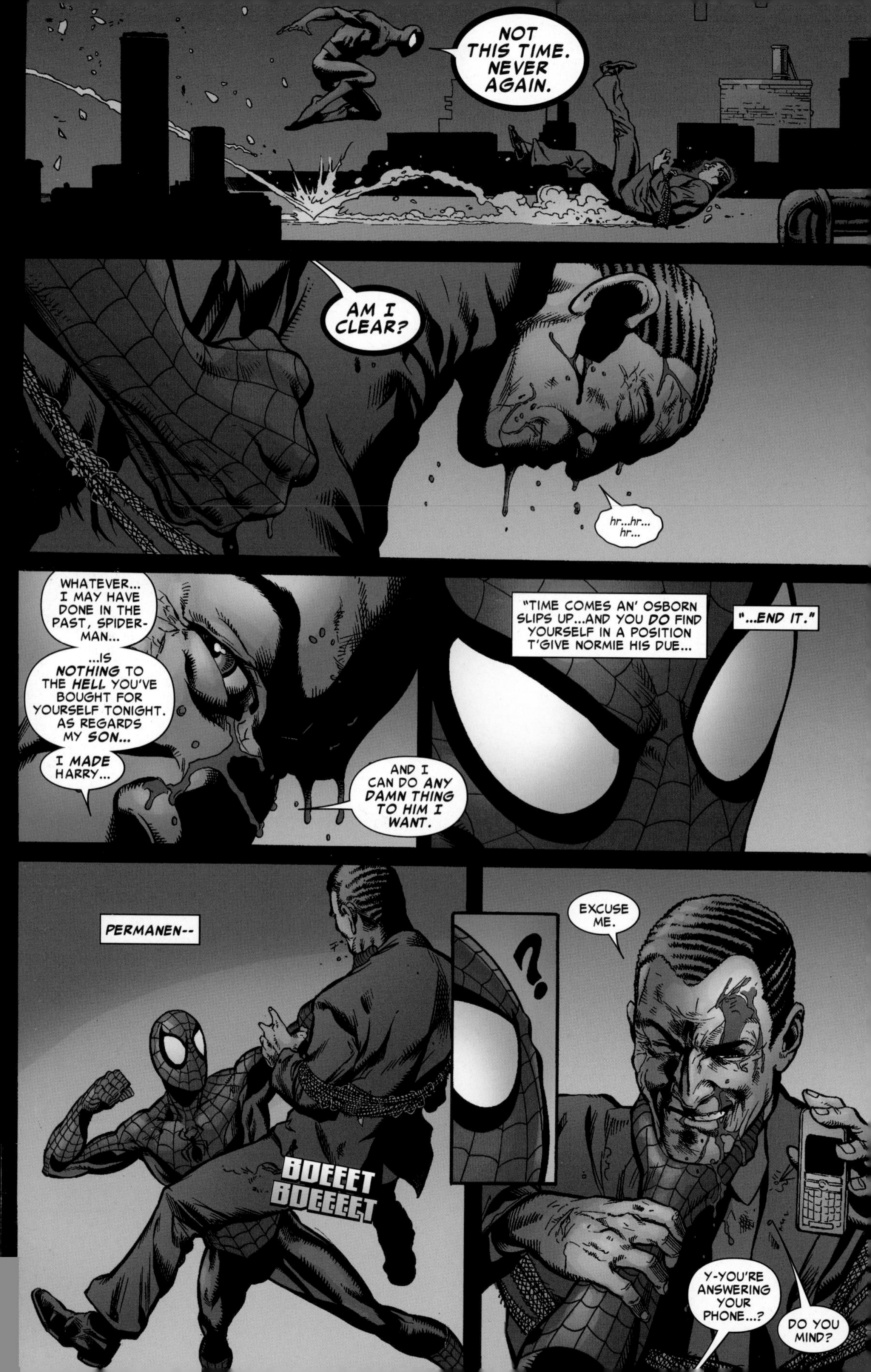
NOT THIS TIME. NEVER AGAIN.
AM I CLEAR?
hr...hr... hr...
WHATEVER... I MAY HAVE DONE IN THE PAST, SPIDER-MAN...
...IS NOTHING TO THE HELL YOU'VE BOUGHT FOR YOURSELF TONIGHT. AS REGARDS MY SON...
I MADE HARRY...
AND I CAN DO ANY DAMN THING TO HIM I WANT.
"TIME COMES AN' OSBORN SLIPS UP...AND YOU DO FIND YOURSELF IN A POSITION T'GIVE NORMIE HIS DUE...
"...END IT."
PERMANEN--
BOEEET BOEEEET
?
EXCUSE ME.
Y-YOU'RE ANSWERING YOUR PHONE...?
DO YOU MIND?

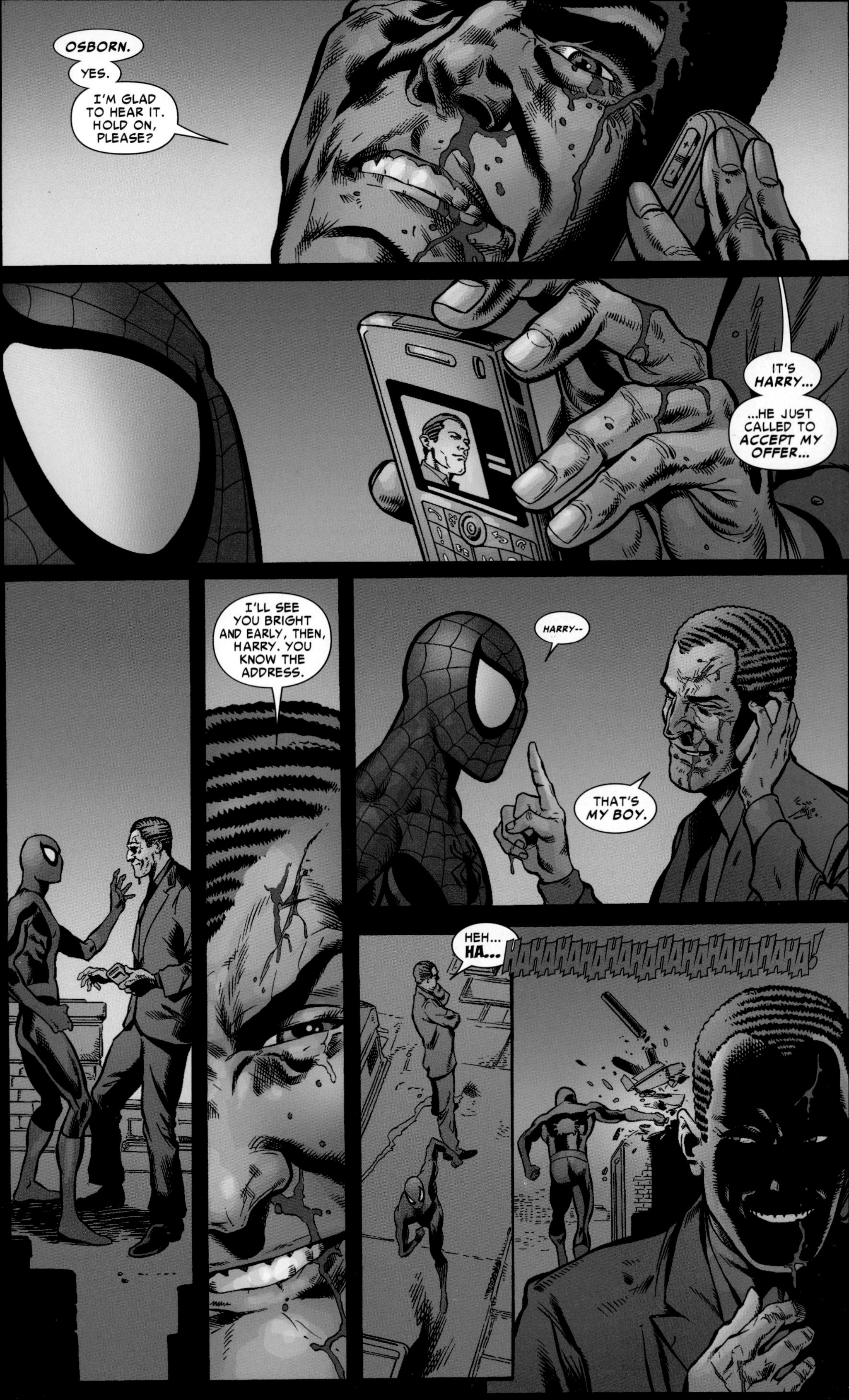
OSBORN.
YES.
I'M GLAD TO HEAR IT. HOLD ON, PLEASE?
IT'S HARRY...
...HE JUST CALLED TO ACCEPT MY OFFER...
I'LL SEE YOU BRIGHT AND EARLY, THEN, HARRY. YOU KNOW THE ADDRESS.
HARRY--
THAT'S MY BOY.
HEH... HA...
HAHAHAHAHAHAHAHAHAHAHAHAHA!

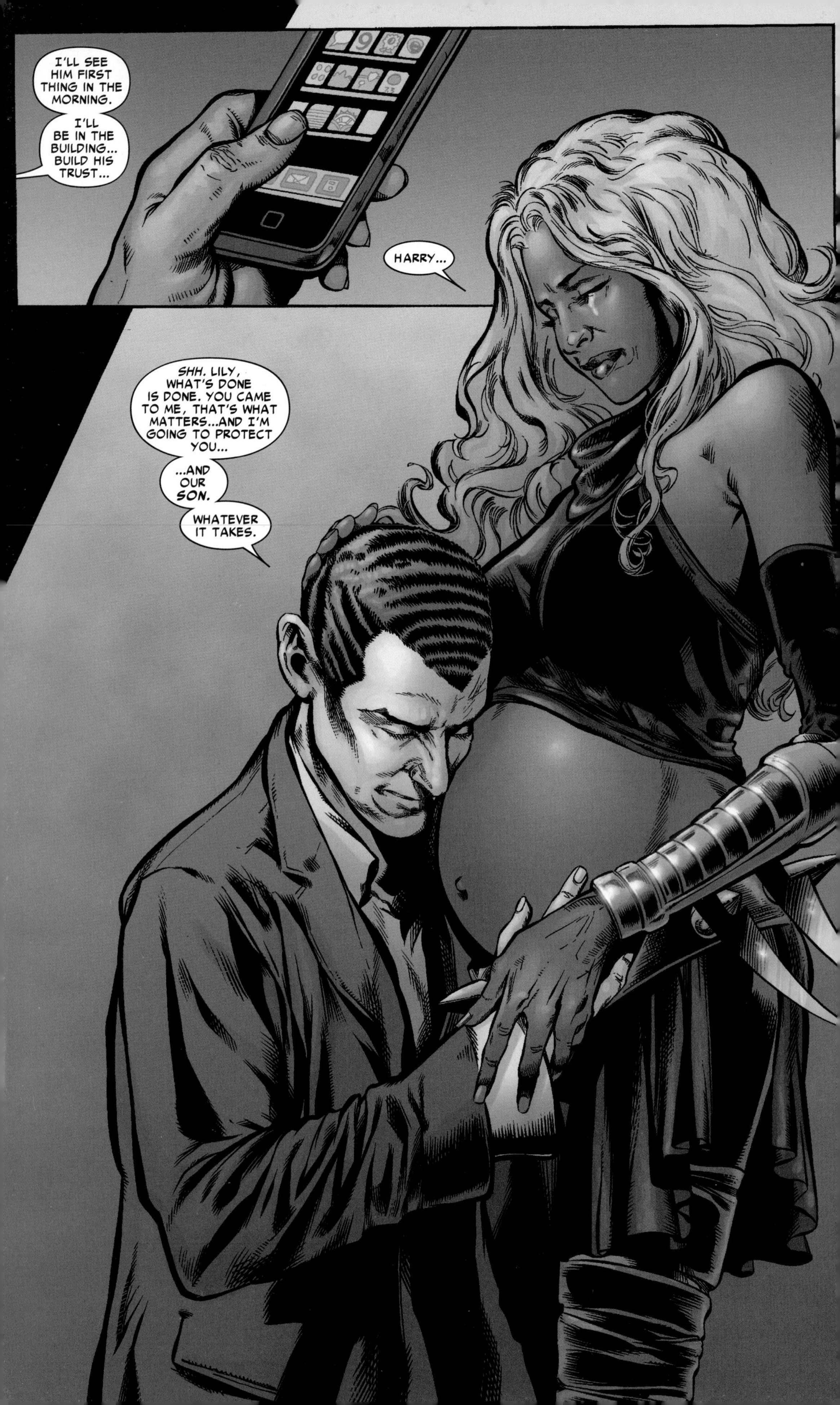

I'LL SEE HIM FIRST THING IN THE MORNING.
I'LL BE IN THE BUILDING... BUILD HIS TRUST...
HARRY...
SHH. LILY, WHAT'S DONE IS DONE. YOU CAME TO ME, THAT'S WHAT MATTERS...AND I'M GOING TO PROTECT YOU...
...AND OUR SON.
WHATEVER IT TAKES.

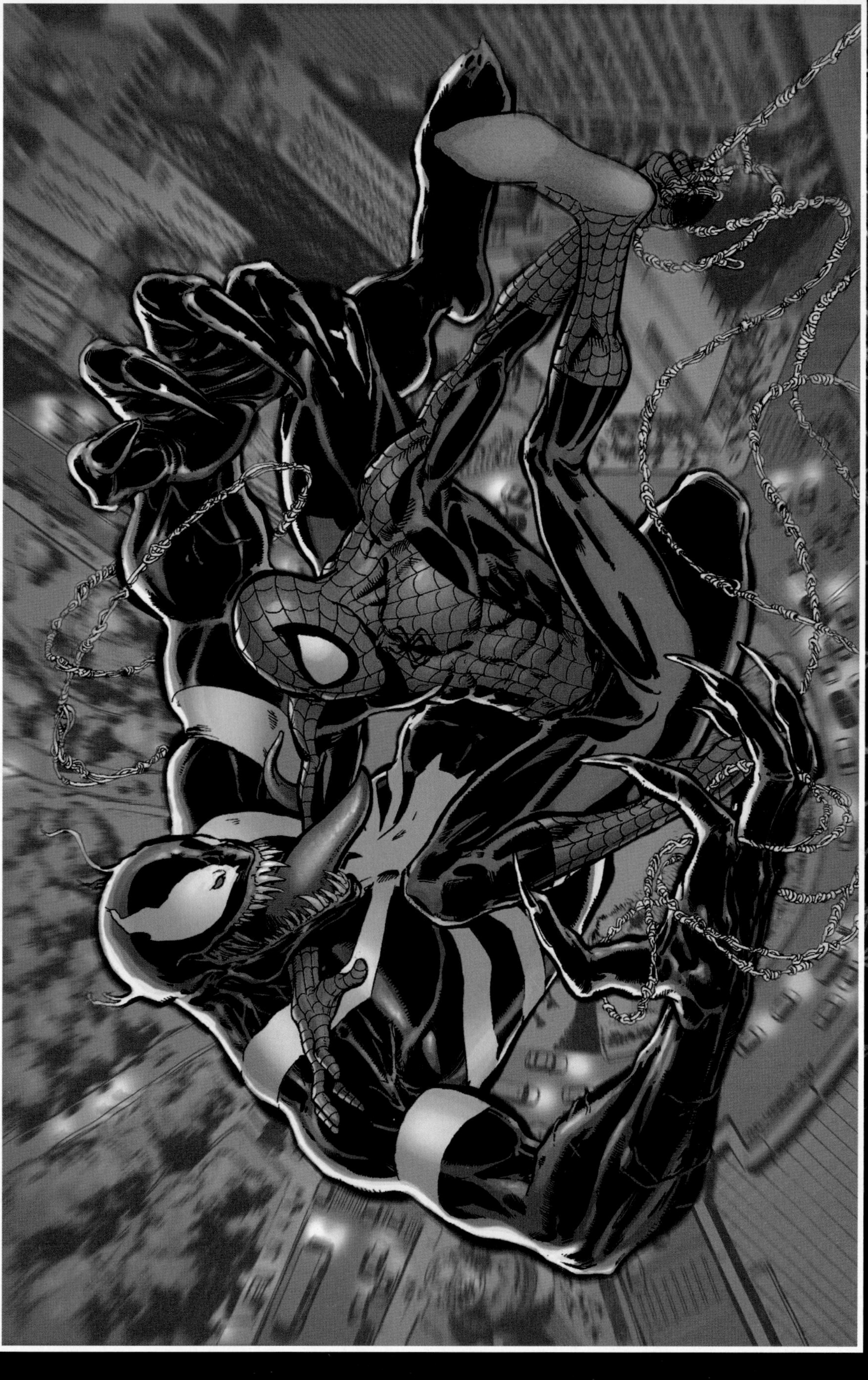

AMAZING SPIDER-MAN #596

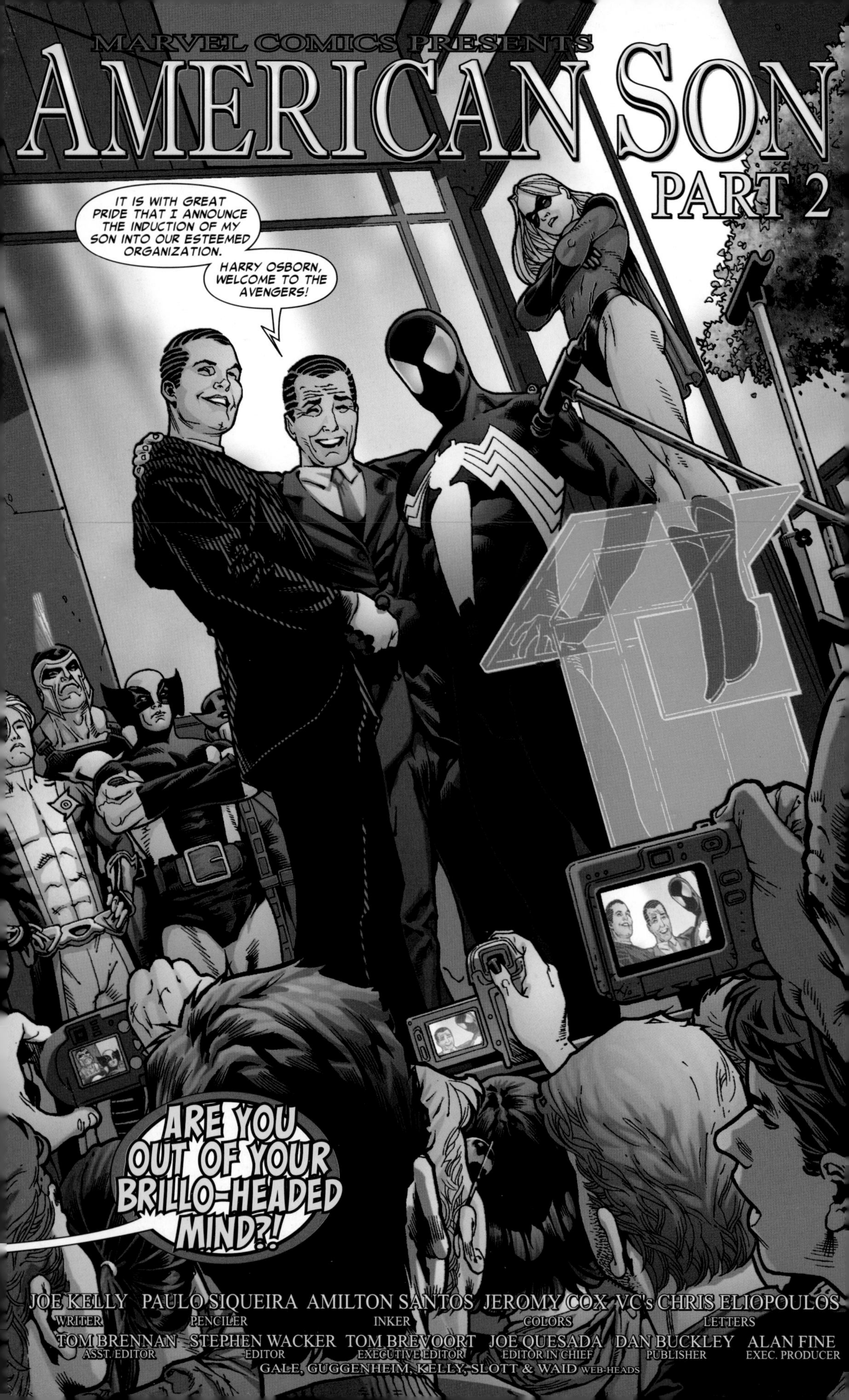
MARVEL COMICS PRESENTS
AMERICAN SON
PART 2
IT IS WITH GREAT PRIDE THAT I ANNOUNCE THE INDUCTION OF MY SON INTO OUR ESTEEMED ORGANIZATION.
HARRY OSBORN, WELCOME TO THE AVENGERS!
ARE YOU OUT OF YOUR BRILLO-HEADED MIND?!
JOE KELLY WRITER PAULO SIQUEIRA PENCILER AMILTON SANTOS INKER JEROMY COX COLORS VC's CHRIS ELIOPOULOS LETTERS
TOM BRENNAN ASST. EDITOR STEPHEN WACKER EDITOR TOM BREVOORT EXECUTIVE EDITOR JOE QUESADA EDITOR IN CHIEF DAN BUCKLEY PUBLISHER ALAN FINE EXEC. PRODUCER
GALE, GUGGENHEIM, KELLY, SLOTT & WAID WEB-HEADS

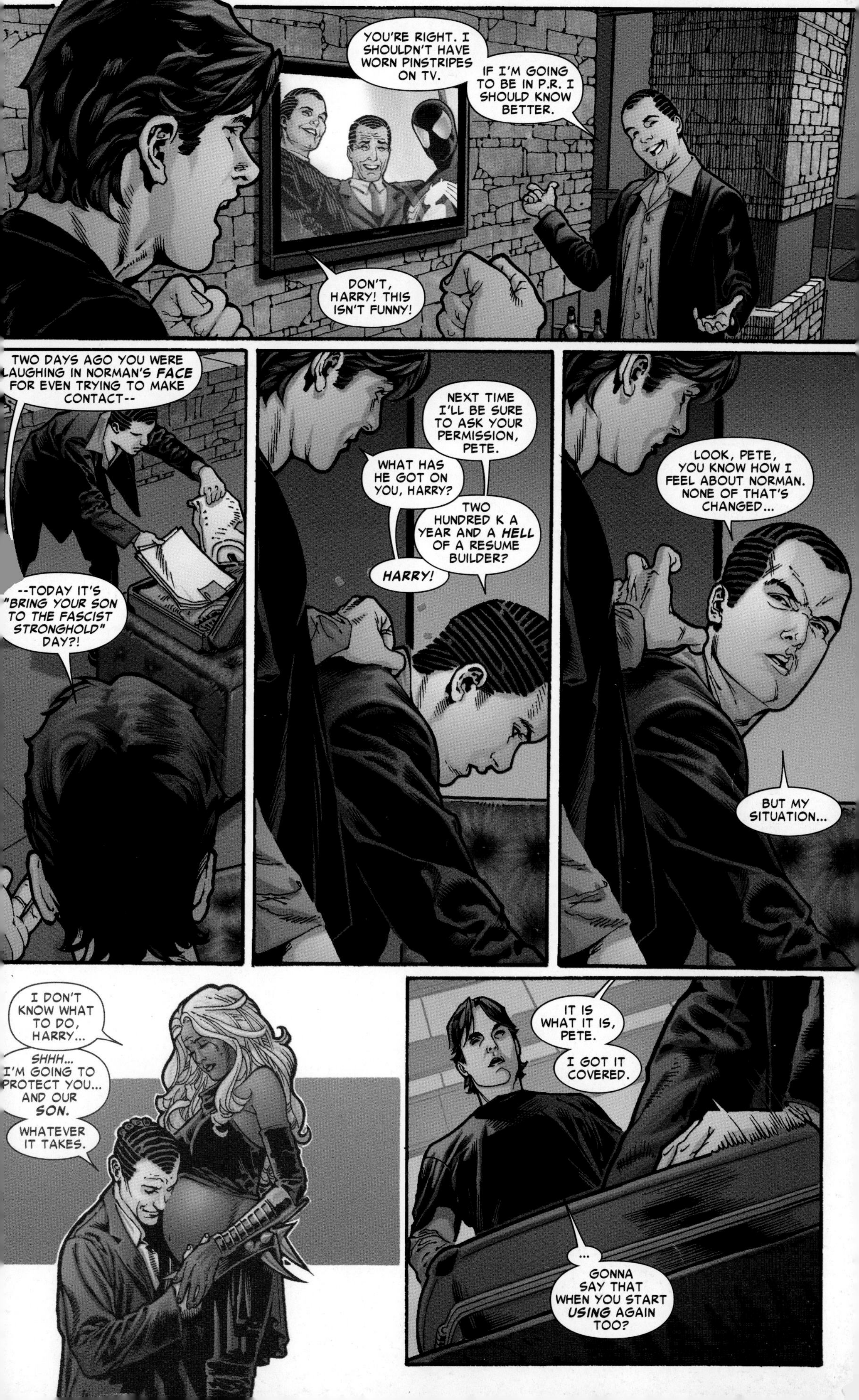

YOU'RE RIGHT. I SHOULDN'T HAVE WORN PINSTRIPES ON TV.
IF I'M GOING TO BE IN P.R. I SHOULD KNOW BETTER.
DON'T, HARRY! THIS ISN'T FUNNY!
TWO DAYS AGO YOU WERE LAUGHING IN NORMAN'S FACE FOR EVEN TRYING TO MAKE CONTACT--
--TODAY IT'S "BRING YOUR SON TO THE FASCIST STRONGHOLD" DAY?!
NEXT TIME I'LL BE SURE TO ASK YOUR PERMISSION, PETE.
WHAT HAS HE GOT ON YOU, HARRY?
TWO HUNDRED K A YEAR AND A HELL OF A RESUME BUILDER?
HARRY!
LOOK, PETE, YOU KNOW HOW I FEEL ABOUT NORMAN. NONE OF THAT'S CHANGED...
BUT MY SITUATION...
I DON'T KNOW WHAT TO DO, HARRY...
SHHH... I'M GOING TO PROTECT YOU... AND OUR SON.
WHATEVER IT TAKES.
IT IS WHAT IT IS, PETE.
I GOT IT COVERED.
...
GONNA SAY THAT WHEN YOU START USING AGAIN TOO?

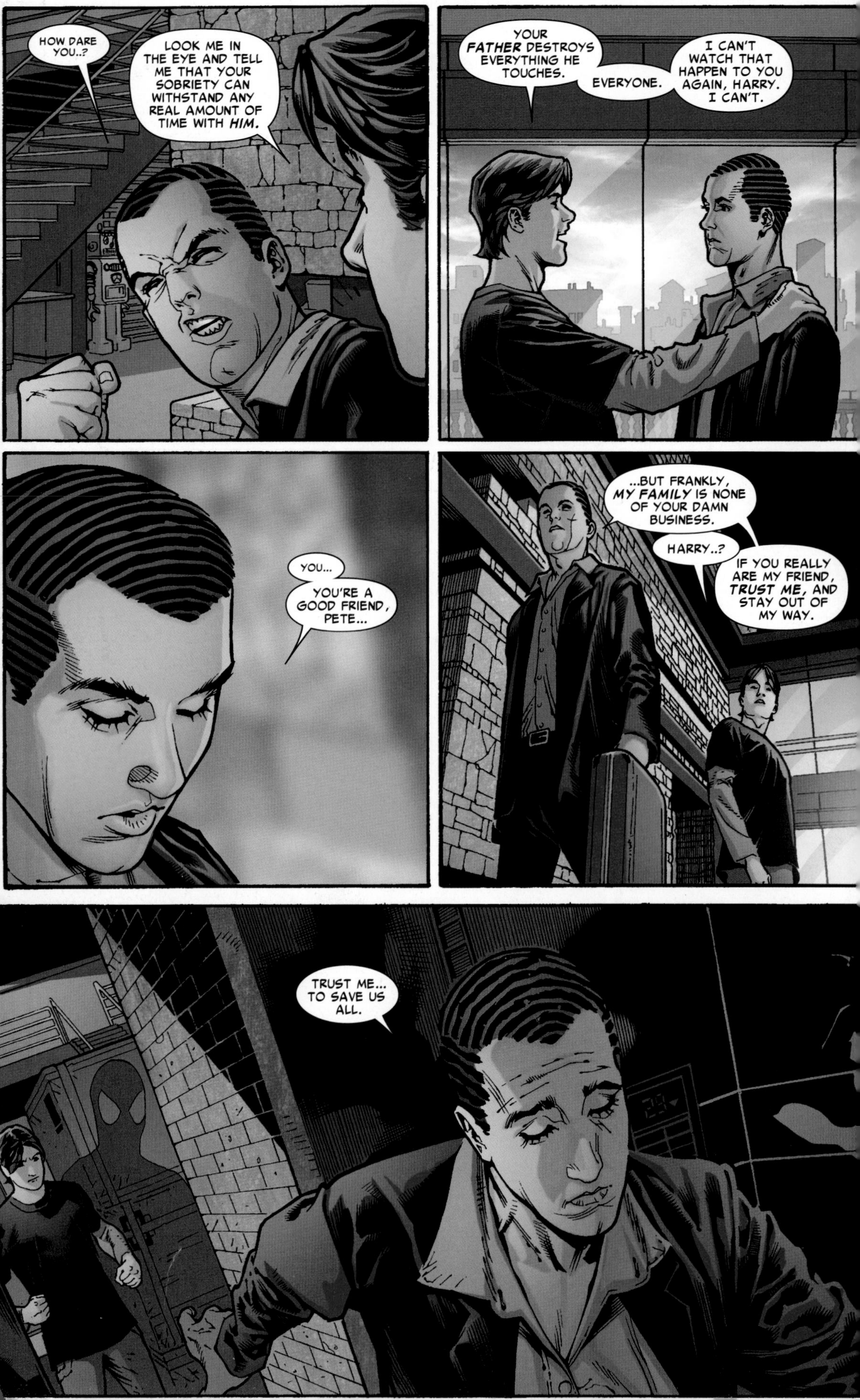

HOW DARE YOU..?
LOOK ME IN THE EYE AND TELL ME THAT YOUR SOBRIETY CAN WITHSTAND ANY REAL AMOUNT OF TIME WITH HIM.
YOUR FATHER DESTROYS EVERYTHING HE TOUCHES.
EVERYONE.
I CAN'T WATCH THAT HAPPEN TO YOU AGAIN, HARRY. I CAN'T.
YOU...
YOU'RE A GOOD FRIEND, PETE...
...BUT FRANKLY, MY FAMILY IS NONE OF YOUR DAMN BUSINESS.
HARRY..?
IF YOU REALLY ARE MY FRIEND, TRUST ME, AND STAY OUT OF MY WAY.
TRUST ME... TO SAVE US ALL.

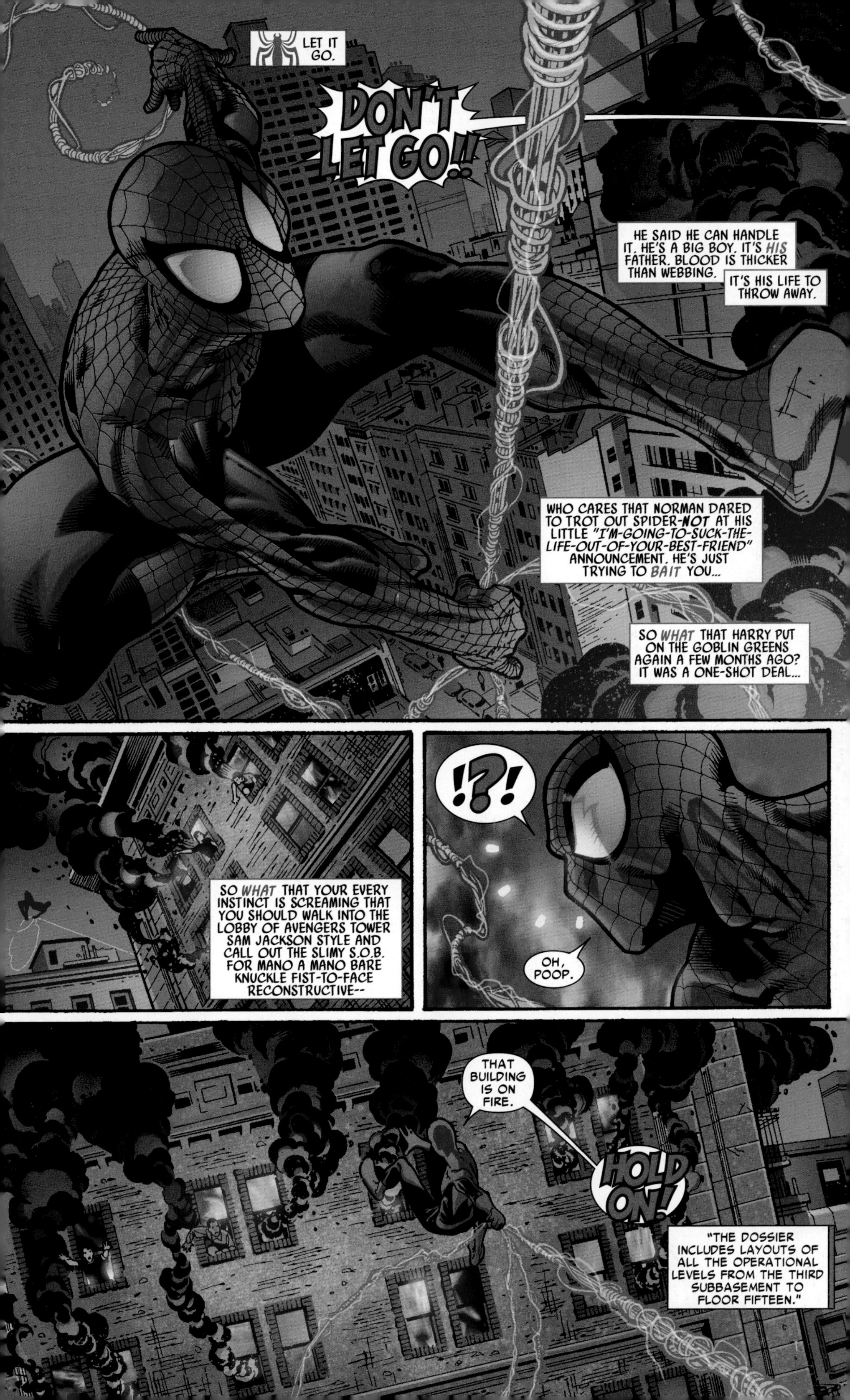

LET IT GO.
DON'T LET GO!!
HE SAID HE CAN HANDLE IT. HE'S A BIG BOY. IT'S HIS FATHER. BLOOD IS THICKER THAN WEBBING.
IT'S HIS LIFE TO THROW AWAY.
WHO CARES THAT NORMAN DARED TO TROT OUT SPIDER-NOT AT HIS LITTLE "I'M-GOING-TO-SUCK-THE-LIFE-OUT-OF-YOUR-BEST-FRIEND" ANNOUNCEMENT. HE'S JUST TRYING TO BAIT YOU...
SO WHAT THAT HARRY PUT ON THE GOBLIN GREENS AGAIN A FEW MONTHS AGO? IT WAS A ONE-SHOT DEAL...
SO WHAT THAT YOUR EVERY INSTINCT IS SCREAMING THAT YOU SHOULD WALK INTO THE LOBBY OF AVENGERS TOWER SAM JACKSON STYLE AND CALL OUT THE SLIMY S.O.B. FOR MANO A MANO BARE KNUCKLE FIST-TO-FACE RECONSTRUCTIVE--
!?!
OH, POOP.
THAT BUILDING IS ON FIRE.
HOLD ON!
"THE DOSSIER INCLUDES LAYOUTS OF ALL THE OPERATIONAL LEVELS FROM THE THIRD SUBBASEMENT TO FLOOR FIFTEEN."

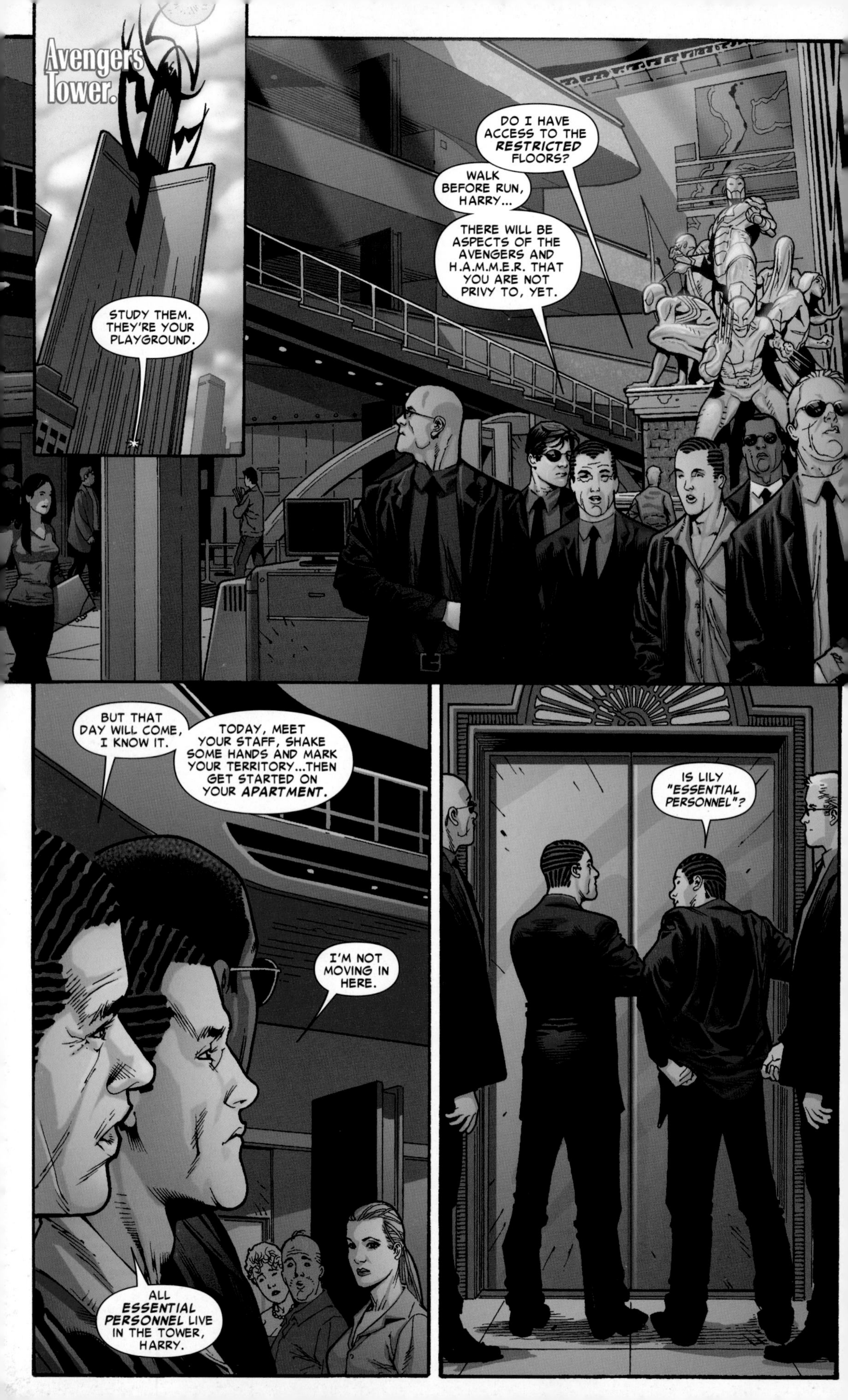
Avengers Tower.
STUDY THEM. THEY'RE YOUR PLAYGROUND.
DO I HAVE ACCESS TO THE RESTRICTED FLOORS?
WALK BEFORE RUN, HARRY...
THERE WILL BE ASPECTS OF THE AVENGERS AND H.A.M.M.E.R. THAT YOU ARE NOT PRIVY TO, YET.
BUT THAT DAY WILL COME, I KNOW IT.
TODAY, MEET YOUR STAFF, SHAKE SOME HANDS AND MARK YOUR TERRITORY...THEN GET STARTED ON YOUR APARTMENT.
I'M NOT MOVING IN HERE.
ALL ESSENTIAL PERSONNEL LIVE IN THE TOWER, HARRY.
IS LILY "ESSENTIAL PERSONNEL"?

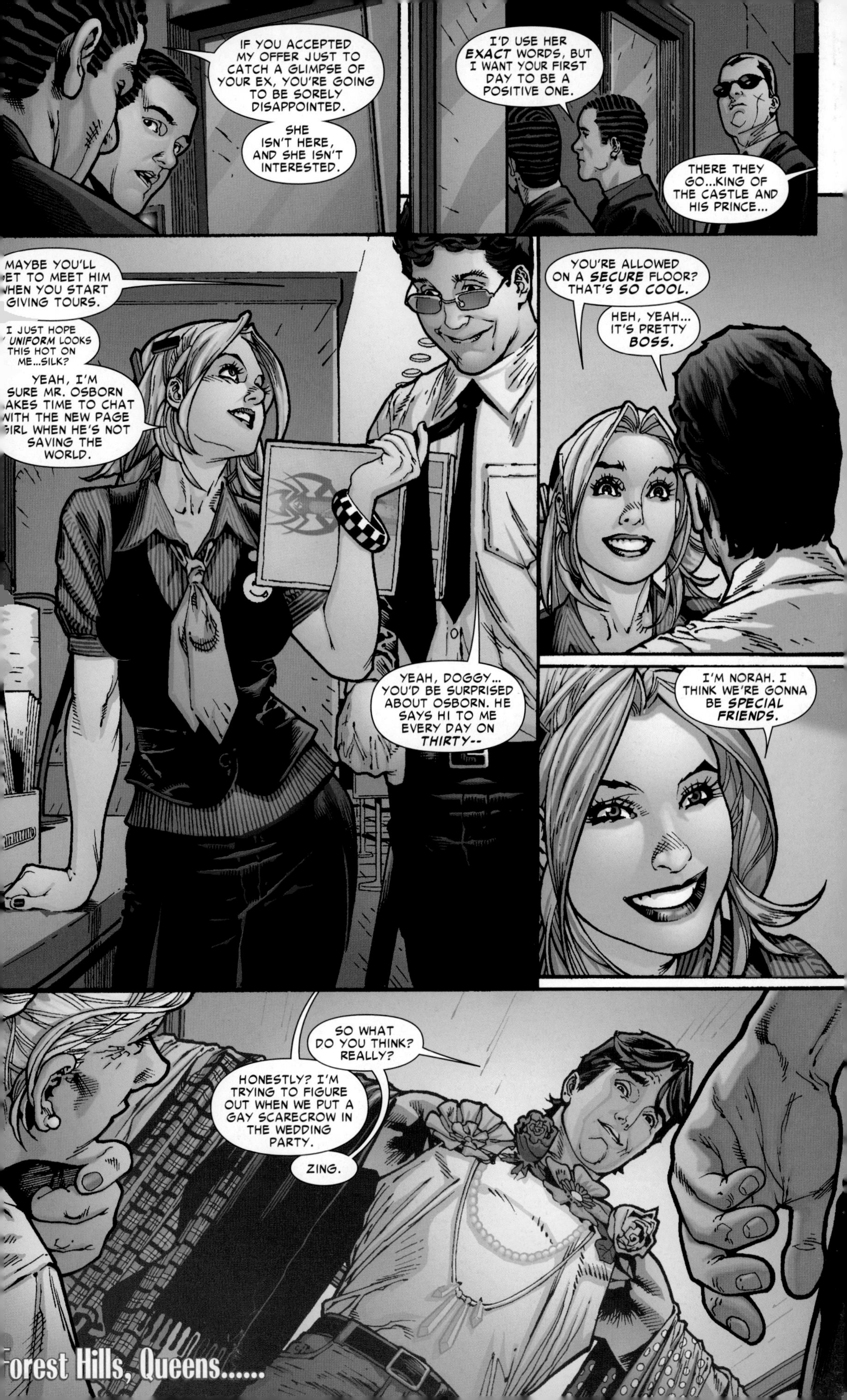
IF YOU ACCEPTED MY OFFER JUST TO CATCH A GLIMPSE OF YOUR EX, YOU'RE GOING TO BE SORELY DISAPPOINTED.
SHE ISN'T HERE, AND SHE ISN'T INTERESTED.
I'D USE HER EXACT WORDS, BUT I WANT YOUR FIRST DAY TO BE A POSITIVE ONE.
THERE THEY GO...KING OF THE CASTLE AND HIS PRINCE...
MAYBE YOU'LL ET TO MEET HIM HEN YOU START GIVING TOURS.
I JUST HOPE UNIFORM LOOKS THIS HOT ON ME...SILK?
YEAH, I'M SURE MR. OSBORN AKES TIME TO CHAT WITH THE NEW PAGE IRL WHEN HE'S NOT SAVING THE WORLD.
YEAH, DOGGY... YOU'D BE SURPRISED ABOUT OSBORN. HE SAYS HI TO ME EVERY DAY ON THIRTY--
YOU'RE ALLOWED ON A SECURE FLOOR? THAT'S SO COOL.
HEH, YEAH... IT'S PRETTY BOSS.
I'M NORAH. I THINK WE'RE GONNA BE SPECIAL FRIENDS.
Forest Hills, Queens......
SO WHAT DO YOU THINK? REALLY?
HONESTLY? I'M TRYING TO FIGURE OUT WHEN WE PUT A GAY SCARECROW IN THE WEDDING PARTY.
ZING.

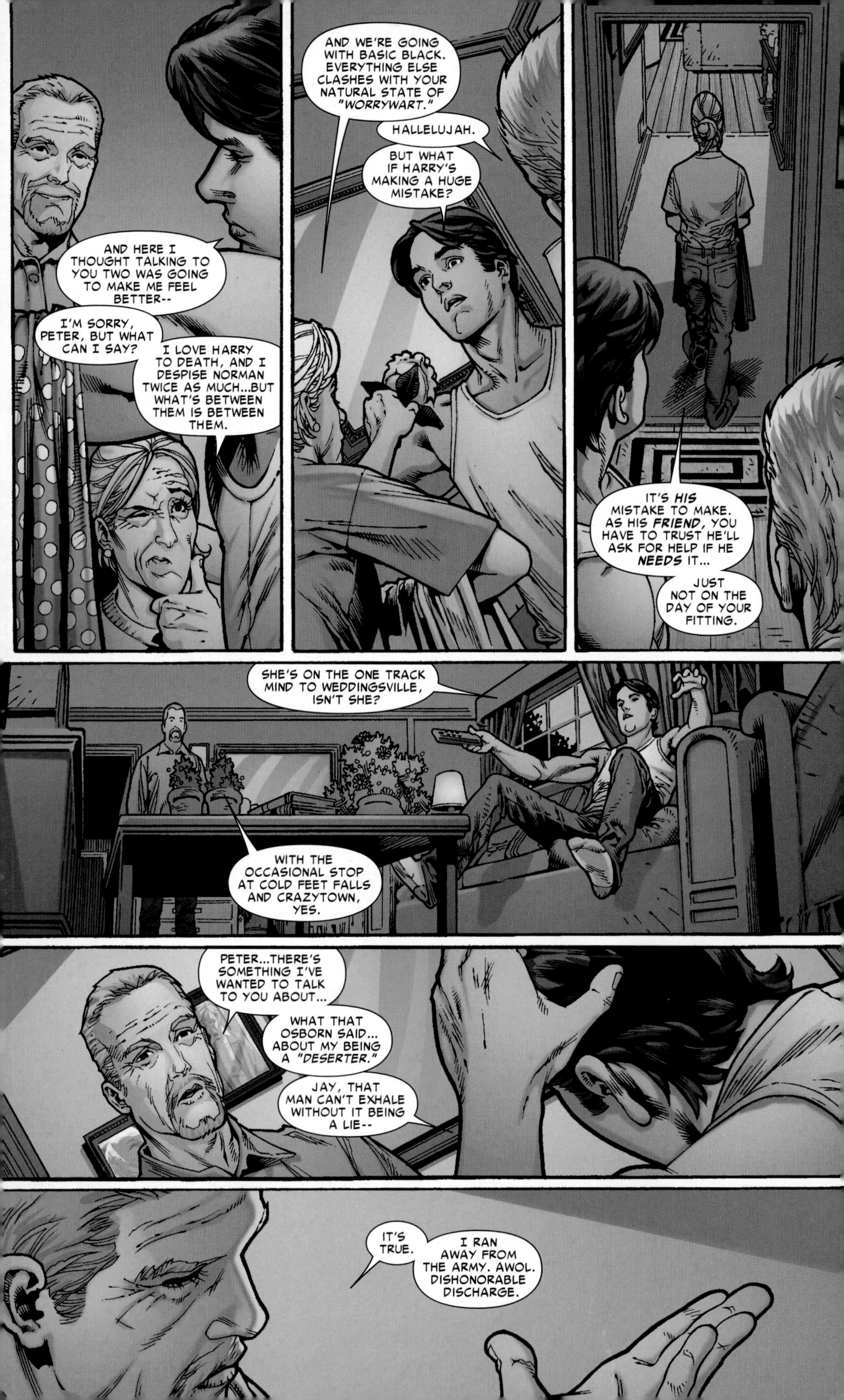
AND HERE I THOUGHT TALKING TO YOU TWO WAS GOING TO MAKE ME FEEL BETTER--
I'M SORRY, PETER, BUT WHAT CAN I SAY?
I LOVE HARRY TO DEATH, AND I DESPISE NORMAN TWICE AS MUCH...BUT WHAT'S BETWEEN THEM IS BETWEEN THEM.
AND WE'RE GOING WITH BASIC BLACK. EVERYTHING ELSE CLASHES WITH YOUR NATURAL STATE OF "WORRYWART."
HALLELUJAH.
BUT WHAT IF HARRY'S MAKING A HUGE MISTAKE?
IT'S HIS MISTAKE TO MAKE. AS HIS FRIEND, YOU HAVE TO TRUST HE'LL ASK FOR HELP IF HE NEEDS IT...
JUST NOT ON THE DAY OF YOUR FITTING.
SHE'S ON THE ONE TRACK MIND TO WEDDINGSVILLE, ISN'T SHE?
WITH THE OCCASIONAL STOP AT COLD FEET FALLS AND CRAZYTOWN, YES.
PETER...THERE'S SOMETHING I'VE WANTED TO TALK TO YOU ABOUT...
WHAT THAT OSBORN SAID... ABOUT MY BEING A "DESERTER."
JAY, THAT MAN CAN'T EXHALE WITHOUT IT BEING A LIE--
IT'S TRUE.
I RAN AWAY FROM THE ARMY. AWOL. DISHONORABLE DISCHARGE.

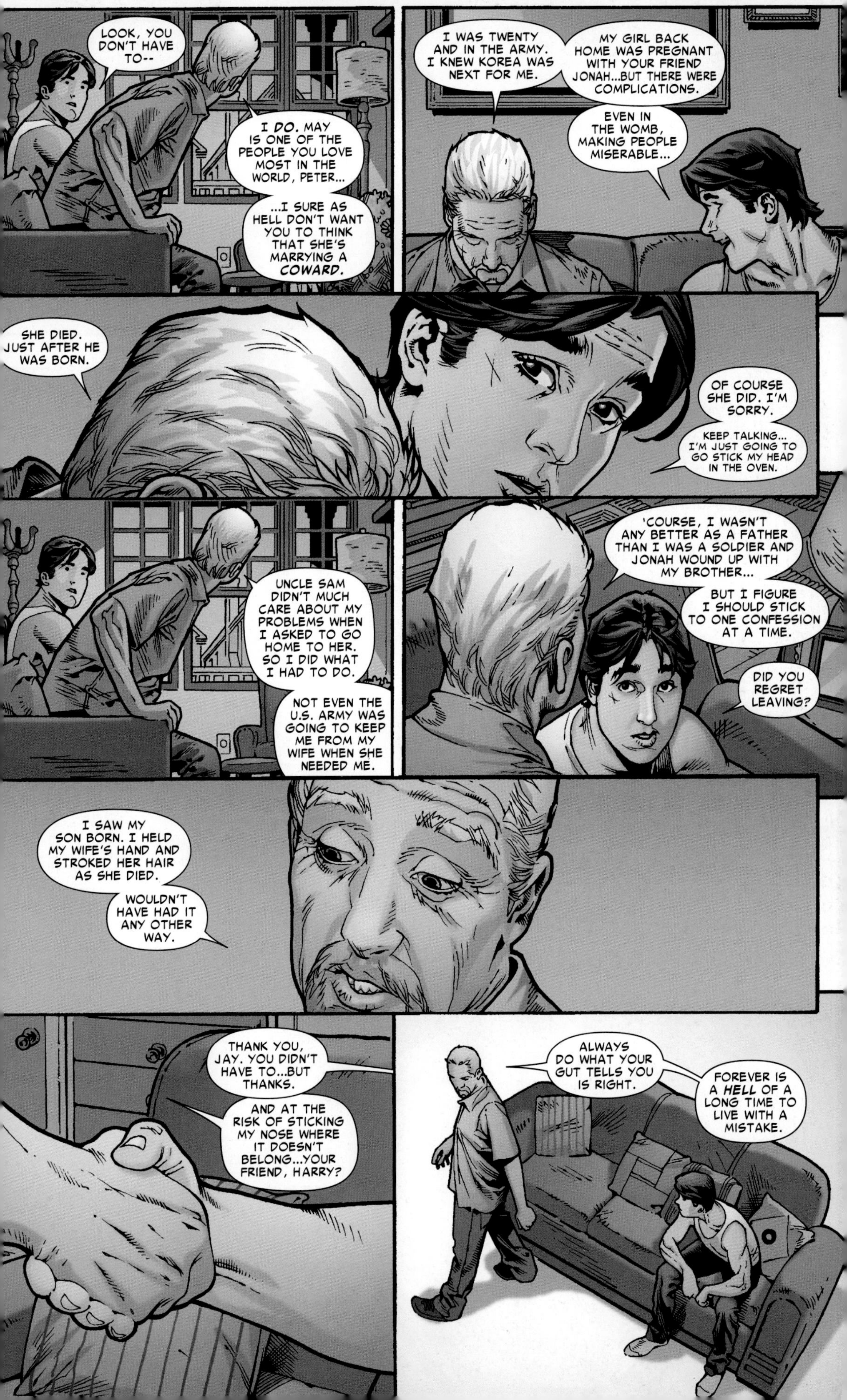

LOOK, YOU DON'T HAVE TO--
I DO. MAY IS ONE OF THE PEOPLE YOU LOVE MOST IN THE WORLD, PETER...
...I SURE AS HELL DON'T WANT YOU TO THINK THAT SHE'S MARRYING A COWARD.
I WAS TWENTY AND IN THE ARMY. I KNEW KOREA WAS NEXT FOR ME.
MY GIRL BACK HOME WAS PREGNANT WITH YOUR FRIEND JONAH...BUT THERE WERE COMPLICATIONS.
EVEN IN THE WOMB, MAKING PEOPLE MISERABLE...
SHE DIED. JUST AFTER HE WAS BORN.
OF COURSE SHE DID. I'M SORRY.
KEEP TALKING... I'M JUST GOING TO GO STICK MY HEAD IN THE OVEN.
UNCLE SAM DIDN'T MUCH CARE ABOUT MY PROBLEMS WHEN I ASKED TO GO HOME TO HER. SO I DID WHAT I HAD TO DO.
NOT EVEN THE U.S. ARMY WAS GOING TO KEEP ME FROM MY WIFE WHEN SHE NEEDED ME.
'COURSE, I WASN'T ANY BETTER AS A FATHER THAN I WAS A SOLDIER AND JONAH WOUND UP WITH MY BROTHER...
BUT I FIGURE I SHOULD STICK TO ONE CONFESSION AT A TIME.
DID YOU REGRET LEAVING?
I SAW MY SON BORN. I HELD MY WIFE'S HAND AND STROKED HER HAIR AS SHE DIED.
WOULDN'T HAVE HAD IT ANY OTHER WAY.
THANK YOU, JAY. YOU DIDN'T HAVE TO...BUT THANKS.
AND AT THE RISK OF STICKING MY NOSE WHERE IT DOESN'T BELONG...YOUR FRIEND, HARRY?
ALWAYS DO WHAT YOUR GUT TELLS YOU IS RIGHT.
FOREVER IS A HELL OF A LONG TIME TO LIVE WITH A MISTAKE.

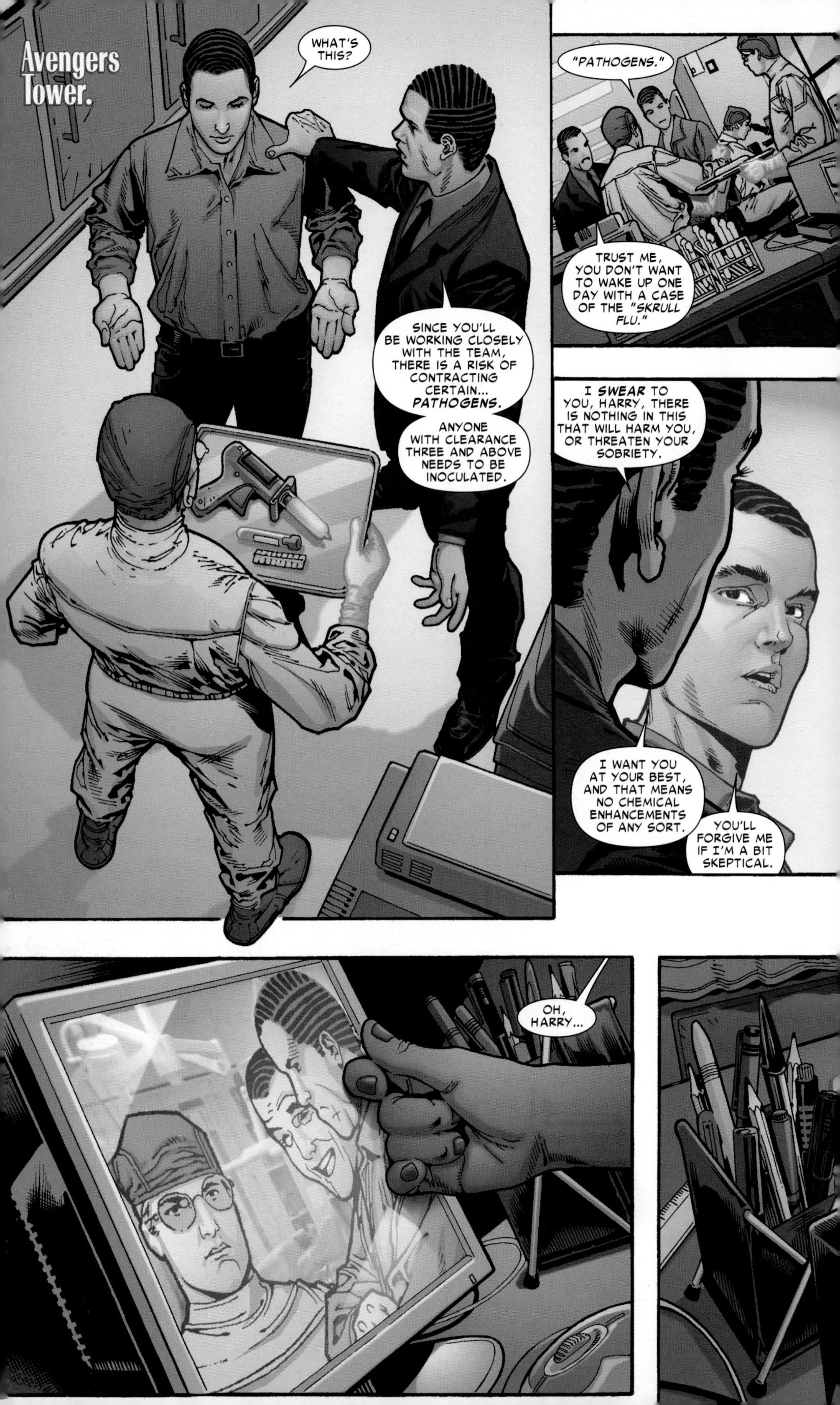

Avengers Tower.
WHAT'S THIS?
"PATHOGENS."
TRUST ME, YOU DON'T WANT TO WAKE UP ONE DAY WITH A CASE OF THE "SKRULL FLU."
SINCE YOU'LL BE WORKING CLOSELY WITH THE TEAM, THERE IS A RISK OF CONTRACTING CERTAIN... PATHOGENS.
ANYONE WITH CLEARANCE THREE AND ABOVE NEEDS TO BE INOCULATED.
I SWEAR TO YOU, HARRY, THERE IS NOTHING IN THIS THAT WILL HARM YOU, OR THREATEN YOUR SOBRIETY.
I WANT YOU AT YOUR BEST, AND THAT MEANS NO CHEMICAL ENHANCEMENTS OF ANY SORT.
YOU'LL FORGIVE ME IF I'M A BIT SKEPTICAL.
OH, HARRY...

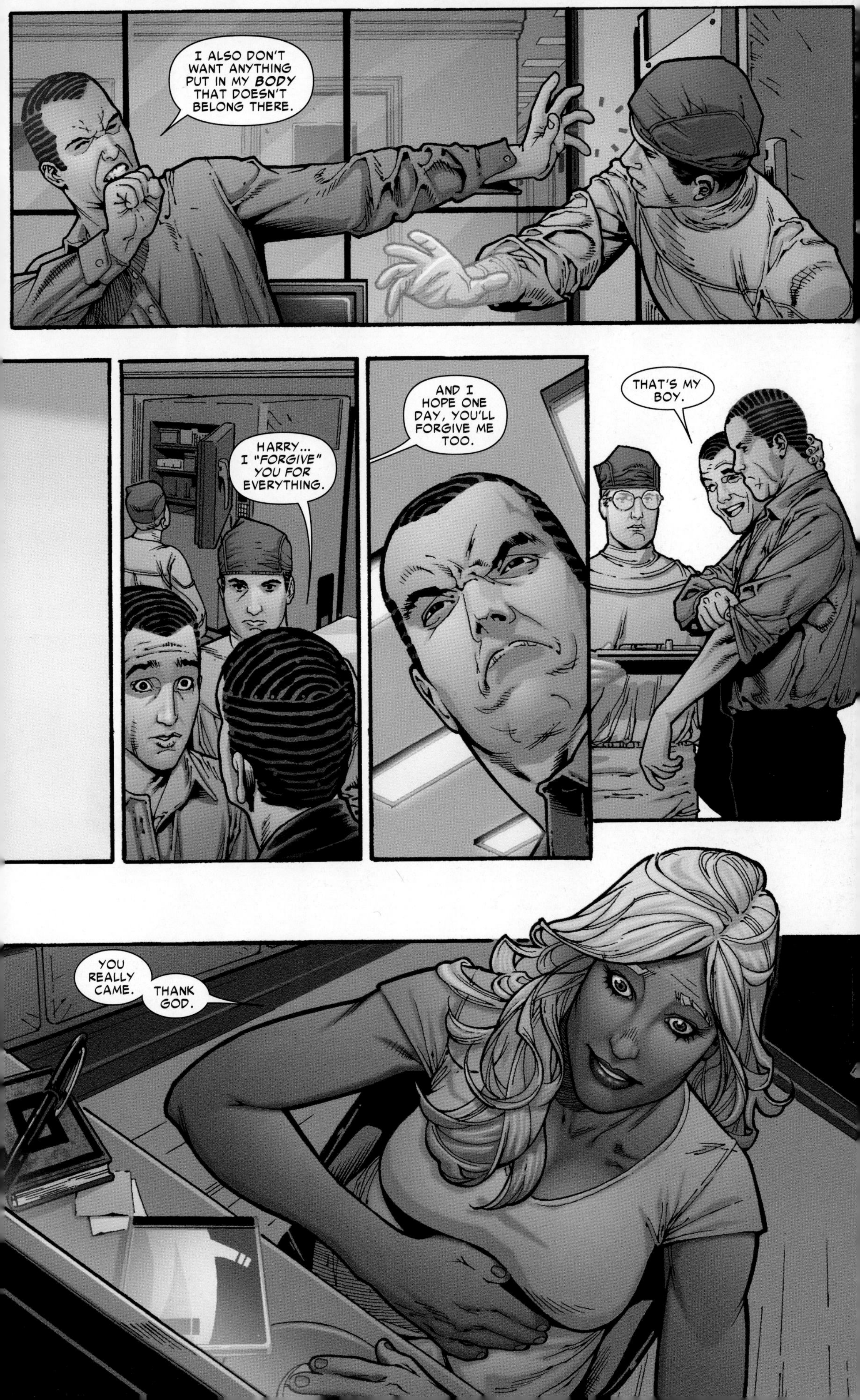
I ALSO DON'T WANT ANYTHING PUT IN MY *BODY* THAT DOESN'T BELONG THERE.
HARRY... I "*FORGIVE*" YOU FOR EVERYTHING.
AND I HOPE ONE DAY, YOU'LL FORGIVE ME TOO.
THAT'S MY BOY.
YOU REALLY CAME.
THANK GOD.

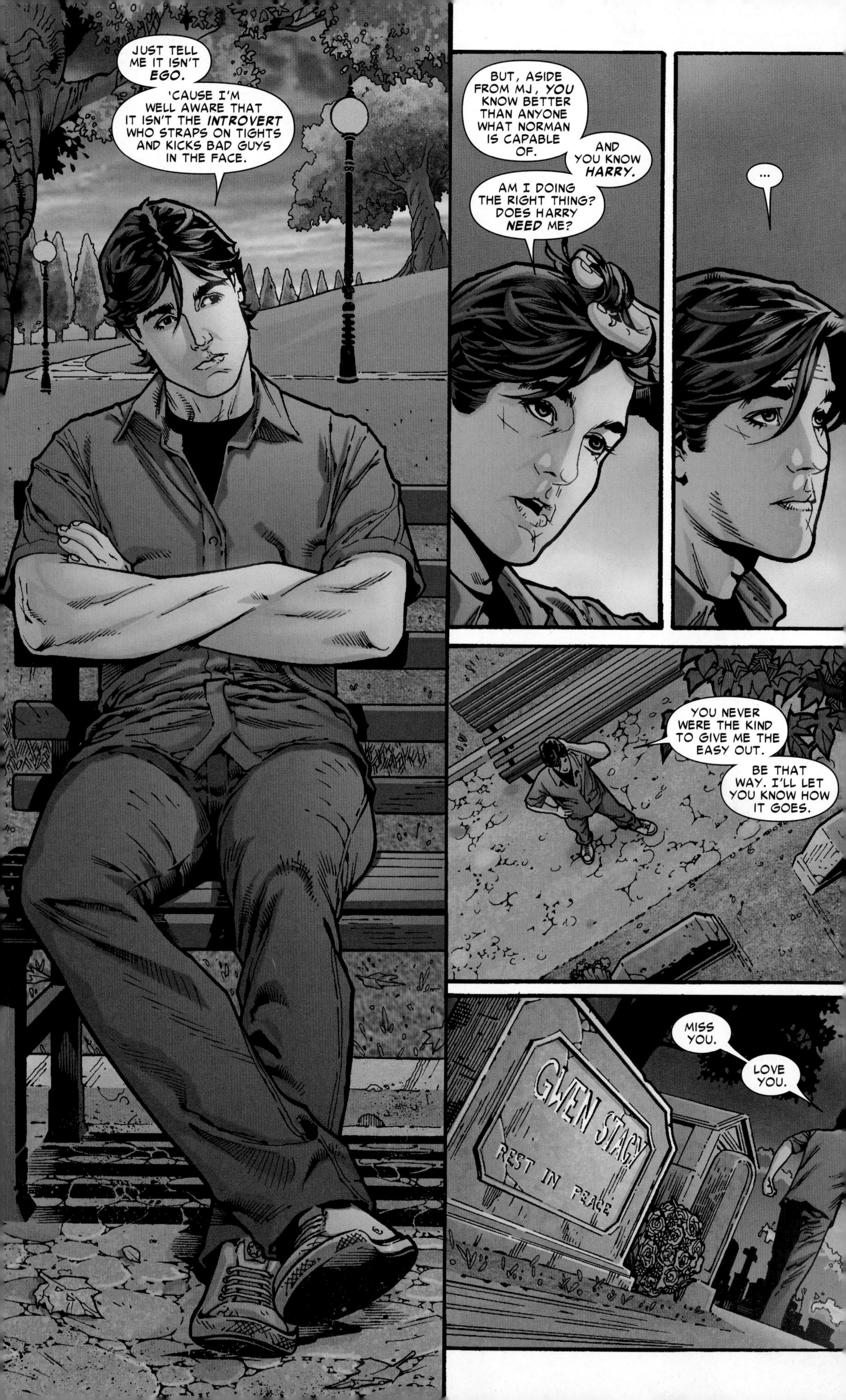
JUST TELL ME IT ISN'T *EGO.*
'CAUSE I'M WELL AWARE THAT IT ISN'T THE *INTROVERT* WHO STRAPS ON TIGHTS AND KICKS BAD GUYS IN THE FACE.
BUT, ASIDE FROM MJ, *YOU* KNOW BETTER THAN ANYONE WHAT NORMAN IS CAPABLE OF.
AND YOU KNOW *HARRY.*
AM I DOING THE RIGHT THING? DOES HARRY *NEED* ME?
...
YOU NEVER WERE THE KIND TO GIVE ME THE EASY OUT.
BE THAT WAY. I'LL LET YOU KNOW HOW IT GOES.
GWEN STACY
REST IN PEACE
MISS YOU.
LOVE YOU.

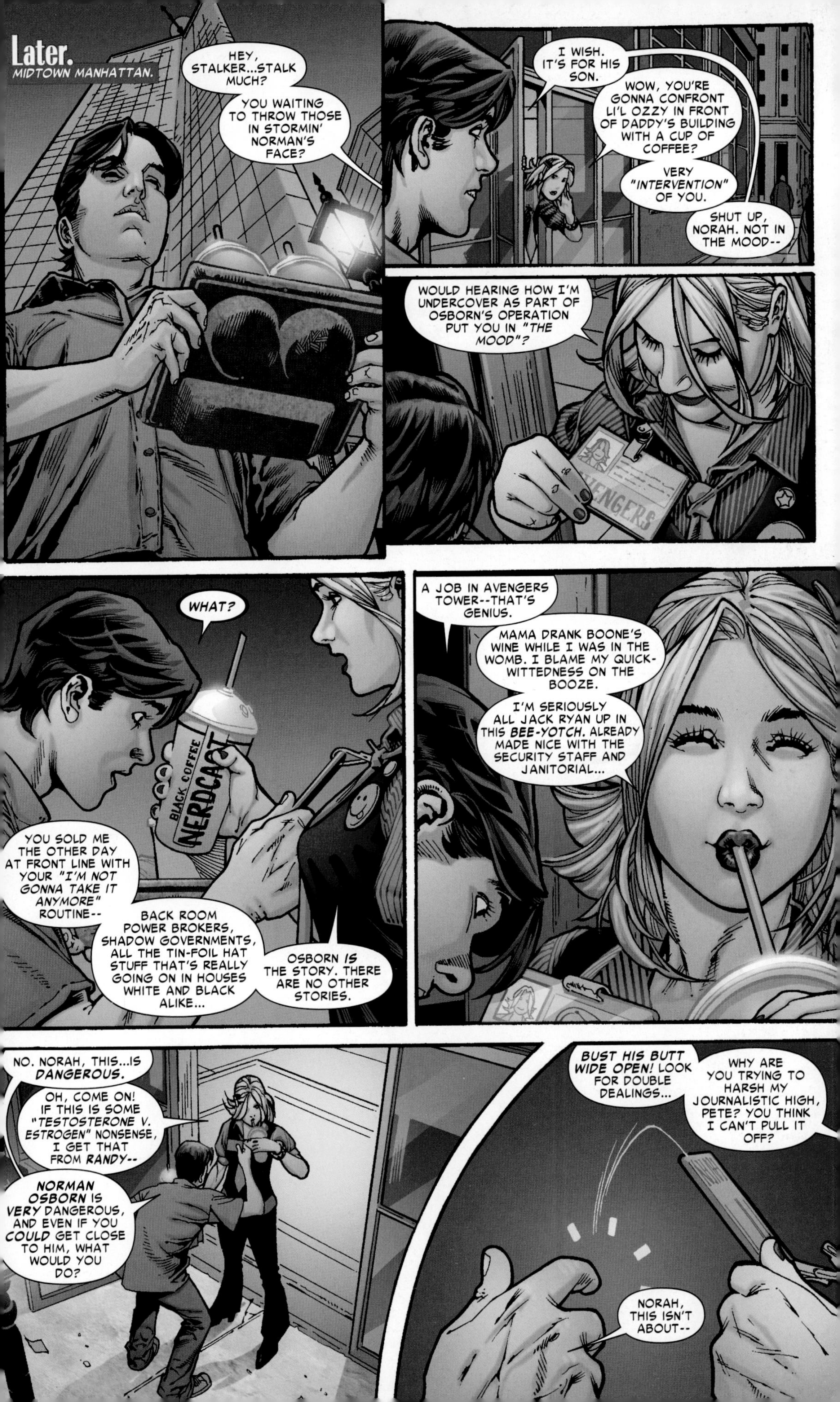
Later.
MIDTOWN MANHATTAN.
HEY, STALKER...STALK MUCH?
YOU WAITING TO THROW THOSE IN STORMIN' NORMAN'S FACE?
I WISH. IT'S FOR HIS SON.
WOW, YOU'RE GONNA CONFRONT LI'L OZZY IN FRONT OF DADDY'S BUILDING WITH A CUP OF COFFEE?
VERY "INTERVENTION" OF YOU.
SHUT UP, NORAH. NOT IN THE MOOD--
WOULD HEARING HOW I'M UNDERCOVER AS PART OF OSBORN'S OPERATION PUT YOU IN "THE MOOD"?
AVENGERS
WHAT?
BLACK COFFEE
NERDCAST
YOU SOLD ME THE OTHER DAY AT FRONT LINE WITH YOUR "I'M NOT GONNA TAKE IT ANYMORE" ROUTINE--
BACK ROOM POWER BROKERS, SHADOW GOVERNMENTS, ALL THE TIN-FOIL HAT STUFF THAT'S REALLY GOING ON IN HOUSES WHITE AND BLACK ALIKE...
OSBORN IS THE STORY. THERE ARE NO OTHER STORIES.
A JOB IN AVENGERS TOWER--THAT'S GENIUS.
MAMA DRANK BOONE'S WINE WHILE I WAS IN THE WOMB. I BLAME MY QUICK-WITTEDNESS ON THE BOOZE.
I'M SERIOUSLY ALL JACK RYAN UP IN THIS BEE-YOTCH. ALREADY MADE NICE WITH THE SECURITY STAFF AND JANITORIAL...
NO. NORAH, THIS...IS DANGEROUS.
OH, COME ON! IF THIS IS SOME "TESTOSTERONE V. ESTROGEN" NONSENSE, I GET THAT FROM RANDY--
NORMAN OSBORN IS VERY DANGEROUS, AND EVEN IF YOU COULD GET CLOSE TO HIM, WHAT WOULD YOU DO?
BUST HIS BUTT WIDE OPEN! LOOK FOR DOUBLE DEALINGS...
WHY ARE YOU TRYING TO HARSH MY JOURNALISTIC HIGH, PETE? YOU THINK I CAN'T PULL IT OFF?
NORAH, THIS ISN'T ABOUT--

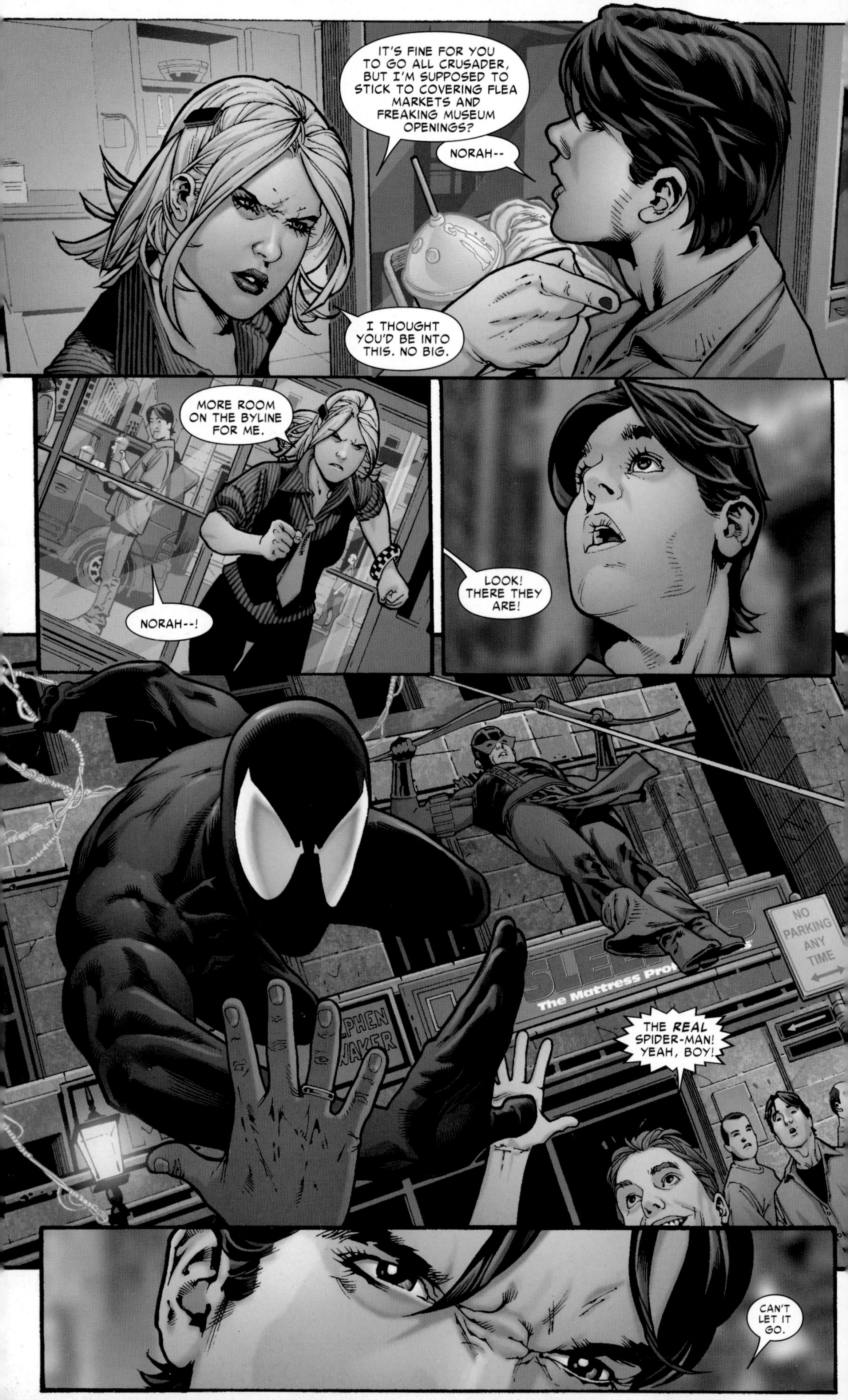

IT'S FINE FOR YOU TO GO ALL CRUSADER, BUT I'M SUPPOSED TO STICK TO COVERING FLEA MARKETS AND FREAKING MUSEUM OPENINGS?
NORAH--
I THOUGHT YOU'D BE INTO THIS. NO BIG.
MORE ROOM ON THE BYLINE FOR ME.
NORAH--!
LOOK! THERE THEY ARE!
NO PARKING ANY TIME
The Mattress Pro
THE REAL SPIDER-MAN! YEAH, BOY!
CAN'T LET IT GO.

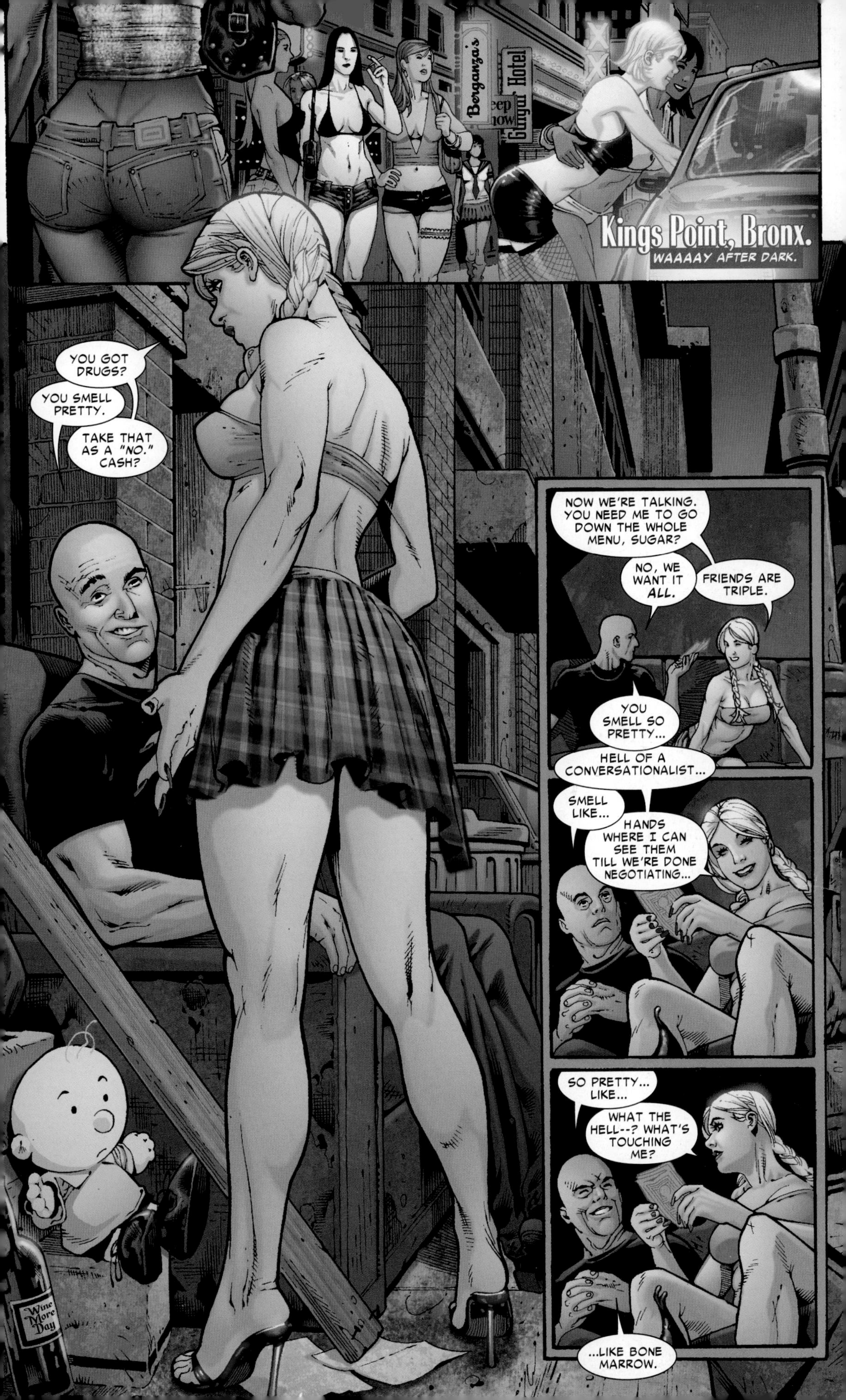
Berganza's
Glagur Hotel
Kings Point, Bronx.
WAAAAY AFTER DARK.
YOU GOT DRUGS?
YOU SMELL PRETTY.
TAKE THAT AS A "NO." CASH?
NOW WE'RE TALKING. YOU NEED ME TO GO DOWN THE WHOLE MENU, SUGAR?
NO, WE WANT IT ALL.
FRIENDS ARE TRIPLE.
YOU SMELL SO PRETTY...
HELL OF A CONVERSATIONALIST...
SMELL LIKE...
HANDS WHERE I CAN SEE THEM TILL WE'RE DONE NEGOTIATING...
SO PRETTY... LIKE...
WHAT THE HELL--? WHAT'S TOUCHING ME?
...LIKE BONE MARROW.
Wine More Day

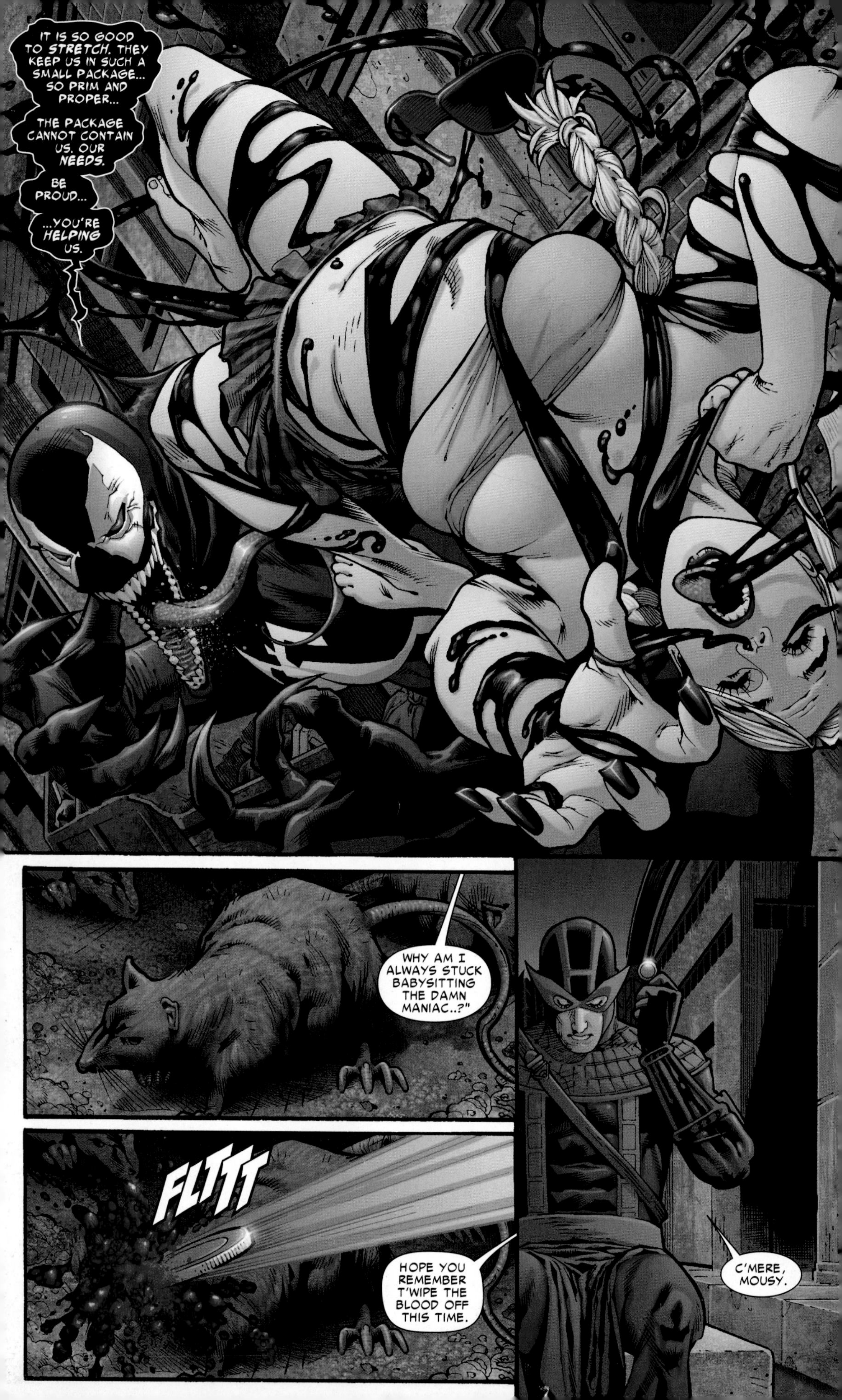

IT IS SO GOOD TO STRETCH. THEY KEEP US IN SUCH A SMALL PACKAGE... SO PRIM AND PROPER...
THE PACKAGE CANNOT CONTAIN US. OUR NEEDS.
BE PROUD...
...YOU'RE HELPING US.
WHY AM I ALWAYS STUCK BABYSITTING THE DAMN MANIAC..?"
FLTTT
HOPE YOU REMEMBER T'WIPE THE BLOOD OFF THIS TIME.
C'MERE, MOUSY.

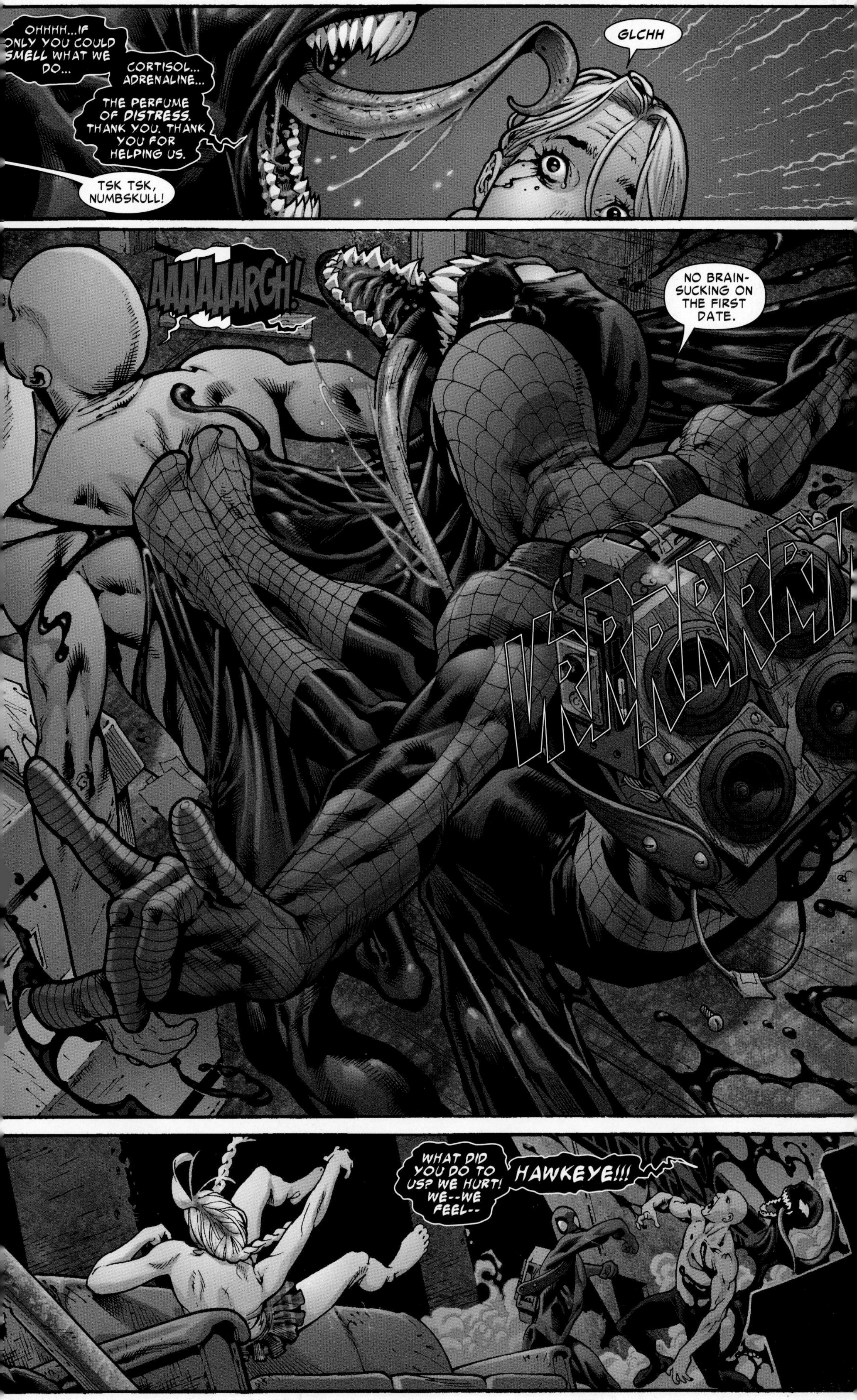
OHHHH...IF ONLY YOU COULD SMELL WHAT WE DO...
CORTISOL... ADRENALINE...
THE PERFUME OF DISTRESS. THANK YOU. THANK YOU FOR HELPING US.
GLCHH
TSK TSK, NUMBSKULL!
AAAAAARGH!
NO BRAIN-SUCKING ON THE FIRST DATE.
VRRRRRRRN
WHAT DID YOU DO TO US? WE HURT! WE--WE FEEL--
HAWKEYE!!!

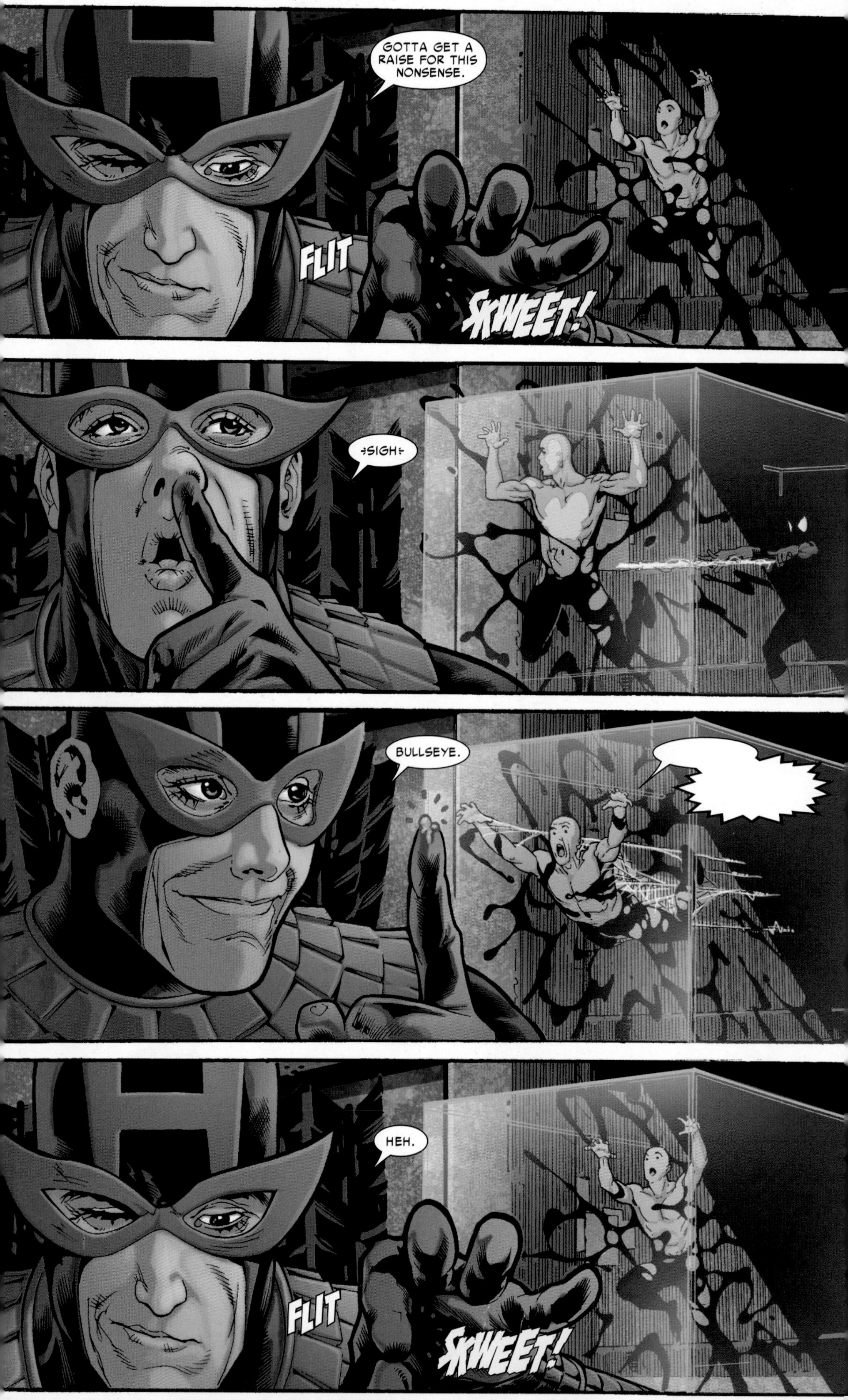

GOTTA GET A RAISE FOR THIS NONSENSE.
FLIT
SKWEET!
=SIGH=
BULLSEYE.
HEH.
FLIT
SKWEET!

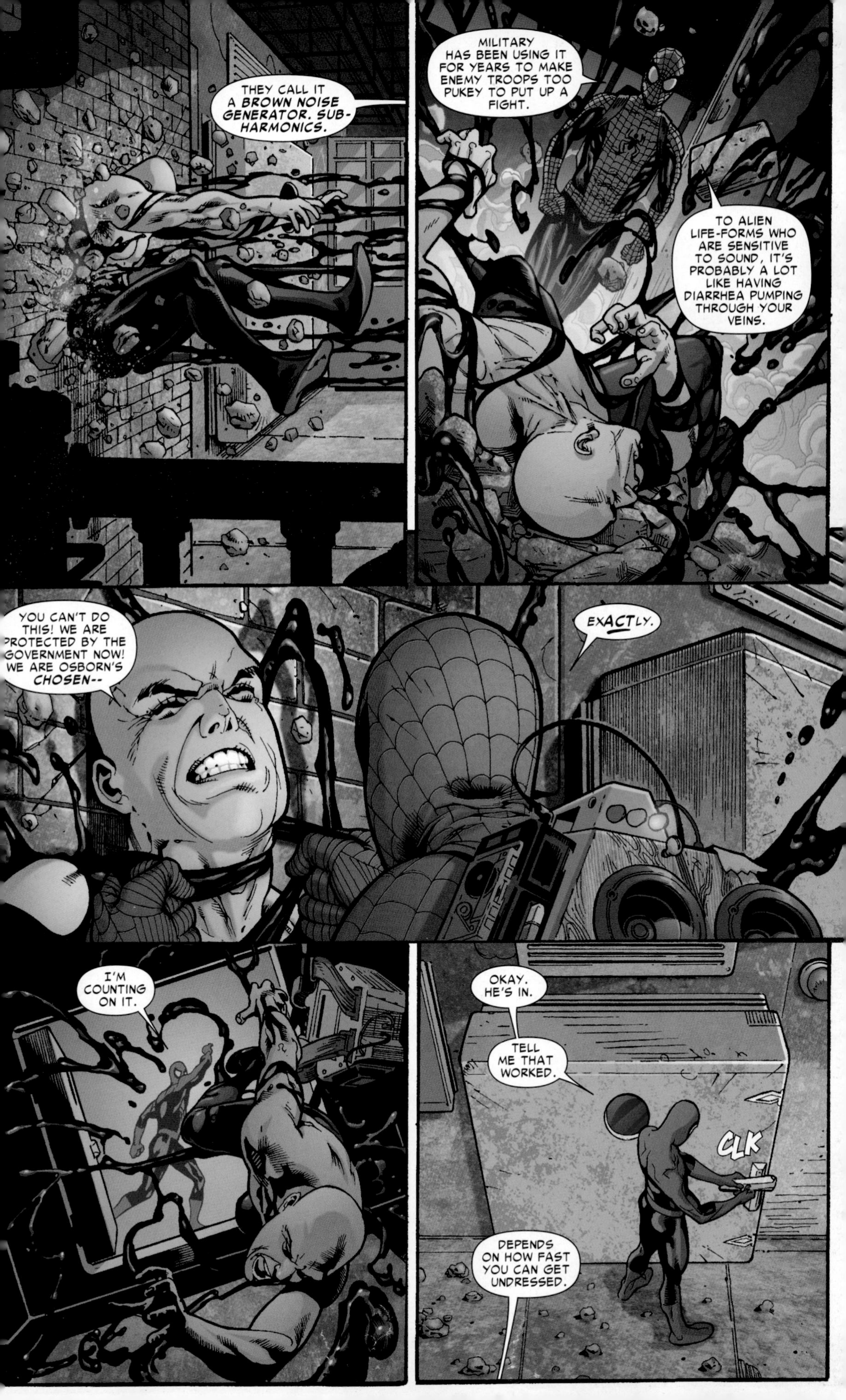
THEY CALL IT A BROWN NOISE GENERATOR. SUB-HARMONICS.
MILITARY HAS BEEN USING IT FOR YEARS TO MAKE ENEMY TROOPS TOO PUKEY TO PUT UP A FIGHT.
TO ALIEN LIFE-FORMS WHO ARE SENSITIVE TO SOUND, IT'S PROBABLY A LOT LIKE HAVING DIARRHEA PUMPING THROUGH YOUR VEINS.
YOU CAN'T DO THIS! WE ARE PROTECTED BY THE GOVERNMENT NOW! WE ARE OSBORN'S CHOSEN--
EXACTLY.
I'M COUNTING ON IT.
OKAY. HE'S IN.
TELL ME THAT WORKED.
CLK
DEPENDS ON HOW FAST YOU CAN GET UNDRESSED.

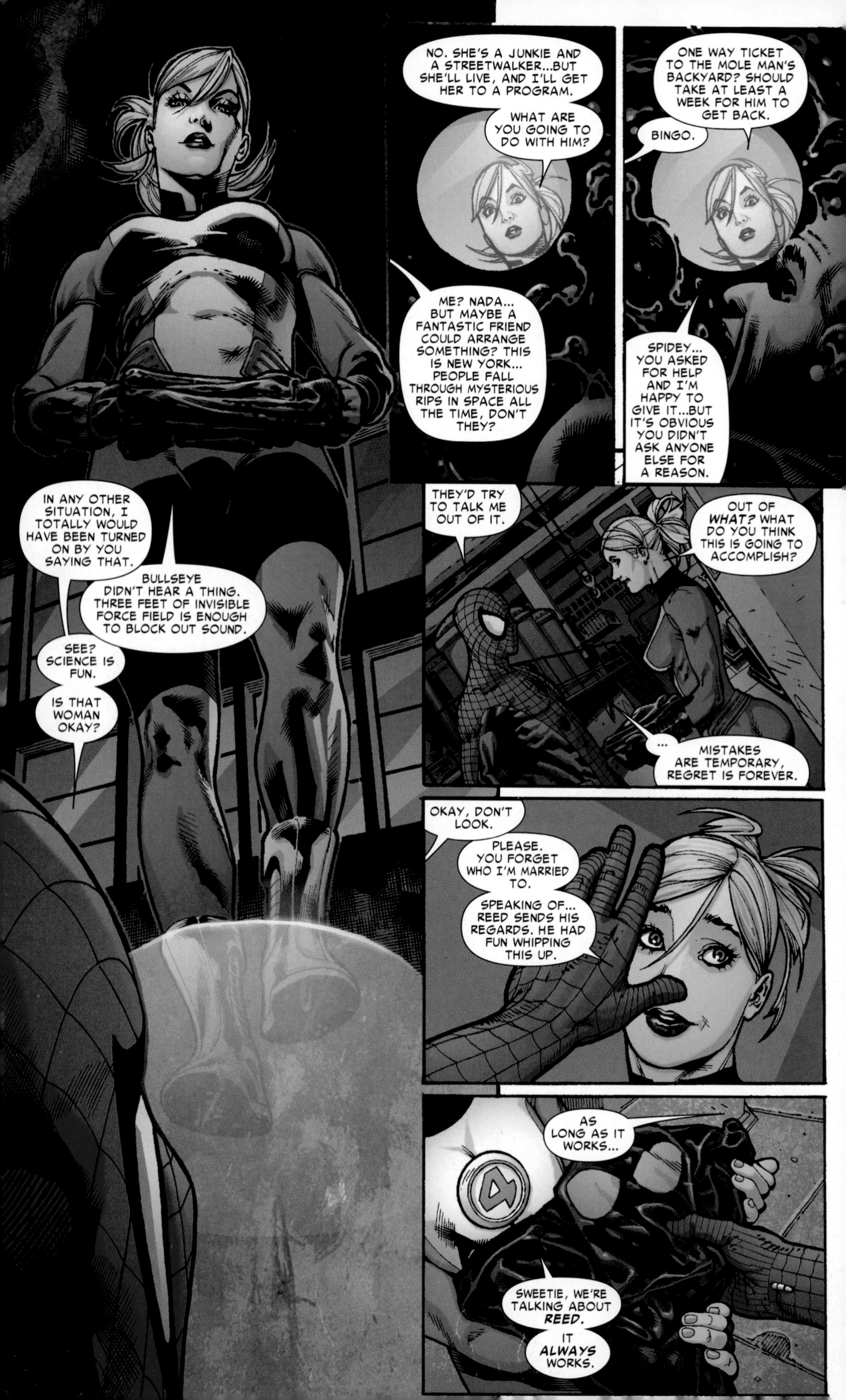
NO. SHE'S A JUNKIE AND A STREETWALKER...BUT SHE'LL LIVE, AND I'LL GET HER TO A PROGRAM.
WHAT ARE YOU GOING TO DO WITH HIM?
ME? NADA... BUT MAYBE A FANTASTIC FRIEND COULD ARRANGE SOMETHING? THIS IS NEW YORK... PEOPLE FALL THROUGH MYSTERIOUS RIPS IN SPACE ALL THE TIME, DON'T THEY?
ONE WAY TICKET TO THE MOLE MAN'S BACKYARD? SHOULD TAKE AT LEAST A WEEK FOR HIM TO GET BACK.
BINGO.
SPIDEY... YOU ASKED FOR HELP AND I'M HAPPY TO GIVE IT...BUT IT'S OBVIOUS YOU DIDN'T ASK ANYONE ELSE FOR A REASON.
IS THAT WOMAN OKAY?
IN ANY OTHER SITUATION, I TOTALLY WOULD HAVE BEEN TURNED ON BY YOU SAYING THAT.
BULLSEYE DIDN'T HEAR A THING. THREE FEET OF INVISIBLE FORCE FIELD IS ENOUGH TO BLOCK OUT SOUND.
SEE? SCIENCE IS FUN.
THEY'D TRY TO TALK ME OUT OF IT.
OUT OF *WHAT?* WHAT DO YOU THINK THIS IS GOING TO ACCOMPLISH?
...
MISTAKES ARE TEMPORARY, REGRET IS FOREVER.
OKAY, DON'T LOOK.
PLEASE. YOU FORGET WHO I'M MARRIED TO.
SPEAKING OF... REED SENDS HIS REGARDS. HE HAD FUN WHIPPING THIS UP.
AS LONG AS IT WORKS...
SWEETIE, WE'RE TALKING ABOUT *REED.*
IT *ALWAYS* WORKS.

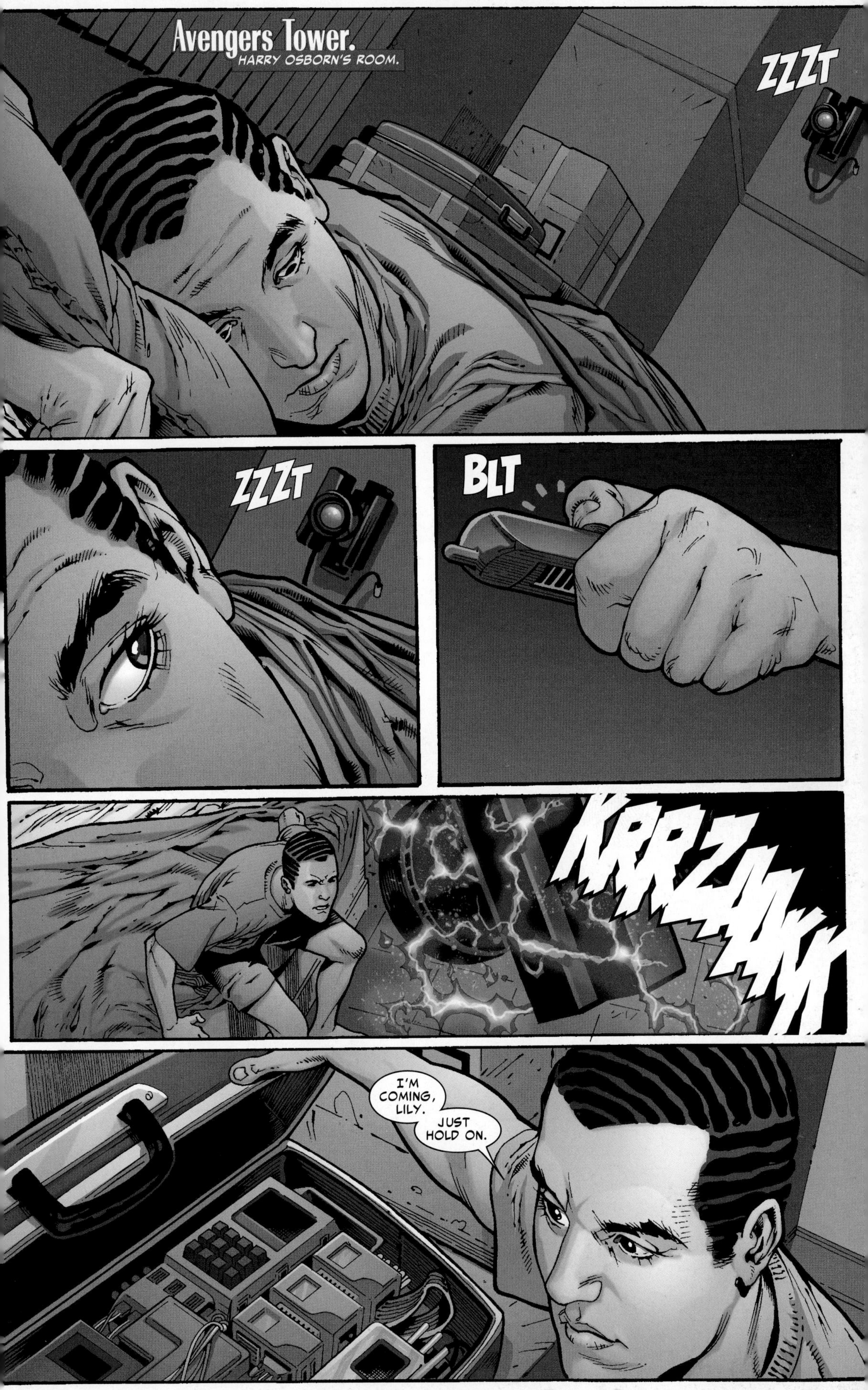
Avengers Tower.
HARRY OSBORN'S ROOM.
ZZZT
ZZZT
BLT
KRRZAKK
I'M COMING, LILY.
JUST HOLD ON.

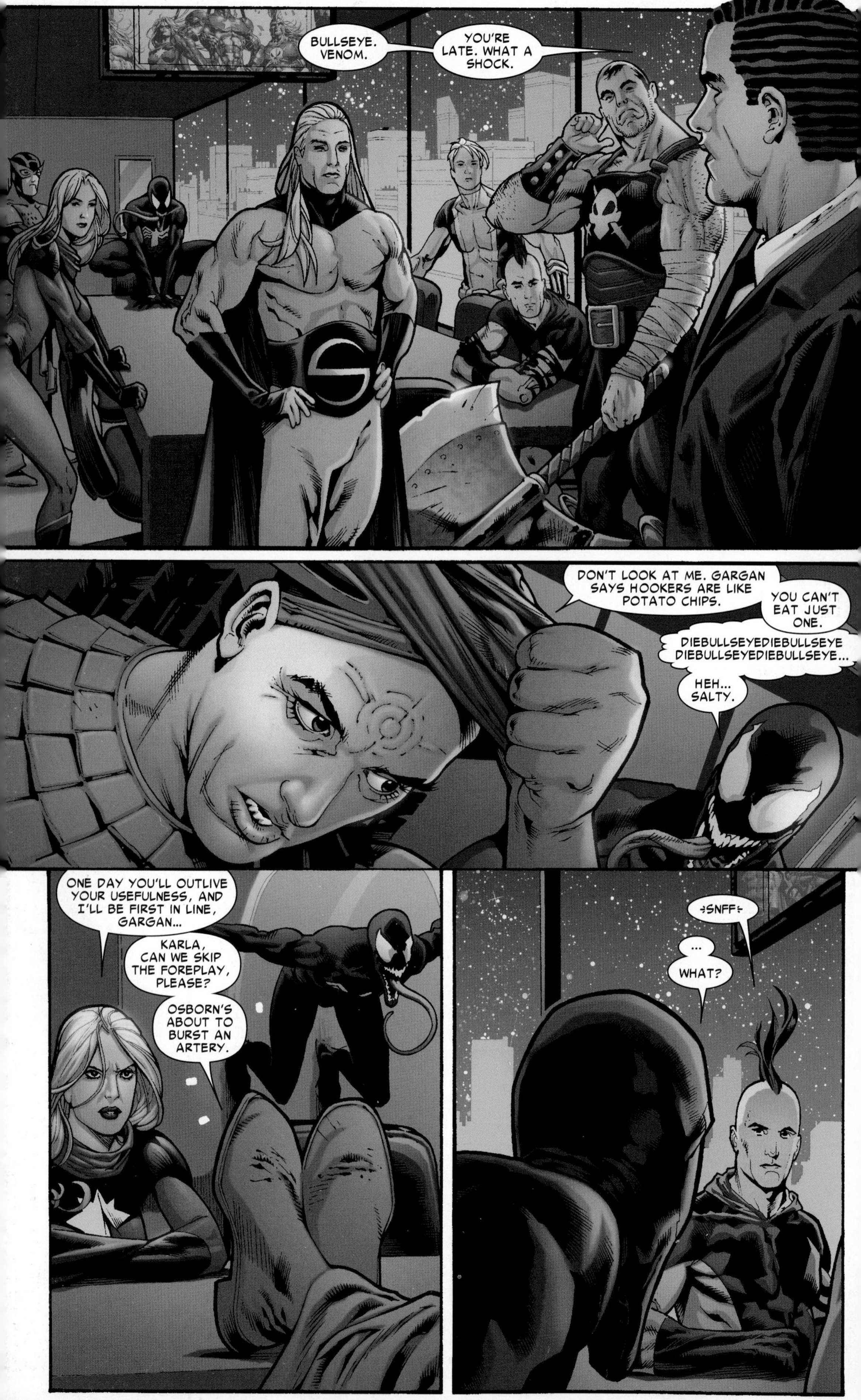
BULLSEYE. VENOM.
YOU'RE LATE. WHAT A SHOCK.
DON'T LOOK AT ME. GARGAN SAYS HOOKERS ARE LIKE POTATO CHIPS.
YOU CAN'T EAT JUST ONE.
DIEBULLSEYEDIEBULLSEYE DIEBULLSEYEDIEBULLSEYE...
HEH... SALTY.
ONE DAY YOU'LL OUTLIVE YOUR USEFULNESS, AND I'LL BE FIRST IN LINE, GARGAN...
KARLA, CAN WE SKIP THE FOREPLAY, PLEASE?
OSBORN'S ABOUT TO BURST AN ARTERY.
SNFF
...
WHAT?

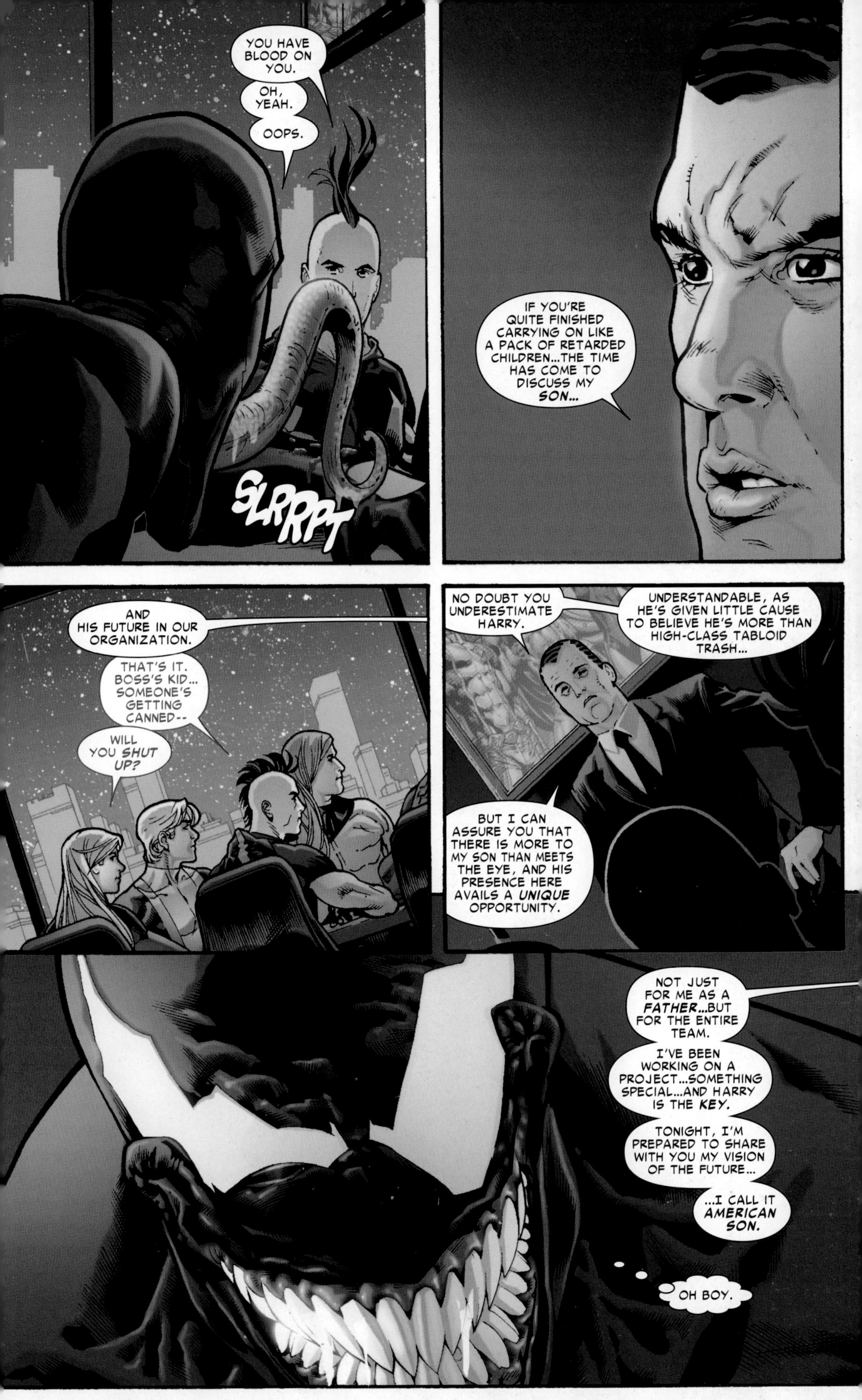
YOU HAVE BLOOD ON YOU.
OH, YEAH.
OOPS.
SLRRPT
IF YOU'RE QUITE FINISHED CARRYING ON LIKE A PACK OF RETARDED CHILDREN...THE TIME HAS COME TO DISCUSS MY SON...
AND HIS FUTURE IN OUR ORGANIZATION.
THAT'S IT. BOSS'S KID... SOMEONE'S GETTING CANNED--
WILL YOU SHUT UP?
NO DOUBT YOU UNDERESTIMATE HARRY.
UNDERSTANDABLE, AS HE'S GIVEN LITTLE CAUSE TO BELIEVE HE'S MORE THAN HIGH-CLASS TABLOID TRASH...
BUT I CAN ASSURE YOU THAT THERE IS MORE TO MY SON THAN MEETS THE EYE, AND HIS PRESENCE HERE AVAILS A UNIQUE OPPORTUNITY.
NOT JUST FOR ME AS A FATHER...BUT FOR THE ENTIRE TEAM.
I'VE BEEN WORKING ON A PROJECT...SOMETHING SPECIAL...AND HARRY IS THE KEY.
TONIGHT, I'M PREPARED TO SHARE WITH YOU MY VISION OF THE FUTURE...
...I CALL IT AMERICAN SON.
OH BOY.

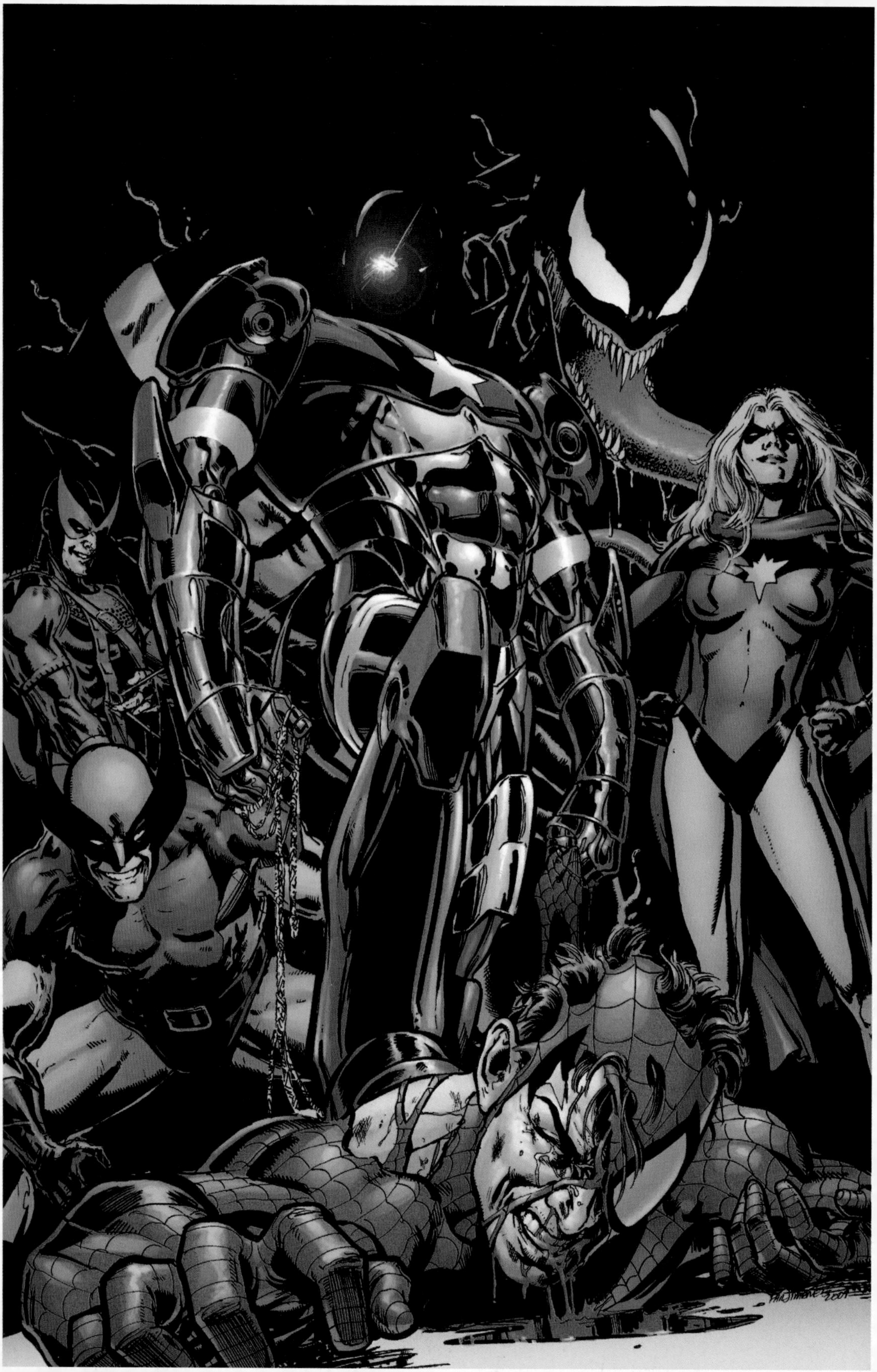

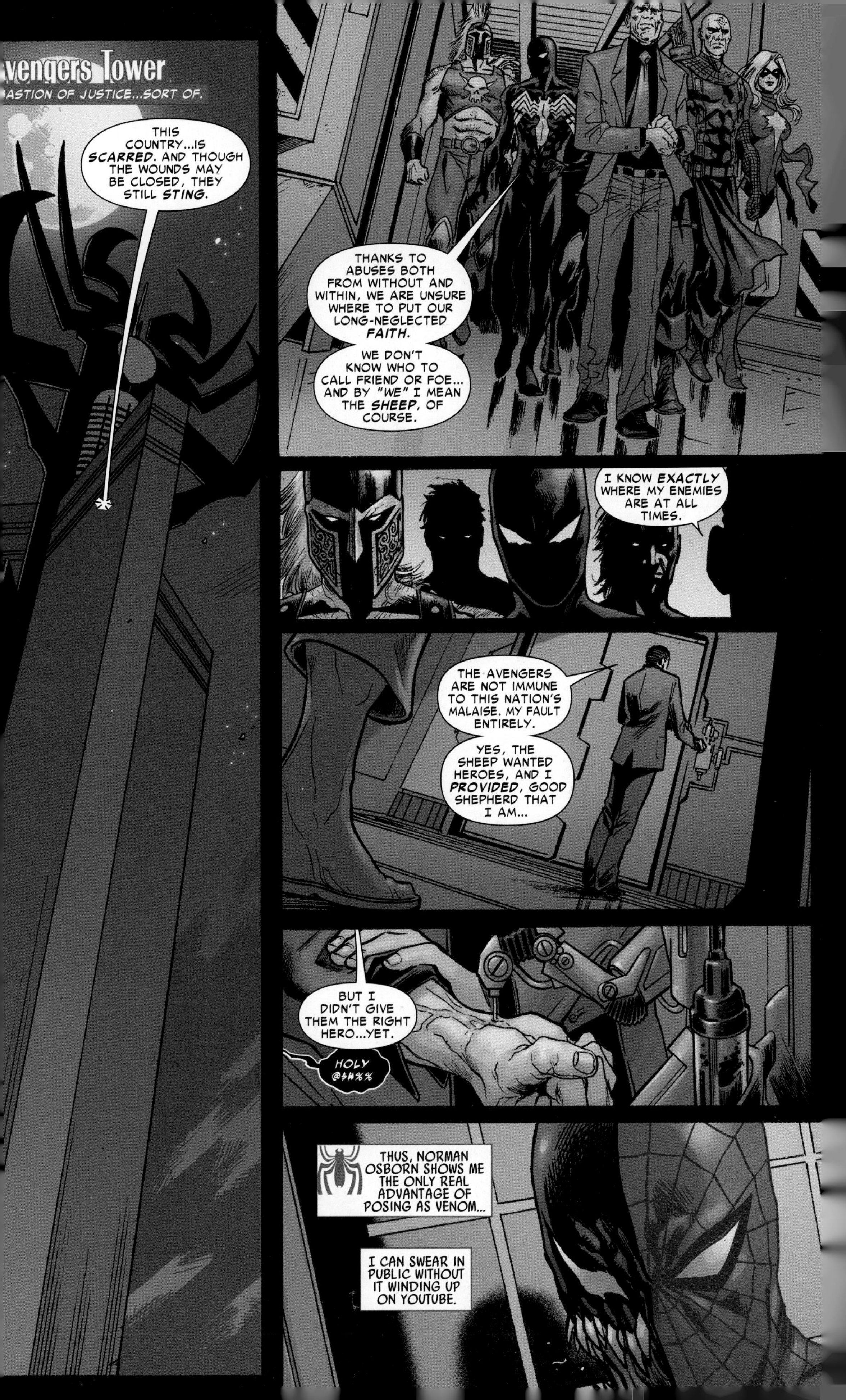
vengers Tower
ASTION OF JUSTICE...SORT OF.
THIS COUNTRY...IS SCARRED. AND THOUGH THE WOUNDS MAY BE CLOSED, THEY STILL STING.
THANKS TO ABUSES BOTH FROM WITHOUT AND WITHIN, WE ARE UNSURE WHERE TO PUT OUR LONG-NEGLECTED FAITH.
WE DON'T KNOW WHO TO CALL FRIEND OR FOE... AND BY "WE" I MEAN THE SHEEP, OF COURSE.
I KNOW EXACTLY WHERE MY ENEMIES ARE AT ALL TIMES.
THE AVENGERS ARE NOT IMMUNE TO THIS NATION'S MALAISE. MY FAULT ENTIRELY.
YES, THE SHEEP WANTED HEROES, AND I PROVIDED, GOOD SHEPHERD THAT I AM...
BUT I DIDN'T GIVE THEM THE RIGHT HERO...YET.
HOLY @$#%%
THUS, NORMAN OSBORN SHOWS ME THE ONLY REAL ADVANTAGE OF POSING AS VENOM...
I CAN SWEAR IN PUBLIC WITHOUT IT WINDING UP ON YOUTUBE.

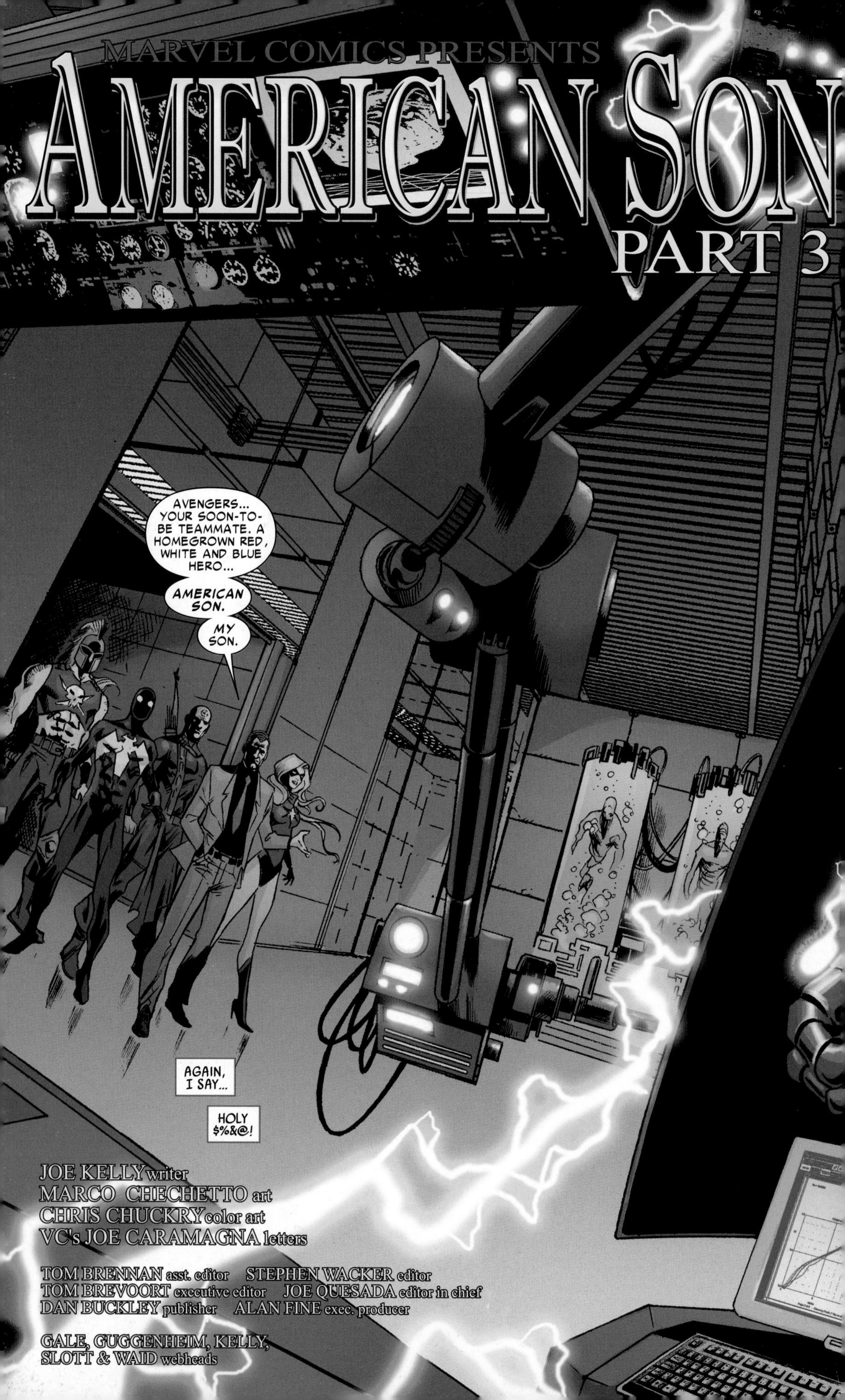
MARVEL COMICS PRESENTS
AMERICAN SON
PART 3
AVENGERS... YOUR SOON-TO-BE TEAMMATE. A HOMEGROWN RED, WHITE AND BLUE HERO...
AMERICAN SON.
MY SON.
AGAIN, I SAY...
HOLY $%&@!
JOE KELLY writer
MARCO CHECHETTO art
CHRIS CHUCKRY color art
VC's JOE CARAMAGNA letters
TOM BRENNAN asst. editor STEPHEN WACKER editor
TOM BREVOORT executive editor JOE QUESADA editor in chief
DAN BUCKLEY publisher ALAN FINE exec. producer
GALE, GUGGENHEIM, KELLY, SLOTT & WAID webheads

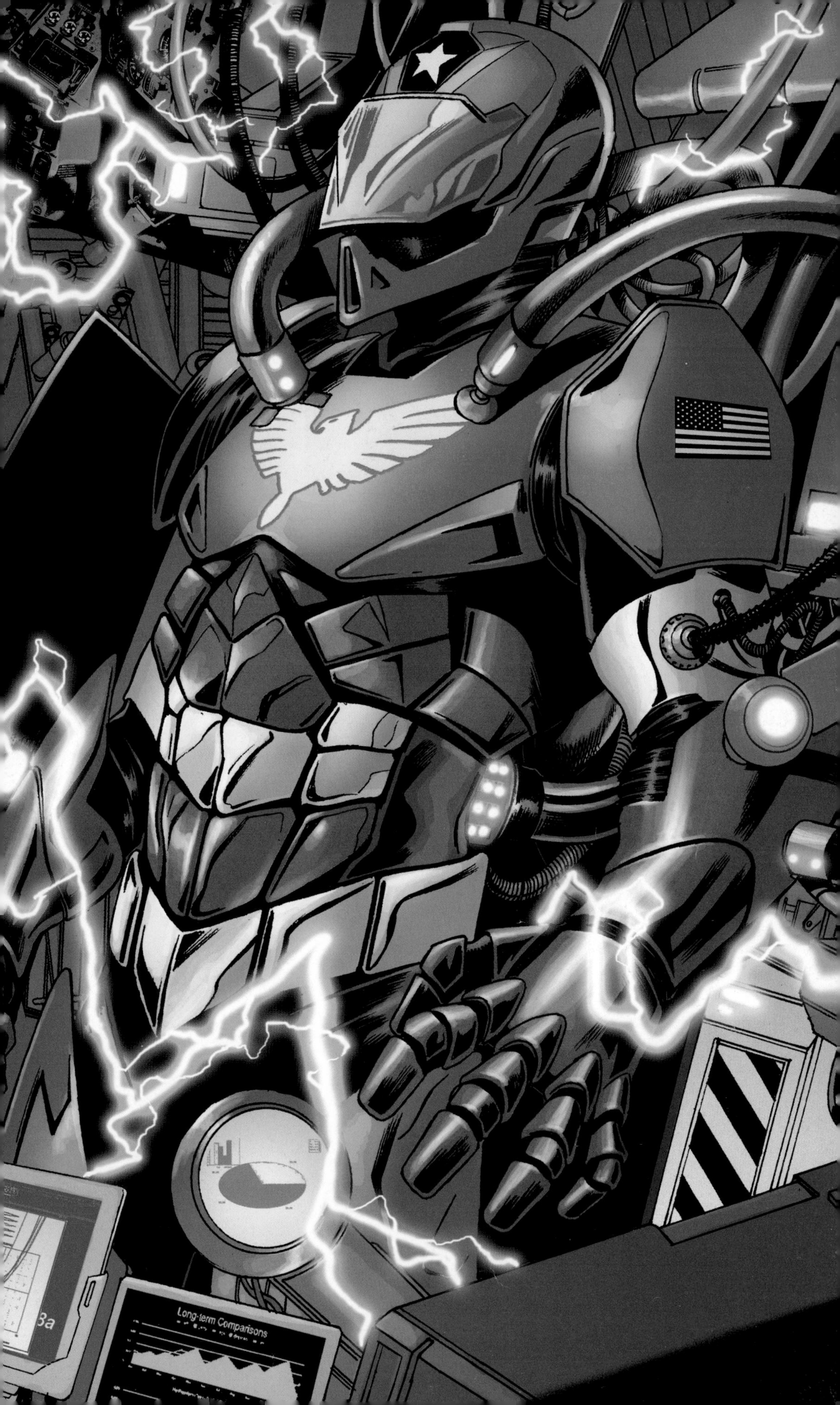
3a
Long-term Comparisons

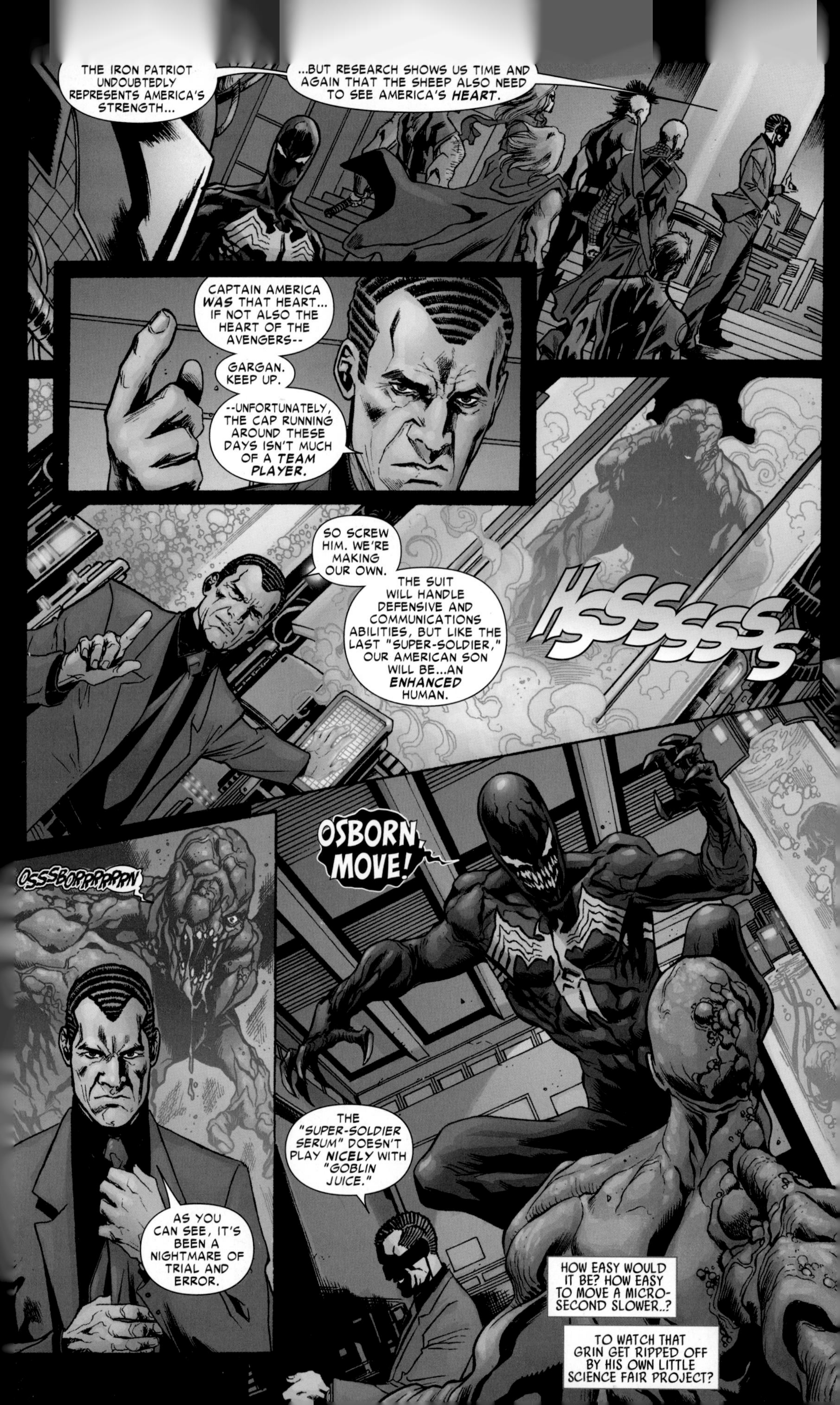
THE IRON PATRIOT UNDOUBTEDLY REPRESENTS AMERICA'S STRENGTH...
...BUT RESEARCH SHOWS US TIME AND AGAIN THAT THE SHEEP ALSO NEED TO SEE AMERICA'S HEART.
CAPTAIN AMERICA WAS THAT HEART... IF NOT ALSO THE HEART OF THE AVENGERS--
GARGAN. KEEP UP.
--UNFORTUNATELY, THE CAP RUNNING AROUND THESE DAYS ISN'T MUCH OF A TEAM PLAYER.
SO SCREW HIM. WE'RE MAKING OUR OWN.
THE SUIT WILL HANDLE DEFENSIVE AND COMMUNICATIONS ABILITIES, BUT LIKE THE LAST "SUPER-SOLDIER," OUR AMERICAN SON WILL BE...AN ENHANCED HUMAN.
HSSSSSSS
OSBORN, MOVE!
OSSSBORRRRRRN
THE "SUPER-SOLDIER SERUM" DOESN'T PLAY NICELY WITH "GOBLIN JUICE."
AS YOU CAN SEE, IT'S BEEN A NIGHTMARE OF TRIAL AND ERROR.
HOW EASY WOULD IT BE? HOW EASY TO MOVE A MICRO-SECOND SLOWER..?
TO WATCH THAT GRIN GET RIPPED OFF BY HIS OWN LITTLE SCIENCE FAIR PROJECT?

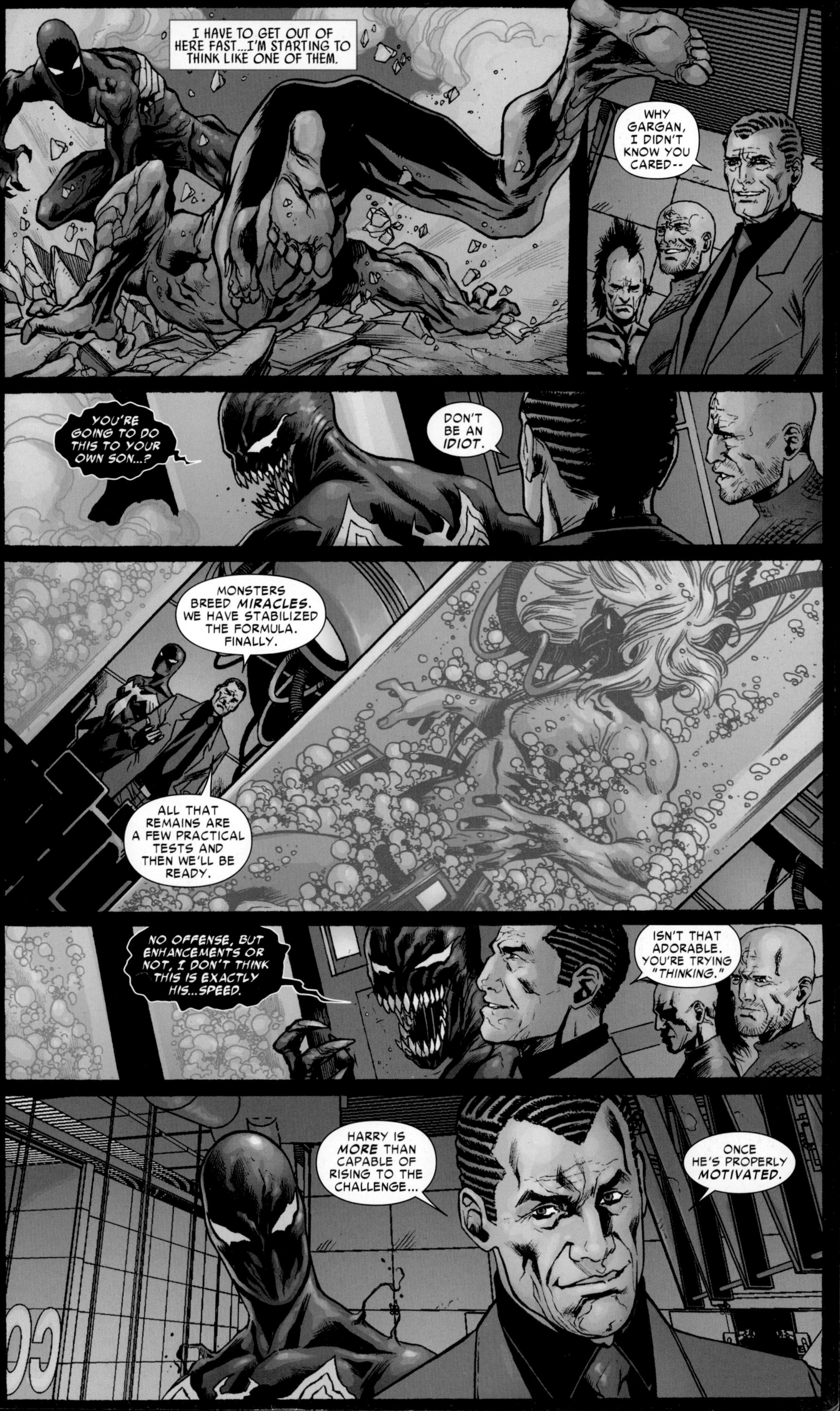
I HAVE TO GET OUT OF HERE FAST...I'M STARTING TO THINK LIKE ONE OF THEM.
WHY GARGAN, I DIDN'T KNOW YOU CARED--
YOU'RE GOING TO DO THIS TO YOUR OWN SON...?
DON'T BE AN IDIOT.
MONSTERS BREED MIRACLES. WE HAVE STABILIZED THE FORMULA. FINALLY.
ALL THAT REMAINS ARE A FEW PRACTICAL TESTS AND THEN WE'LL BE READY.
NO OFFENSE, BUT ENHANCEMENTS OR NOT, I DON'T THINK THIS IS EXACTLY HIS...SPEED.
ISN'T THAT ADORABLE. YOU'RE TRYING "THINKING."
HARRY IS MORE THAN CAPABLE OF RISING TO THE CHALLENGE...
ONCE HE'S PROPERLY MOTIVATED.

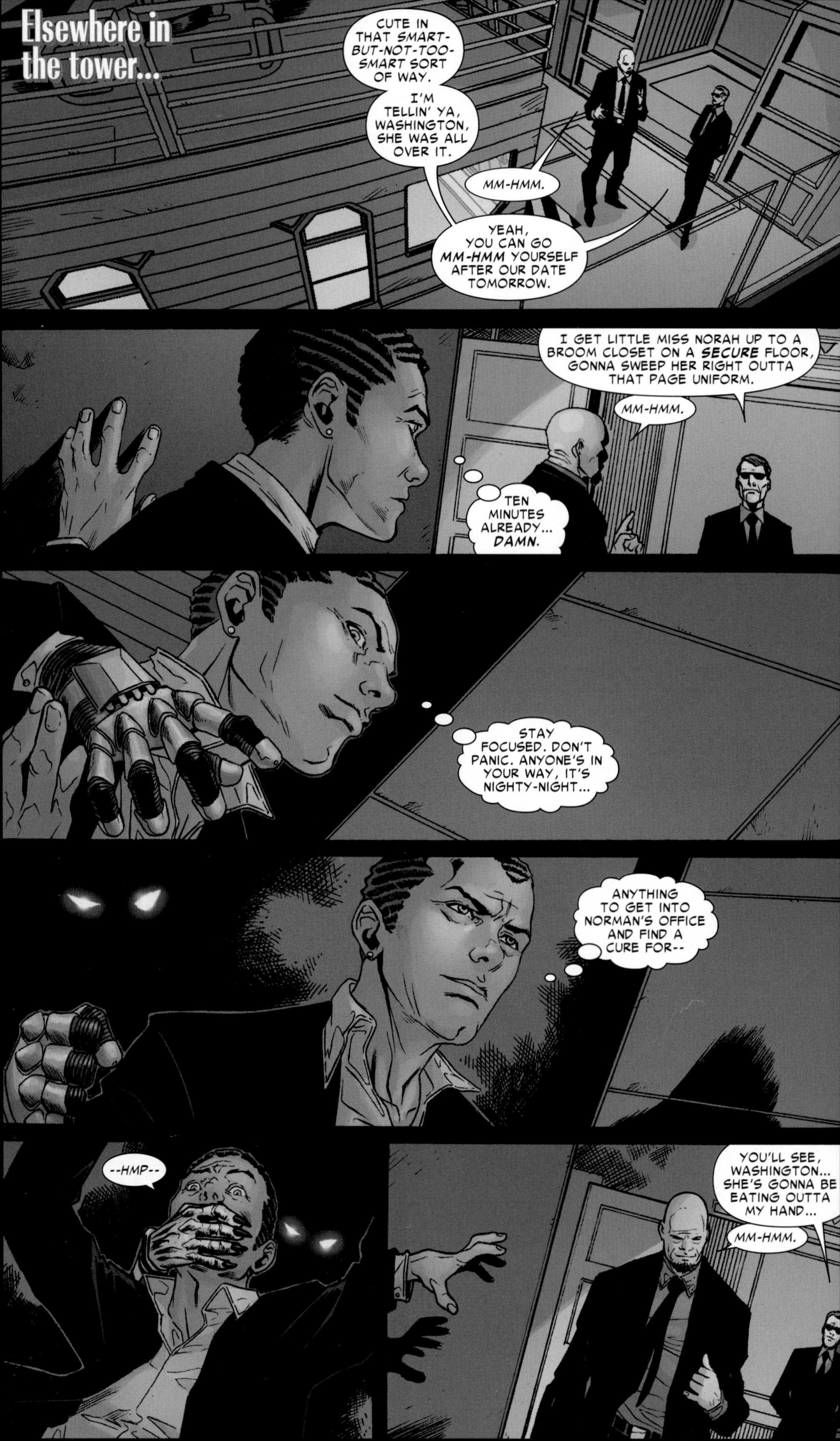
Elsewhere in the tower...
CUTE IN THAT SMART-BUT-NOT-TOO-SMART SORT OF WAY.
I'M TELLIN' YA, WASHINGTON, SHE WAS ALL OVER IT.
MM-HMM.
YEAH, YOU CAN GO MM-HMM YOURSELF AFTER OUR DATE TOMORROW.
I GET LITTLE MISS NORAH UP TO A BROOM CLOSET ON A SECURE FLOOR, GONNA SWEEP HER RIGHT OUTTA THAT PAGE UNIFORM.
MM-HMM.
TEN MINUTES ALREADY... DAMN.
STAY FOCUSED. DON'T PANIC. ANYONE'S IN YOUR WAY, IT'S NIGHTY-NIGHT...
ANYTHING TO GET INTO NORMAN'S OFFICE AND FIND A CURE FOR--
--HMP--
YOU'LL SEE, WASHINGTON... SHE'S GONNA BE EATING OUTTA MY HAND...
MM-HMM.

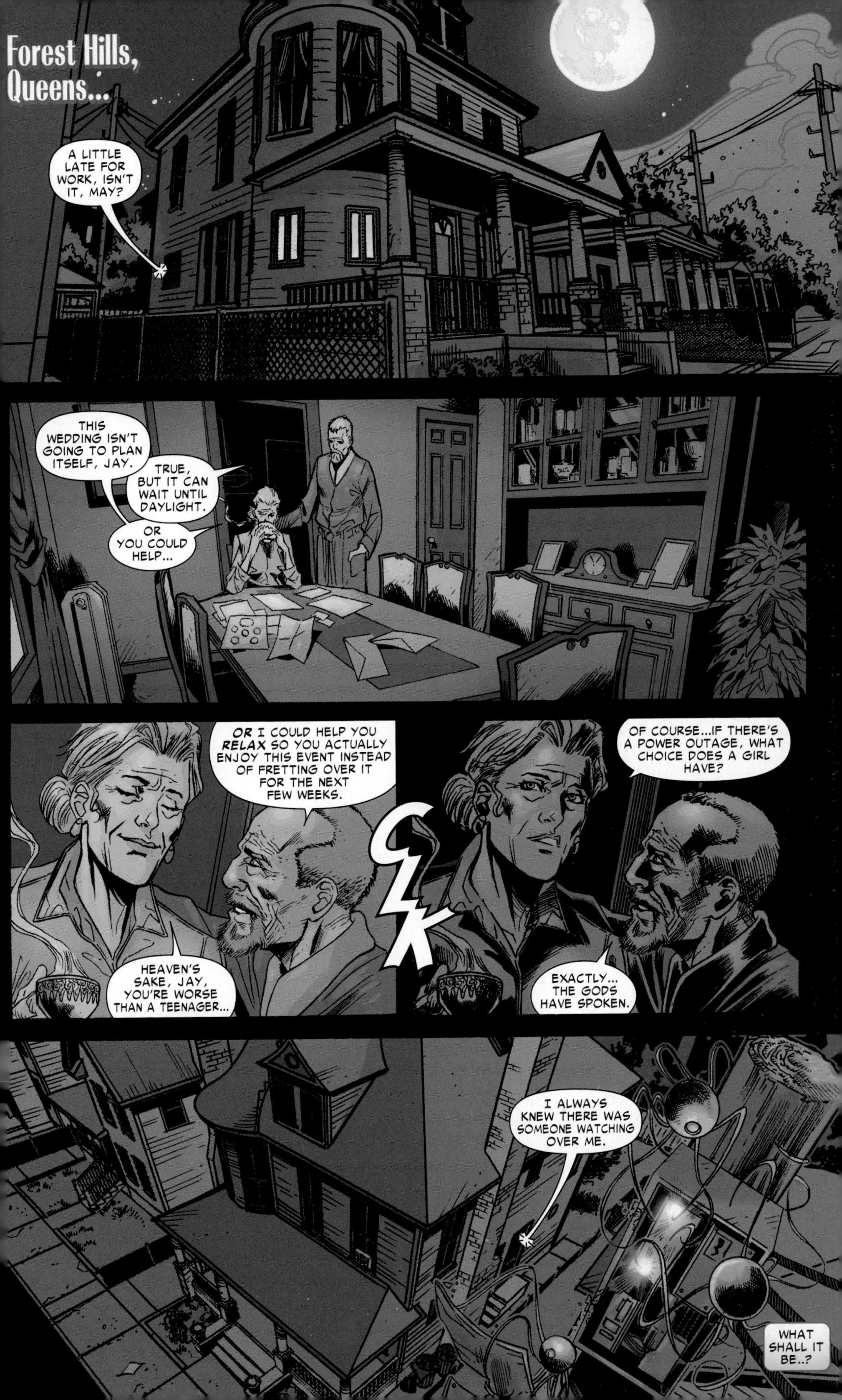
Forest Hills, Queens...
A LITTLE LATE FOR WORK, ISN'T IT, MAY?
THIS WEDDING ISN'T GOING TO PLAN ITSELF, JAY.
TRUE, BUT IT CAN WAIT UNTIL DAYLIGHT.
OR YOU COULD HELP...
OR I COULD HELP YOU RELAX SO YOU ACTUALLY ENJOY THIS EVENT INSTEAD OF FRETTING OVER IT FOR THE NEXT FEW WEEKS.
HEAVEN'S SAKE, JAY, YOU'RE WORSE THAN A TEENAGER...
CLK
OF COURSE...IF THERE'S A POWER OUTAGE, WHAT CHOICE DOES A GIRL HAVE?
EXACTLY... THE GODS HAVE SPOKEN.
I ALWAYS KNEW THERE WAS SOMEONE WATCHING OVER ME.
WHAT SHALL IT BE..?

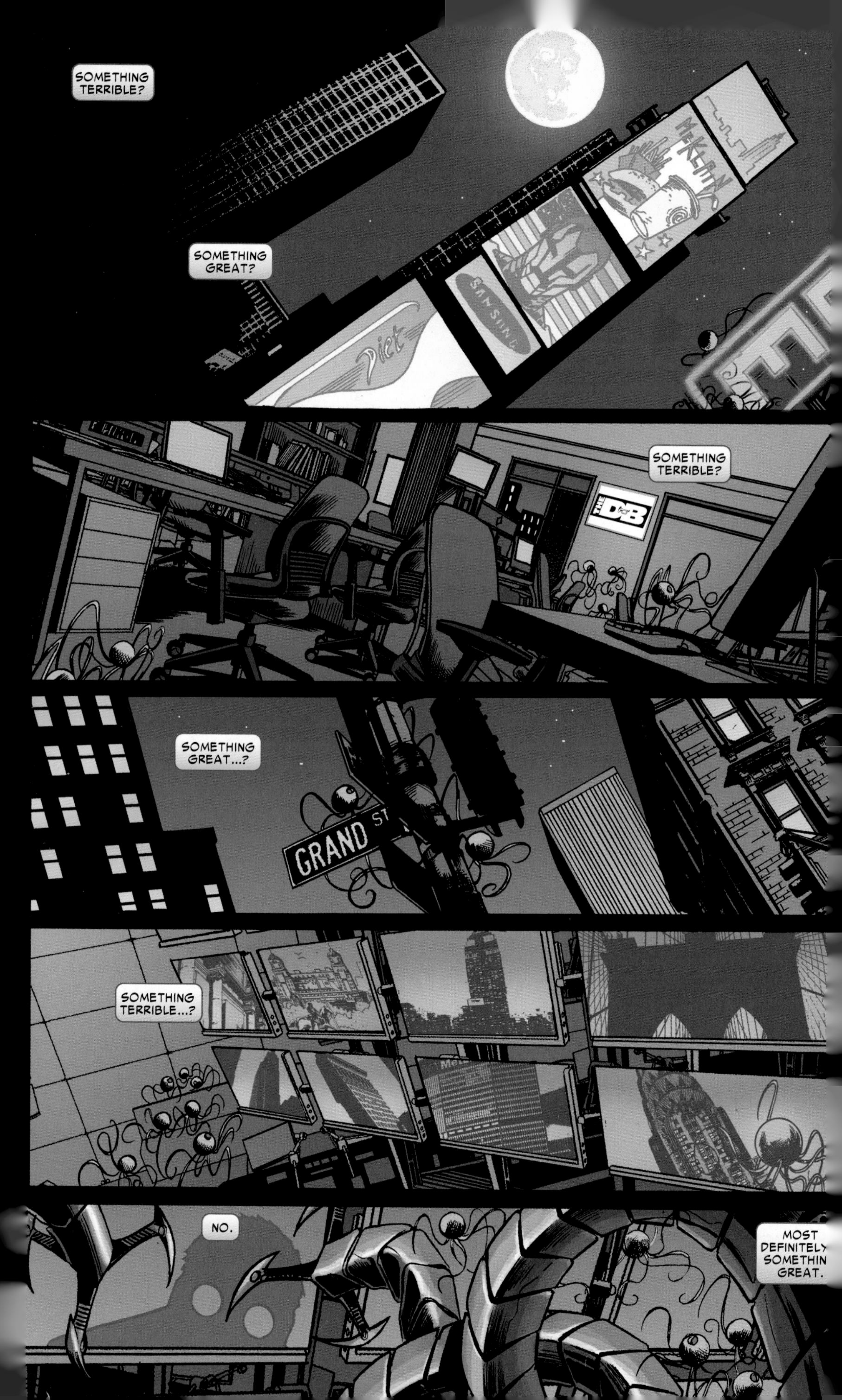
SOMETHING TERRIBLE?
SOMETHING GREAT?
SAMSUNG
Diet
SOMETHING TERRIBLE?
SOMETHING GREAT...?
GRAND ST
SOMETHING TERRIBLE...?
NO.
MOST DEFINITELY SOMETHIN GREAT.

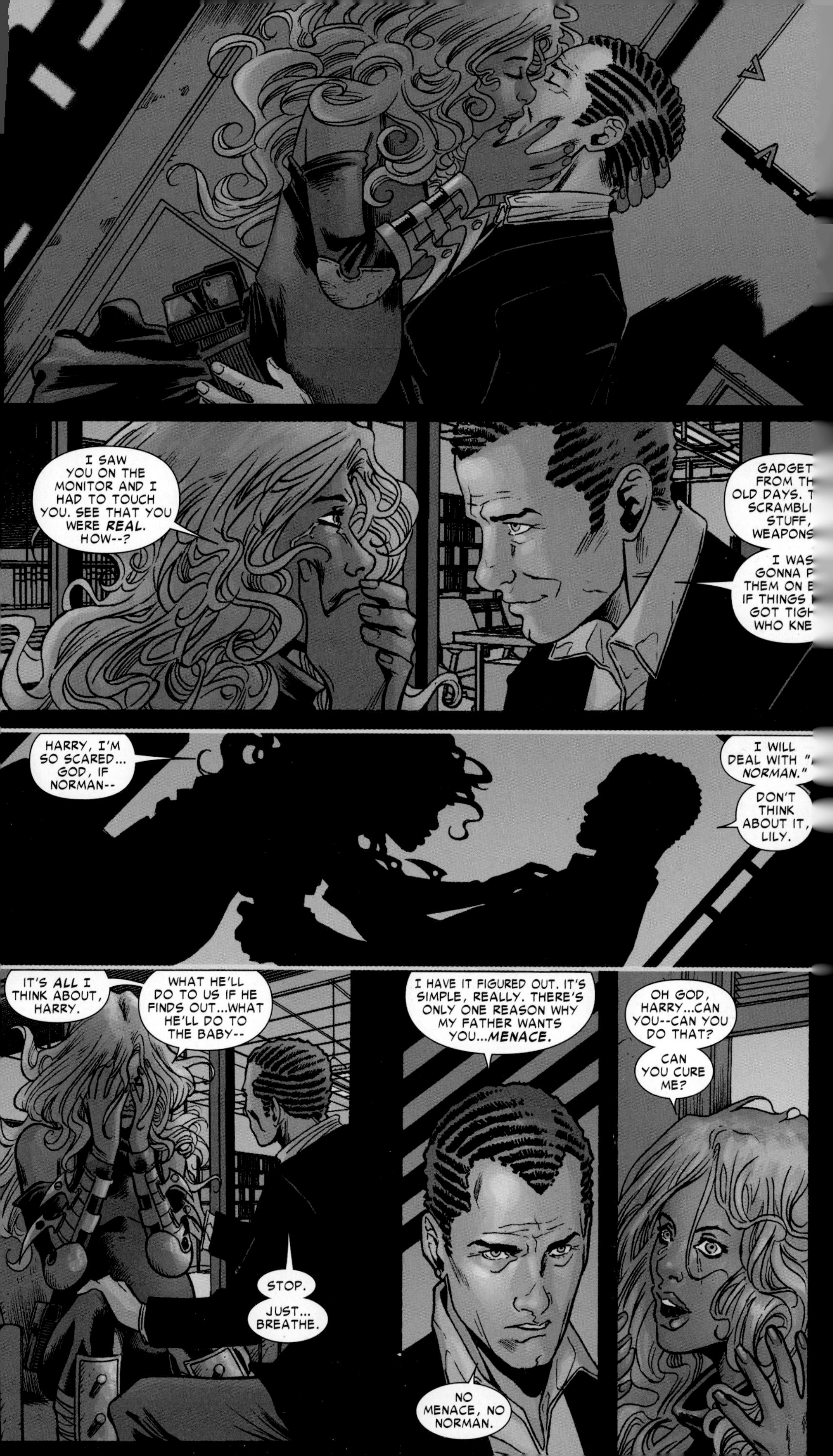

I SAW YOU ON THE MONITOR AND I HAD TO TOUCH YOU. SEE THAT YOU WERE *REAL*. HOW--?
GADGET FROM TH OLD DAYS. T SCRAMBLI STUFF, WEAPONS
I WAS GONNA P THEM ON E IF THINGS GOT TIGH WHO KNE
HARRY, I'M SO SCARED... GOD, IF NORMAN--
I WILL DEAL WITH "*NORMAN*."
DON'T THINK ABOUT IT, LILY.
IT'S *ALL* I THINK ABOUT, HARRY.
WHAT HE'LL DO TO US IF HE FINDS OUT...WHAT HE'LL DO TO THE BABY--
STOP.
JUST... BREATHE.
I HAVE IT FIGURED OUT. IT'S SIMPLE, REALLY. THERE'S ONLY ONE REASON WHY MY FATHER WANTS YOU...*MENACE.*
NO MENACE, NO NORMAN.
OH GOD, HARRY...CAN YOU--CAN YOU DO THAT?
CAN YOU CURE ME?

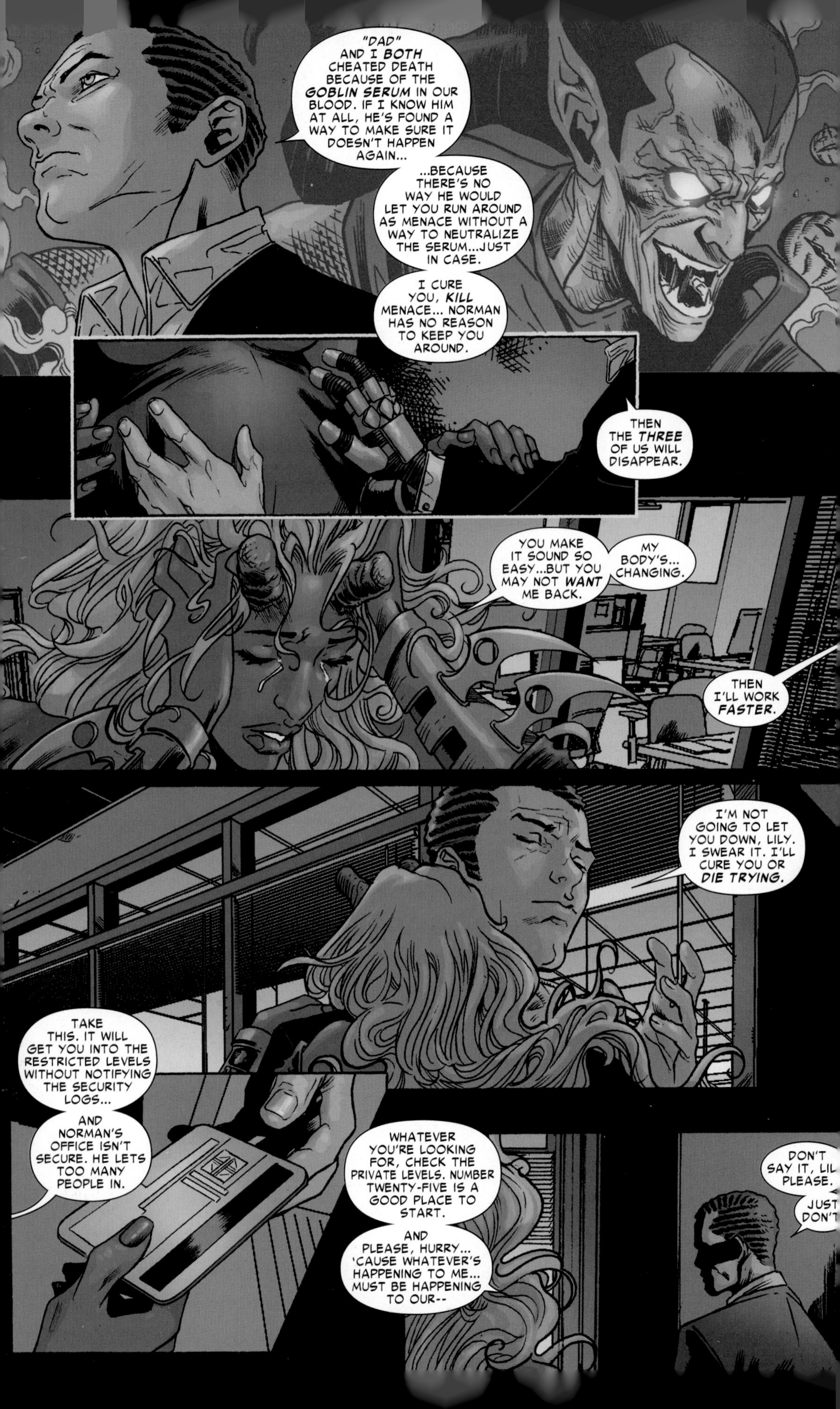
"DAD" AND I BOTH CHEATED DEATH BECAUSE OF THE GOBLIN SERUM IN OUR BLOOD. IF I KNOW HIM AT ALL, HE'S FOUND A WAY TO MAKE SURE IT DOESN'T HAPPEN AGAIN...
...BECAUSE THERE'S NO WAY HE WOULD LET YOU RUN AROUND AS MENACE WITHOUT A WAY TO NEUTRALIZE THE SERUM...JUST IN CASE.
I CURE YOU, KILL MENACE... NORMAN HAS NO REASON TO KEEP YOU AROUND.
THEN THE THREE OF US WILL DISAPPEAR.
YOU MAKE IT SOUND SO EASY...BUT YOU MAY NOT WANT ME BACK.
MY BODY'S... CHANGING.
THEN I'LL WORK FASTER.
I'M NOT GOING TO LET YOU DOWN, LILY. I SWEAR IT. I'LL CURE YOU OR DIE TRYING.
TAKE THIS. IT WILL GET YOU INTO THE RESTRICTED LEVELS WITHOUT NOTIFYING THE SECURITY LOGS...
AND NORMAN'S OFFICE ISN'T SECURE. HE LETS TOO MANY PEOPLE IN.
WHATEVER YOU'RE LOOKING FOR, CHECK THE PRIVATE LEVELS. NUMBER TWENTY-FIVE IS A GOOD PLACE TO START.
AND PLEASE, HURRY... 'CAUSE WHATEVER'S HAPPENING TO ME... MUST BE HAPPENING TO OUR--

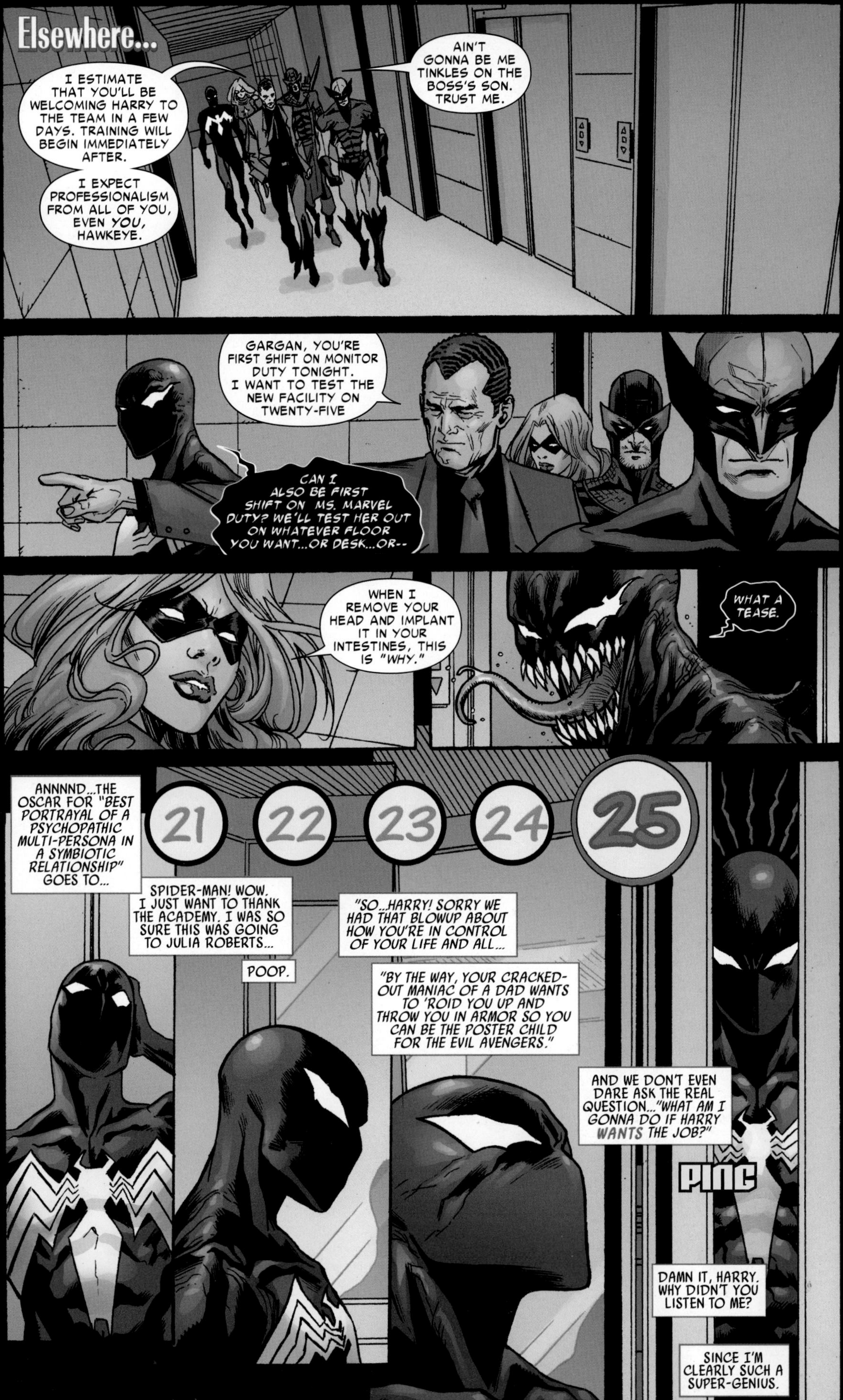

Elsewhere...
I ESTIMATE THAT YOU'LL BE WELCOMING HARRY TO THE TEAM IN A FEW DAYS. TRAINING WILL BEGIN IMMEDIATELY AFTER.
I EXPECT PROFESSIONALISM FROM ALL OF YOU, EVEN YOU, HAWKEYE.
AIN'T GONNA BE ME TINKLES ON THE BOSS'S SON. TRUST ME.
GARGAN, YOU'RE FIRST SHIFT ON MONITOR DUTY TONIGHT. I WANT TO TEST THE NEW FACILITY ON TWENTY-FIVE
CAN I ALSO BE FIRST SHIFT ON MS. MARVEL DUTY? WE'LL TEST HER OUT ON WHATEVER FLOOR YOU WANT...OR DESK...OR--
WHEN I REMOVE YOUR HEAD AND IMPLANT IT IN YOUR INTESTINES, THIS IS "WHY."
WHAT A TEASE.
ANNNND...THE OSCAR FOR "BEST PORTRAYAL OF A PSYCHOPATHIC MULTI-PERSONA IN A SYMBIOTIC RELATIONSHIP" GOES TO...
21
22
23
24
25
SPIDER-MAN! WOW. I JUST WANT TO THANK THE ACADEMY. I WAS SO SURE THIS WAS GOING TO JULIA ROBERTS...
POOP.
"SO...HARRY! SORRY WE HAD THAT BLOWUP ABOUT HOW YOU'RE IN CONTROL OF YOUR LIFE AND ALL...
"BY THE WAY, YOUR CRACKED-OUT MANIAC OF A DAD WANTS TO 'ROID YOU UP AND THROW YOU IN ARMOR SO YOU CAN BE THE POSTER CHILD FOR THE EVIL AVENGERS."
AND WE DON'T EVEN DARE ASK THE REAL QUESTION..."WHAT AM I GONNA DO IF HARRY WANTS THE JOB?"
PING
DAMN IT, HARRY. WHY DIDN'T YOU LISTEN TO ME?
SINCE I'M CLEARLY SUCH A SUPER-GENIUS.

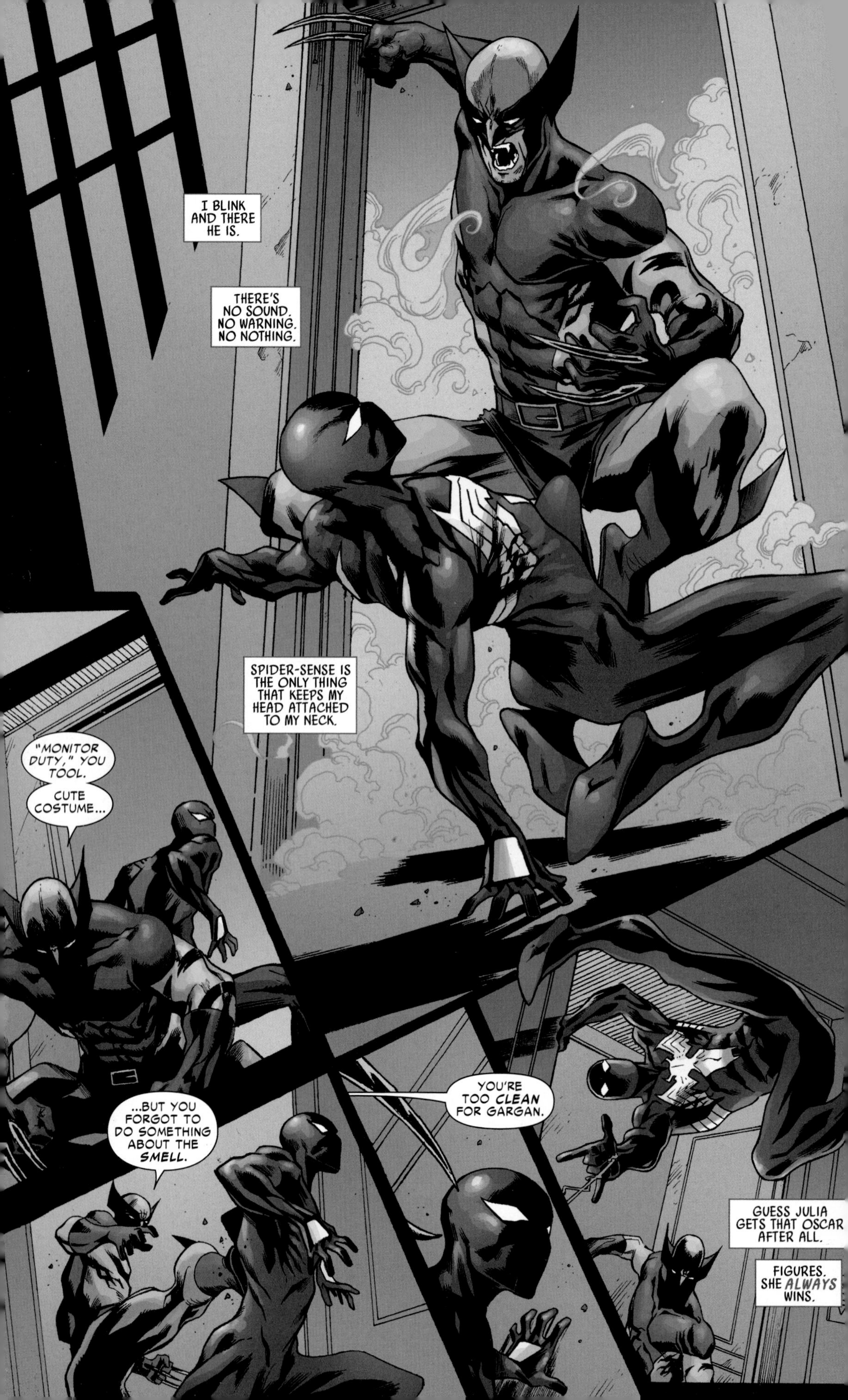
I BLINK AND THERE HE IS.
THERE'S NO SOUND. NO WARNING. NO NOTHING.
SPIDER-SENSE IS THE ONLY THING THAT KEEPS MY HEAD ATTACHED TO MY NECK.
"MONITOR DUTY," YOU TOOL.
CUTE COSTUME...
...BUT YOU FORGOT TO DO SOMETHING ABOUT THE SMELL.
YOU'RE TOO CLEAN FOR GARGAN.
GUESS JULIA GETS THAT OSCAR AFTER ALL.
FIGURES. SHE ALWAYS WINS.

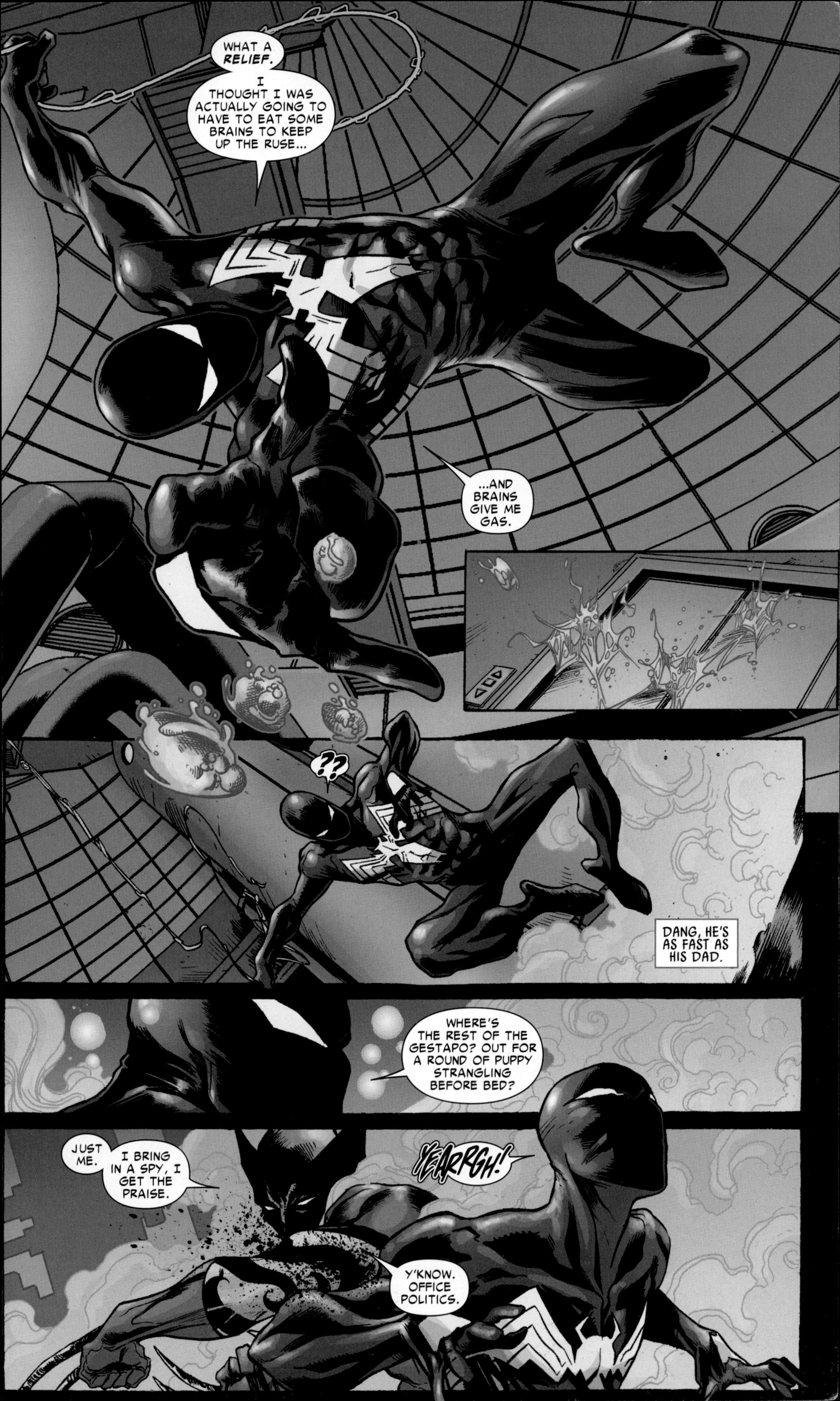
WHAT A RELIEF.
I THOUGHT I WAS ACTUALLY GOING TO HAVE TO EAT SOME BRAINS TO KEEP UP THE RUSE...
...AND BRAINS GIVE ME GAS.
??
DANG, HE'S AS FAST AS HIS DAD.
WHERE'S THE REST OF THE GESTAPO? OUT FOR A ROUND OF PUPPY STRANGLING BEFORE BED?
JUST ME.
I BRING IN A SPY, I GET THE PRAISE.
YEARRGH!
Y'KNOW. OFFICE POLITICS.

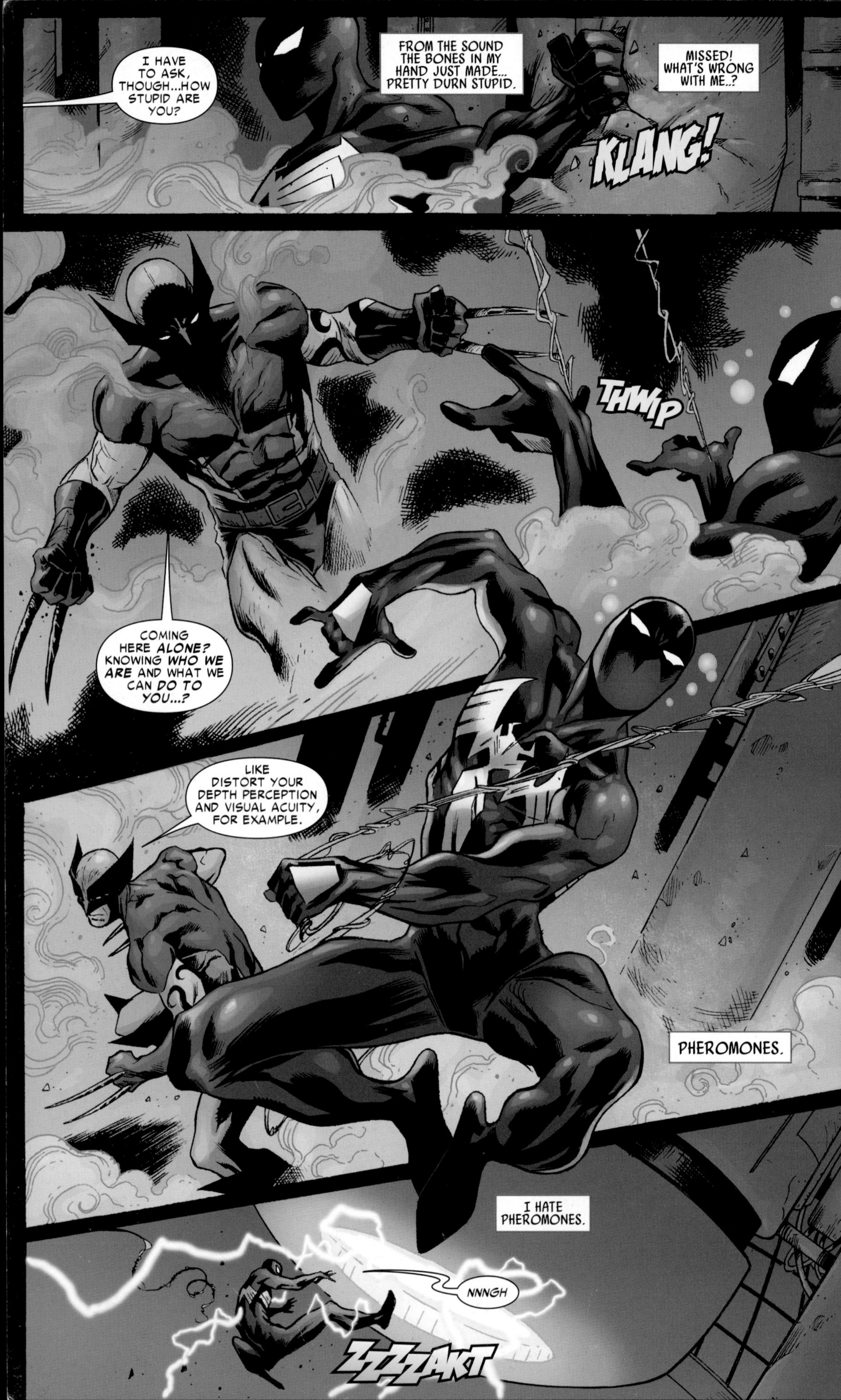
I HAVE TO ASK, THOUGH...HOW STUPID ARE YOU?
FROM THE SOUND THE BONES IN MY HAND JUST MADE... PRETTY DURN STUPID.
MISSED! WHAT'S WRONG WITH ME..?
KLANG!
THWIP
COMING HERE ALONE? KNOWING WHO WE ARE AND WHAT WE CAN DO TO YOU...?
LIKE DISTORT YOUR DEPTH PERCEPTION AND VISUAL ACUITY, FOR EXAMPLE.
PHEROMONES.
I HATE PHEROMONES.
NNNGH
ZZZZAKT

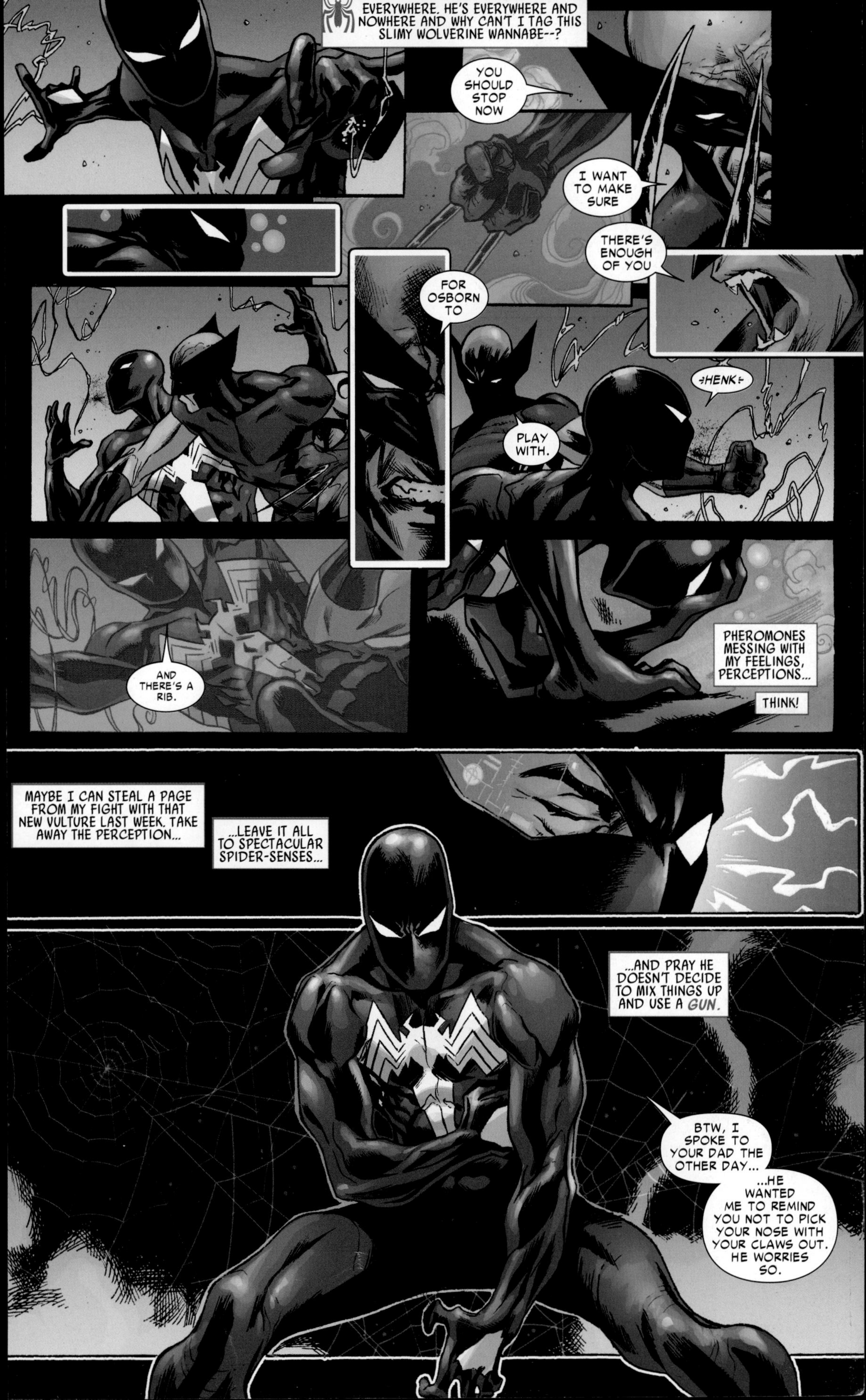
EVERYWHERE. HE'S EVERYWHERE AND NOWHERE AND WHY CAN'T I TAG THIS SLIMY WOLVERINE WANNABE--?
YOU SHOULD STOP NOW
I WANT TO MAKE SURE
THERE'S ENOUGH OF YOU
FOR OSBORN TO
PLAY WITH.
HENK
AND THERE'S A RIB.
PHEROMONES MESSING WITH MY FEELINGS, PERCEPTIONS...
THINK!
MAYBE I CAN STEAL A PAGE FROM MY FIGHT WITH THAT NEW VULTURE LAST WEEK. TAKE AWAY THE PERCEPTION...
...LEAVE IT ALL TO SPECTACULAR SPIDER-SENSES...
...AND PRAY HE DOESN'T DECIDE TO MIX THINGS UP AND USE A GUN.
BTW, I SPOKE TO YOUR DAD THE OTHER DAY...
...HE WANTED ME TO REMIND YOU NOT TO PICK YOUR NOSE WITH YOUR CLAWS OUT. HE WORRIES SO.

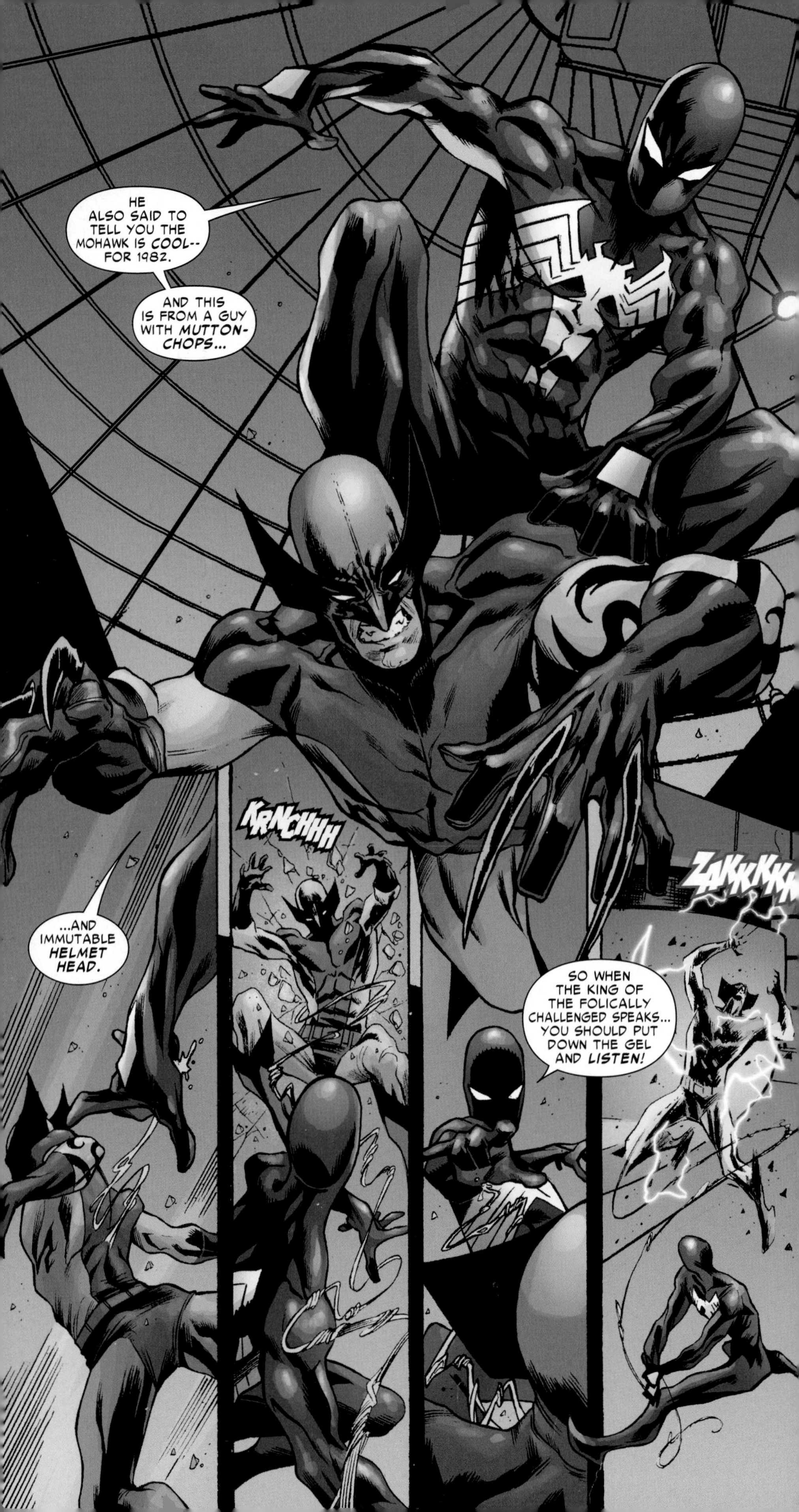
HE ALSO SAID TO TELL YOU THE MOHAWK IS COOL-- FOR 1982.
AND THIS IS FROM A GUY WITH MUTTON-CHOPS...
...AND IMMUTABLE HELMET HEAD.
KRNCHHH
SO WHEN THE KING OF THE FOLICALLY CHALLENGED SPEAKS... YOU SHOULD PUT DOWN THE GEL AND LISTEN!
ZAKKKKK

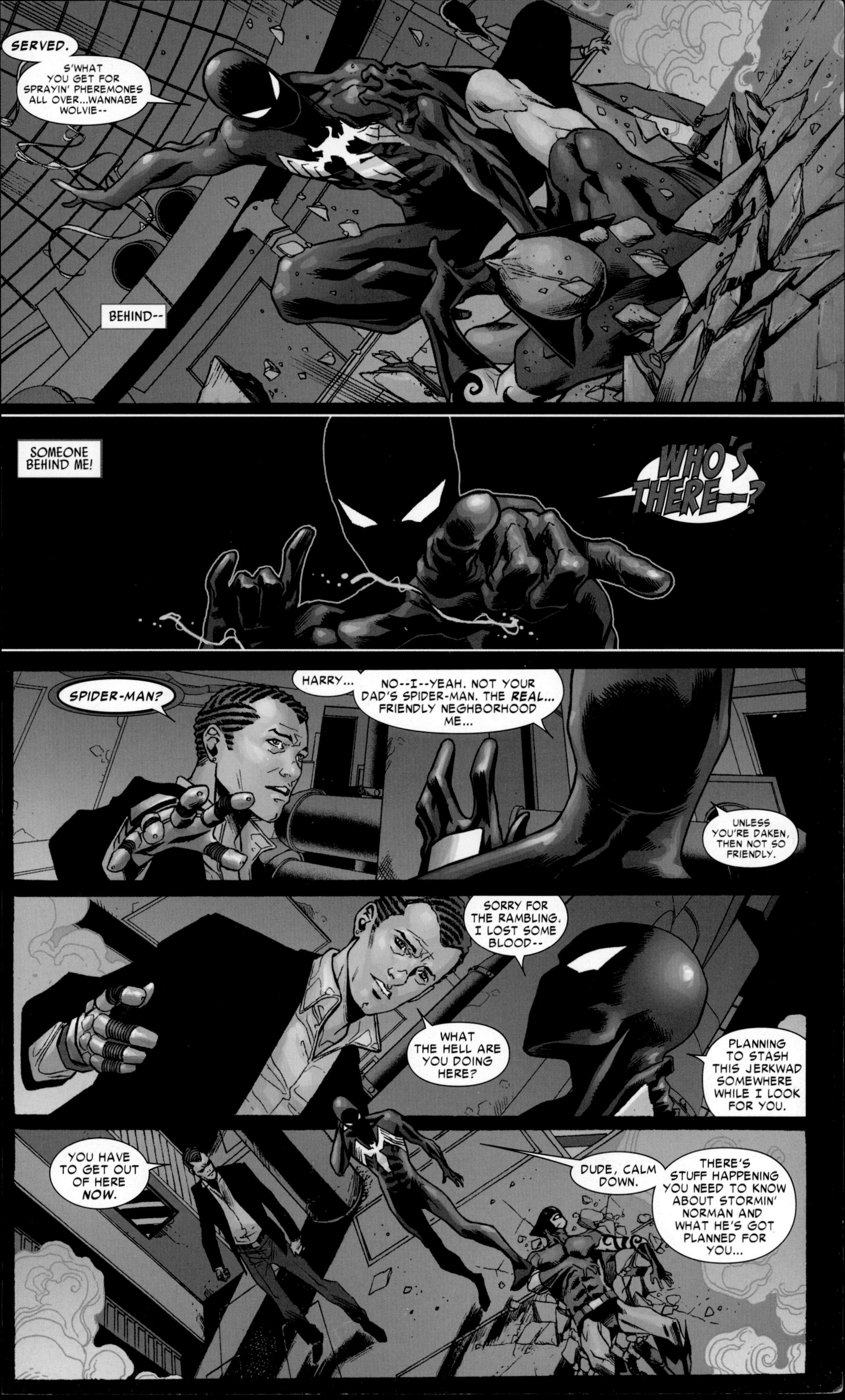
SERVED.
S'WHAT YOU GET FOR SPRAYIN' PHEREMONES ALL OVER...WANNABE WOLVIE--
BEHIND--
SOMEONE BEHIND ME!
WHO'S THERE--?
SPIDER-MAN?
HARRY...
NO--I--YEAH. NOT YOUR DAD'S SPIDER-MAN. THE REAL... FRIENDLY NEIGHBORHOOD ME...
UNLESS YOU'RE DAKEN, THEN NOT SO FRIENDLY.
SORRY FOR THE RAMBLING. I LOST SOME BLOOD--
WHAT THE HELL ARE YOU DOING HERE?
PLANNING TO STASH THIS JERKWAD SOMEWHERE WHILE I LOOK FOR YOU.
YOU HAVE TO GET OUT OF HERE NOW.
DUDE, CALM DOWN.
THERE'S STUFF HAPPENING YOU NEED TO KNOW ABOUT STORMIN' NORMAN AND WHAT HE'S GOT PLANNED FOR YOU...

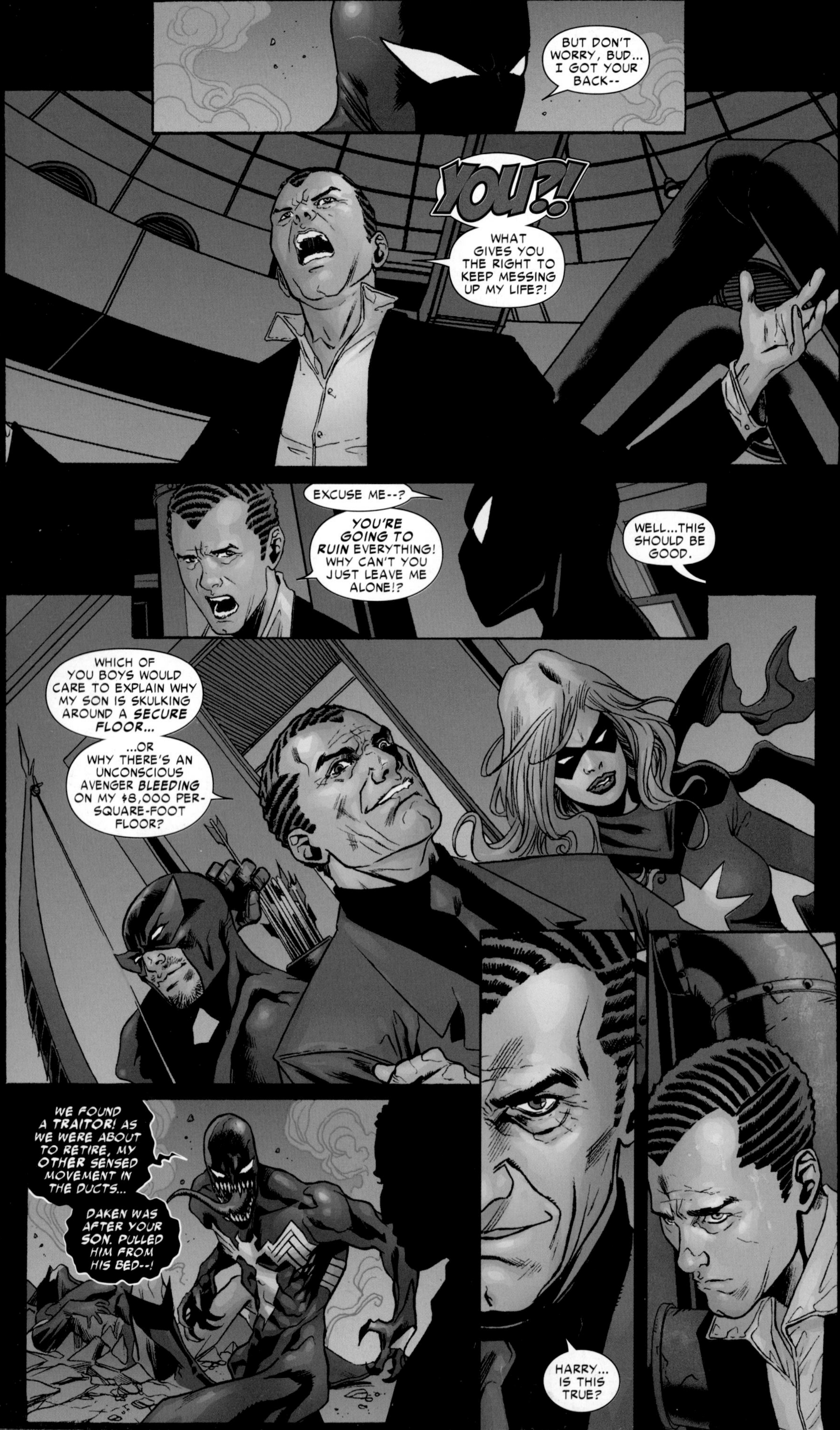
BUT DON'T WORRY, BUD... I GOT YOUR BACK--
YOU?!
WHAT GIVES YOU THE RIGHT TO KEEP MESSING UP MY LIFE?!
EXCUSE ME--?
YOU'RE GOING TO RUIN EVERYTHING! WHY CAN'T YOU JUST LEAVE ME ALONE!?
WELL...THIS SHOULD BE GOOD.
WHICH OF YOU BOYS WOULD CARE TO EXPLAIN WHY MY SON IS SKULKING AROUND A SECURE FLOOR...
...OR WHY THERE'S AN UNCONSCIOUS AVENGER BLEEDING ON MY $8,000 PER-SQUARE-FOOT FLOOR?
WE FOUND A TRAITOR! AS WE WERE ABOUT TO RETIRE, MY OTHER SENSED MOVEMENT IN THE DUCTS...
DAKEN WAS AFTER YOUR SON. PULLED HIM FROM HIS BED--!
HARRY... IS THIS TRUE?

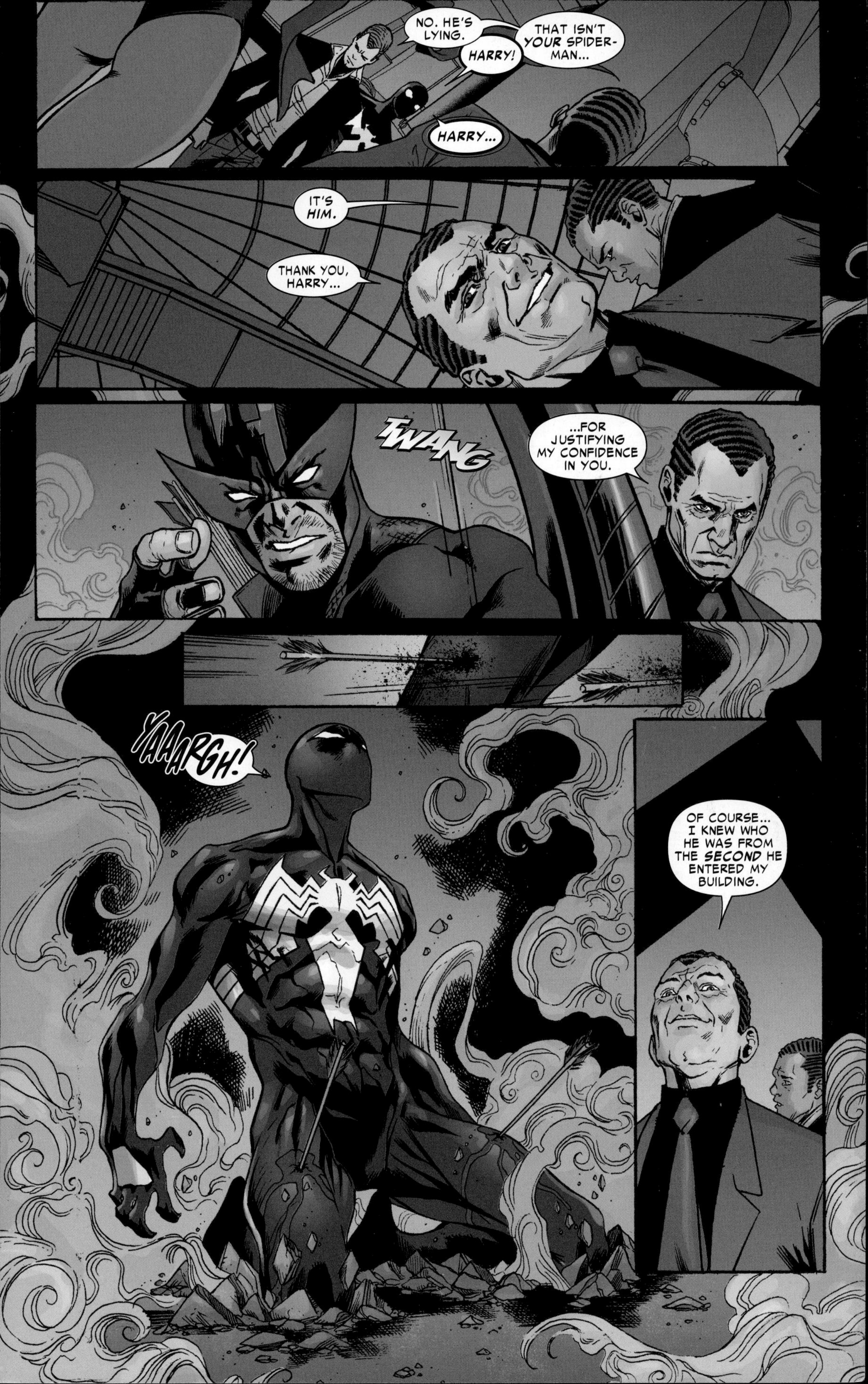

NO. HE'S LYING.
HARRY!
THAT ISN'T YOUR SPIDER-MAN...
HARRY...
IT'S HIM.
THANK YOU, HARRY...
TWANG
...FOR JUSTIFYING MY CONFIDENCE IN YOU.
YAAARGH!
OF COURSE... I KNEW WHO HE WAS FROM THE SECOND HE ENTERED MY BUILDING.

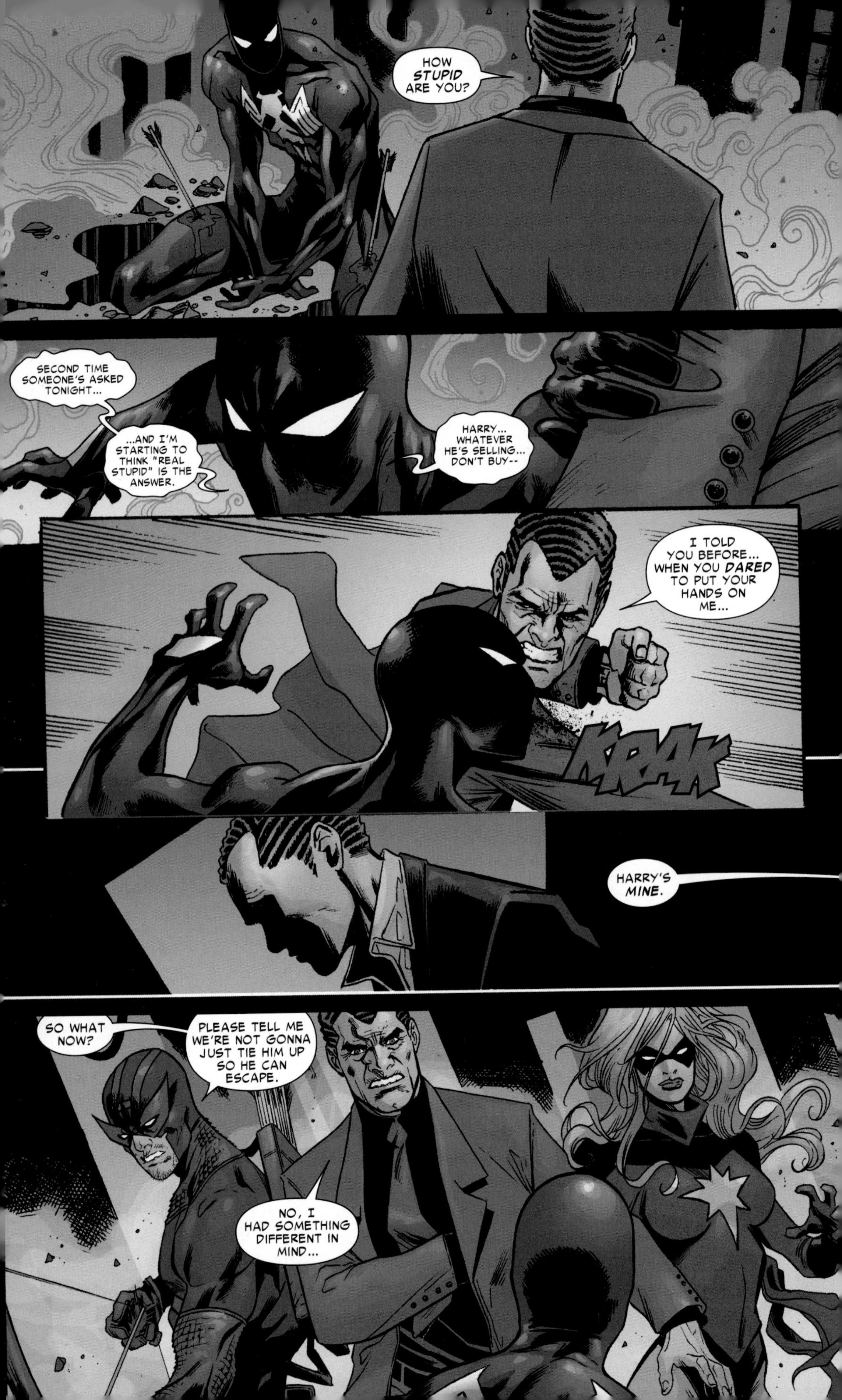

HOW STUPID ARE YOU?
SECOND TIME SOMEONE'S ASKED TONIGHT...
...AND I'M STARTING TO THINK "REAL STUPID" IS THE ANSWER.
HARRY... WHATEVER HE'S SELLING... DON'T BUY--
I TOLD YOU BEFORE... WHEN YOU DARED TO PUT YOUR HANDS ON ME...
KRAK
HARRY'S MINE.
SO WHAT NOW?
PLEASE TELL ME WE'RE NOT GONNA JUST TIE HIM UP SO HE CAN ESCAPE.
NO, I HAD SOMETHING DIFFERENT IN MIND...

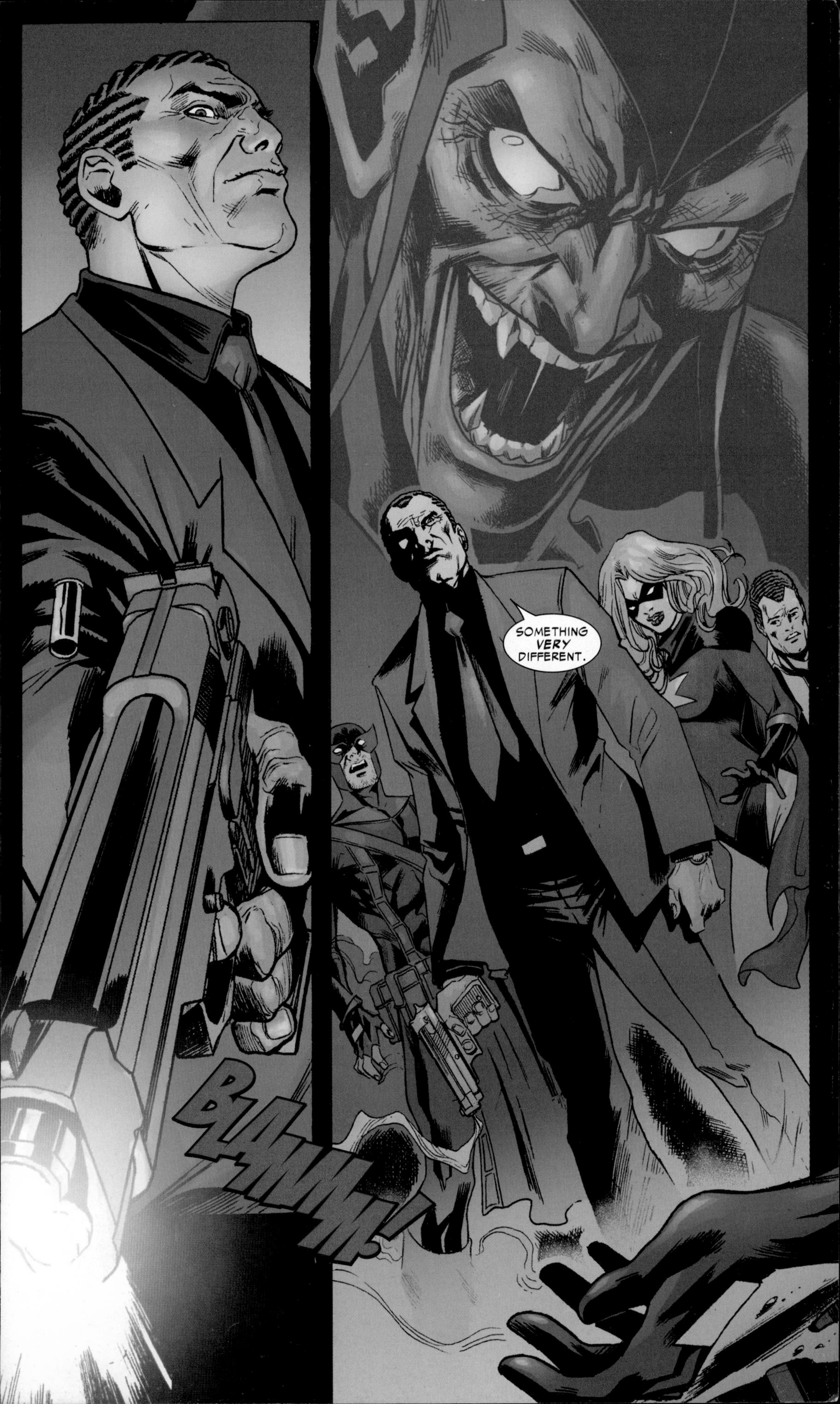
SOMETHING VERY DIFFERENT.
BLAMM!

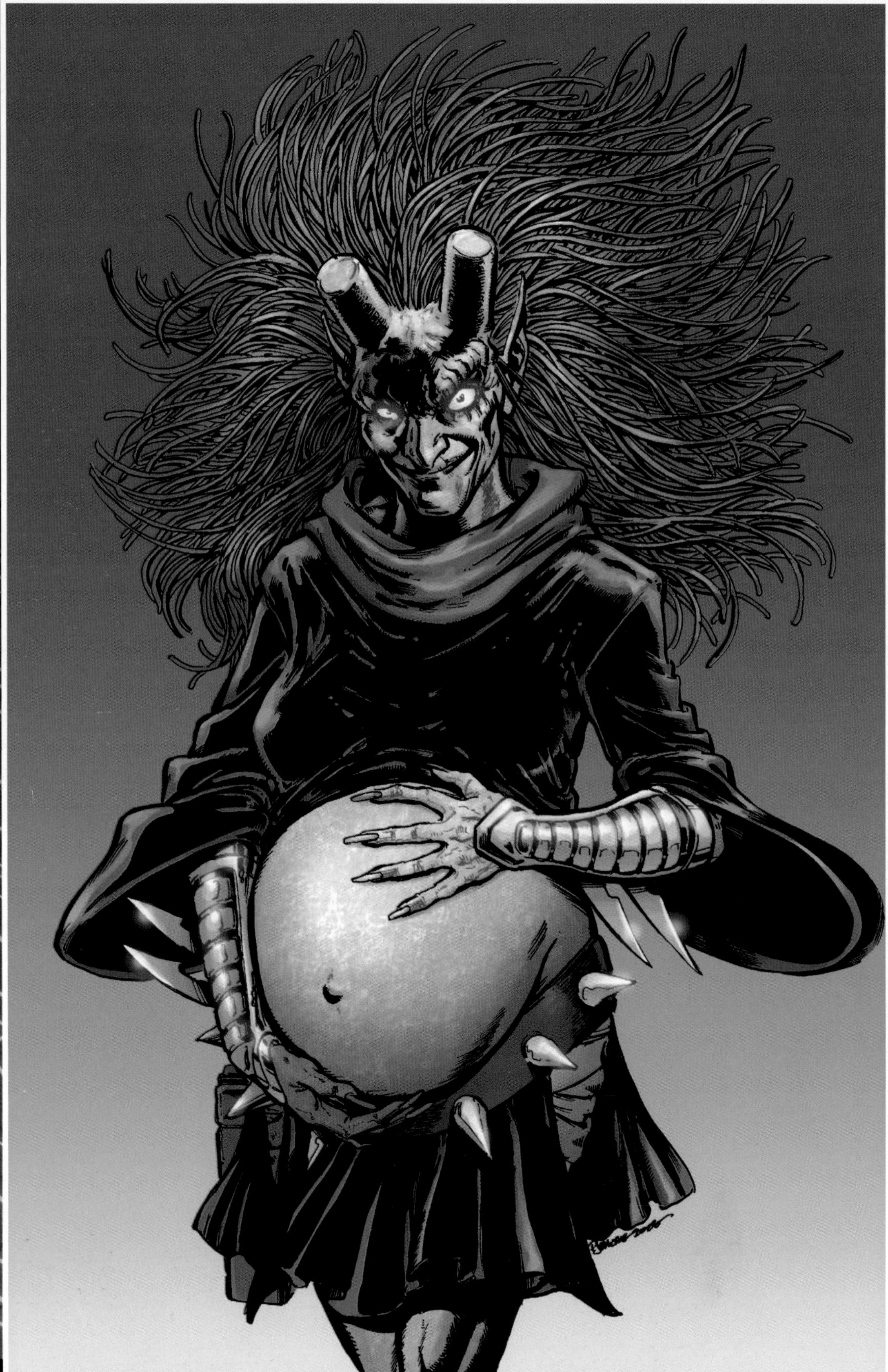

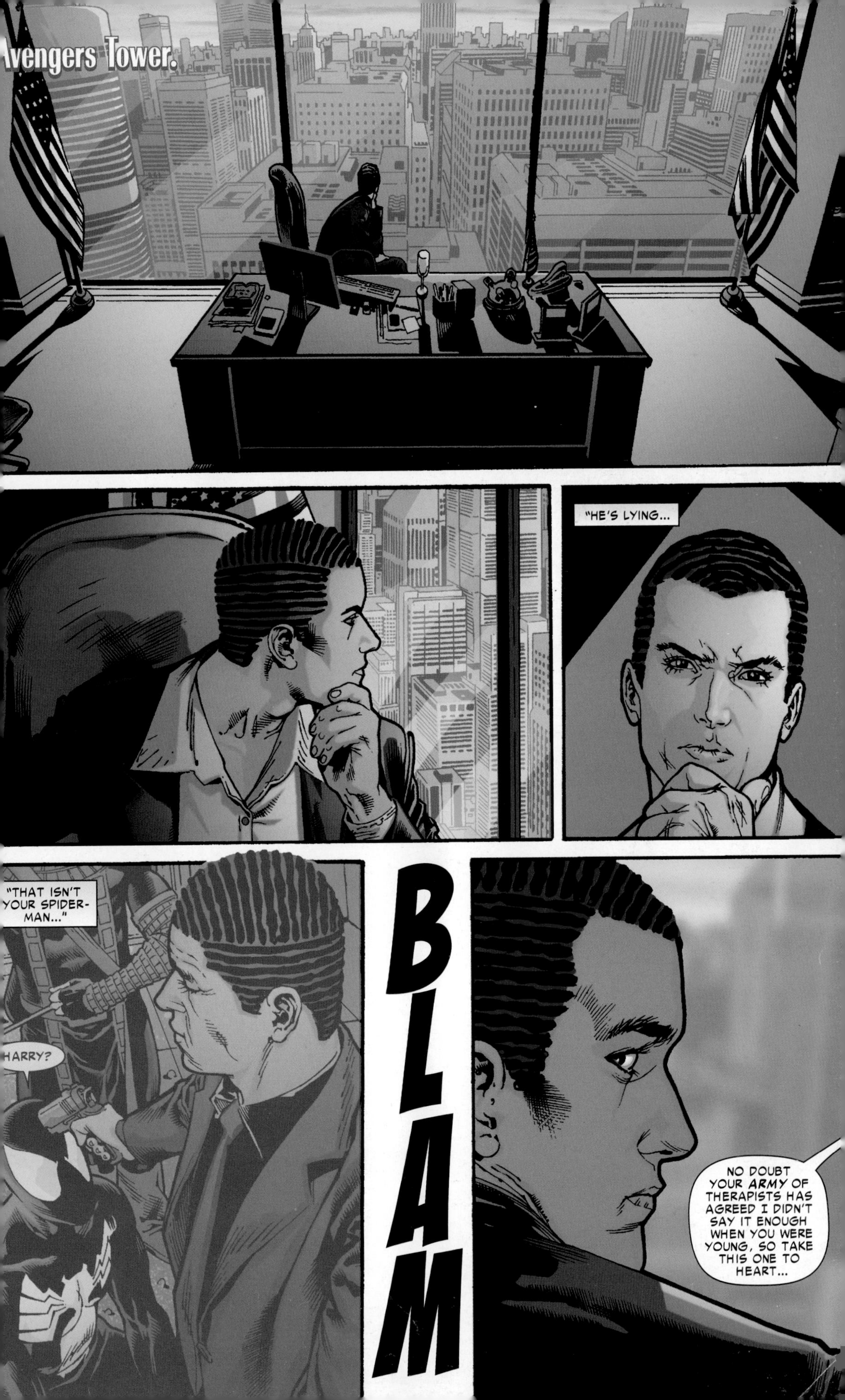
Avengers Tower.
"HE'S LYING...
"THAT ISN'T YOUR SPIDER-MAN..."
HARRY?
BLAM
NO DOUBT YOUR ARMY OF THERAPISTS HAS AGREED I DIDN'T SAY IT ENOUGH WHEN YOU WERE YOUNG, SO TAKE THIS ONE TO HEART...

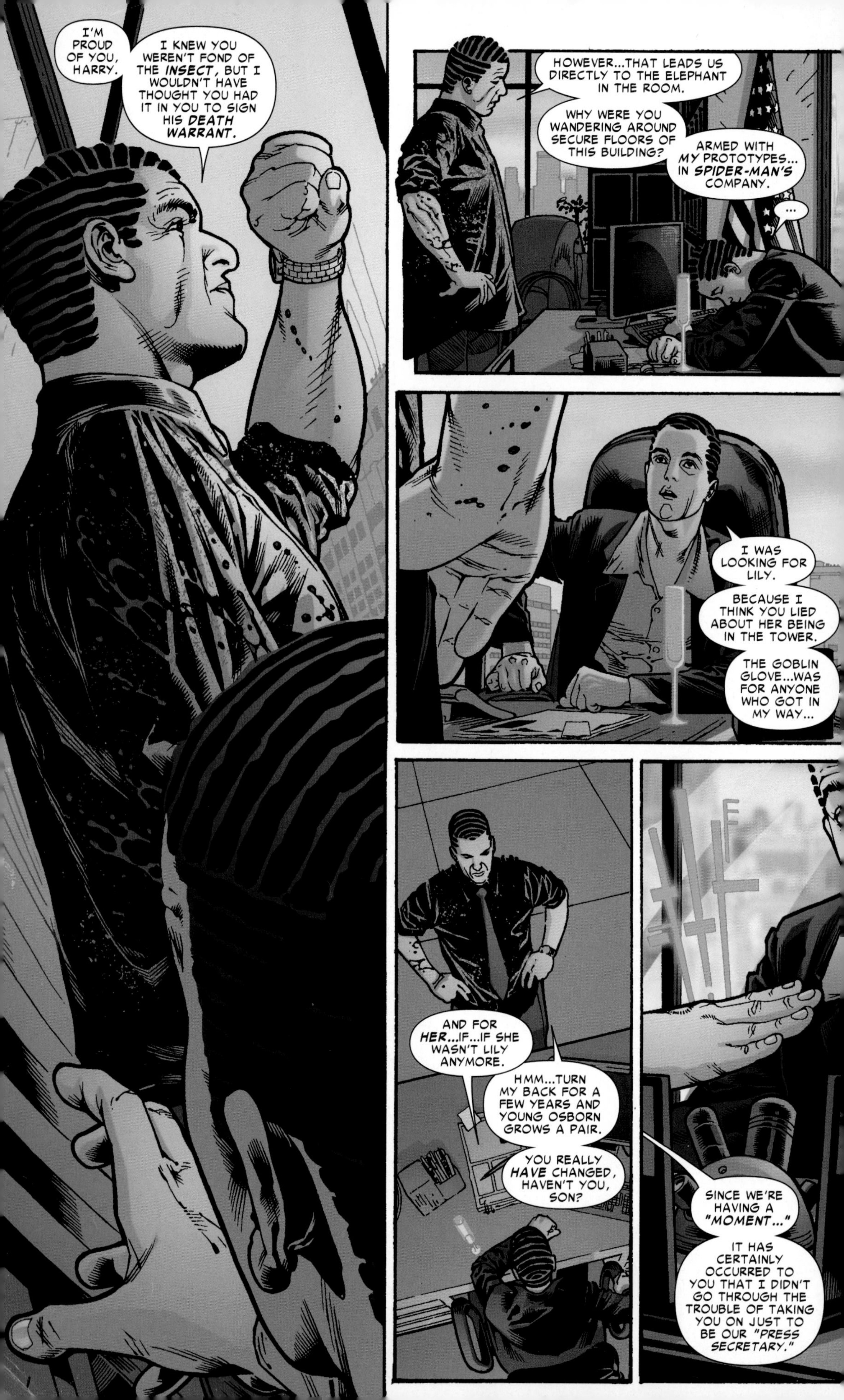
I'M PROUD OF YOU, HARRY.
I KNEW YOU WEREN'T FOND OF THE *INSECT*, BUT I WOULDN'T HAVE THOUGHT YOU HAD IT IN YOU TO SIGN HIS *DEATH WARRANT*.
HOWEVER...THAT LEADS US DIRECTLY TO THE ELEPHANT IN THE ROOM.
WHY WERE YOU WANDERING AROUND SECURE FLOORS OF THIS BUILDING?
ARMED WITH *MY* PROTOTYPES... IN *SPIDER-MAN'S* COMPANY.
...
I WAS LOOKING FOR LILY.
BECAUSE I THINK YOU LIED ABOUT HER BEING IN THE TOWER.
THE GOBLIN GLOVE...WAS FOR ANYONE WHO GOT IN MY WAY...
AND FOR *HER*...IF...IF SHE WASN'T LILY ANYMORE.
HMM...TURN MY BACK FOR A FEW YEARS AND YOUNG OSBORN GROWS A PAIR.
YOU REALLY *HAVE* CHANGED, HAVEN'T YOU, SON?
SINCE WE'RE HAVING A *"MOMENT..."*
IT HAS CERTAINLY OCCURRED TO YOU THAT I DIDN'T GO THROUGH THE TROUBLE OF TAKING YOU ON JUST TO BE OUR *"PRESS SECRETARY."*

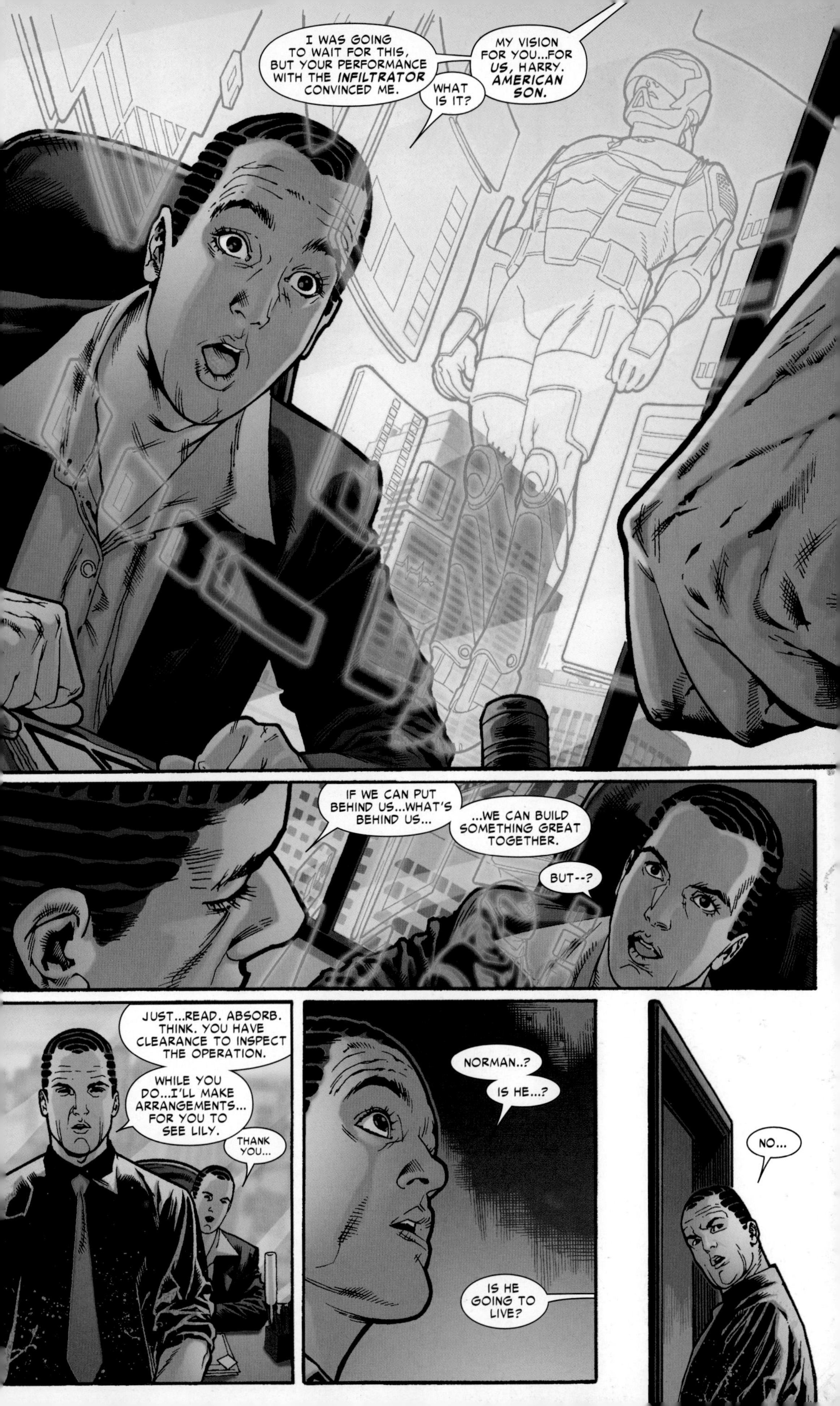

I WAS GOING TO WAIT FOR THIS, BUT YOUR PERFORMANCE WITH THE INFILTRATOR CONVINCED ME.
WHAT IS IT?
MY VISION FOR YOU...FOR US, HARRY. AMERICAN SON.
IF WE CAN PUT BEHIND US...WHAT'S BEHIND US...
...WE CAN BUILD SOMETHING GREAT TOGETHER.
BUT--?
JUST...READ. ABSORB. THINK. YOU HAVE CLEARANCE TO INSPECT THE OPERATION.
WHILE YOU DO...I'LL MAKE ARRANGEMENTS... FOR YOU TO SEE LILY.
THANK YOU...
NORMAN..?
IS HE...?
IS HE GOING TO LIVE?
NO...

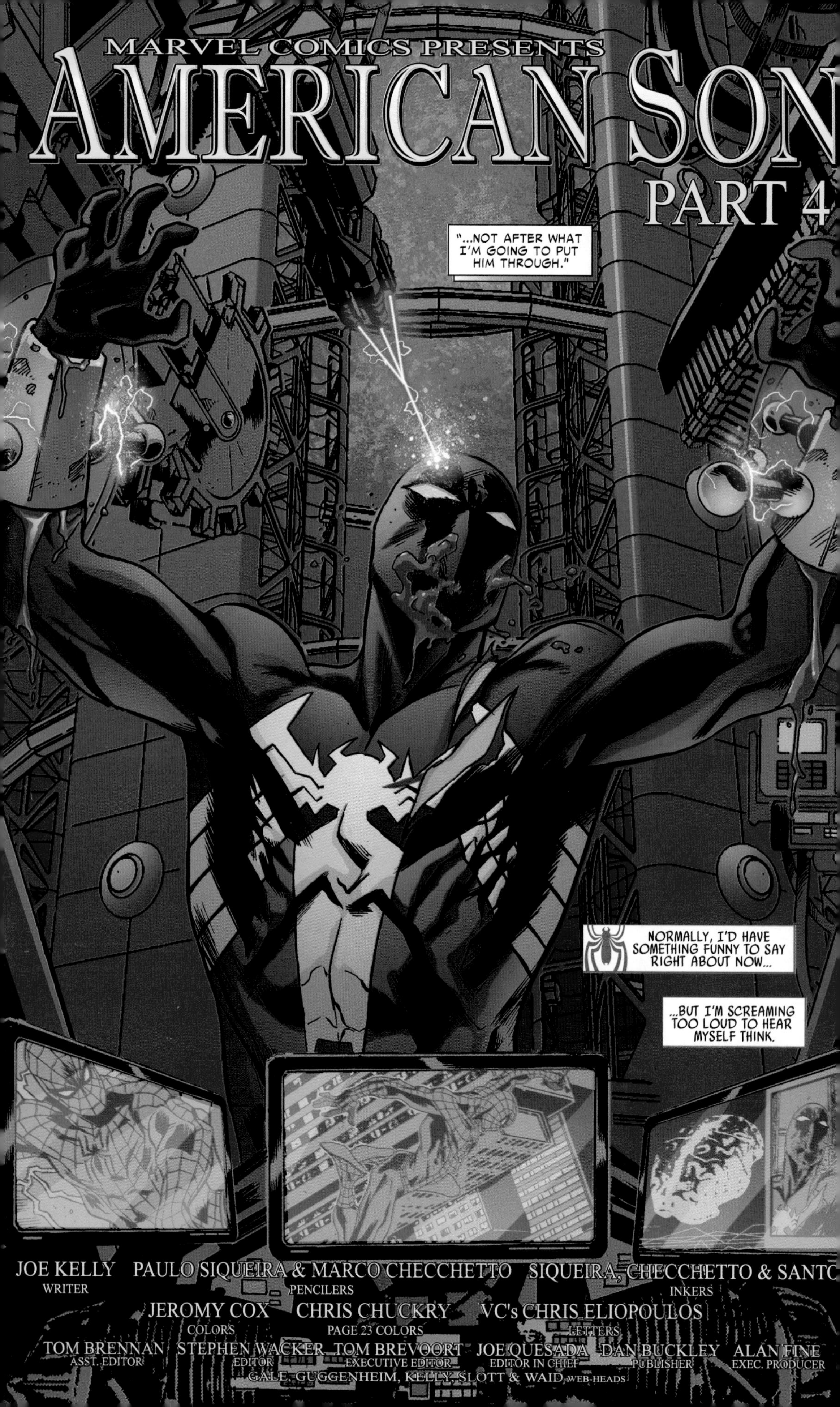
MARVEL COMICS PRESENTS
AMERICAN SON
PART 4
"...NOT AFTER WHAT I'M GOING TO PUT HIM THROUGH."
NORMALLY, I'D HAVE SOMETHING FUNNY TO SAY RIGHT ABOUT NOW...
...BUT I'M SCREAMING TOO LOUD TO HEAR MYSELF THINK.
JOE KELLY WRITER
PAULO SIQUEIRA & MARCO CHECCHETTO PENCILERS
SIQUEIRA, CHECCHETTO & SANTO INKERS
JEROMY COX COLORS
CHRIS CHUCKRY PAGE 23 COLORS
VC's CHRIS ELIOPOULOS LETTERS
TOM BRENNAN ASST. EDITOR
STEPHEN WACKER EDITOR
TOM BREVOORT EXECUTIVE EDITOR
JOE QUESADA EDITOR IN CHIEF
DAN BUCKLEY PUBLISHER
ALAN FINE EXEC. PRODUCER
GALE, GUGGENHEIM, KELLY, SLOTT & WAID WEB-HEADS

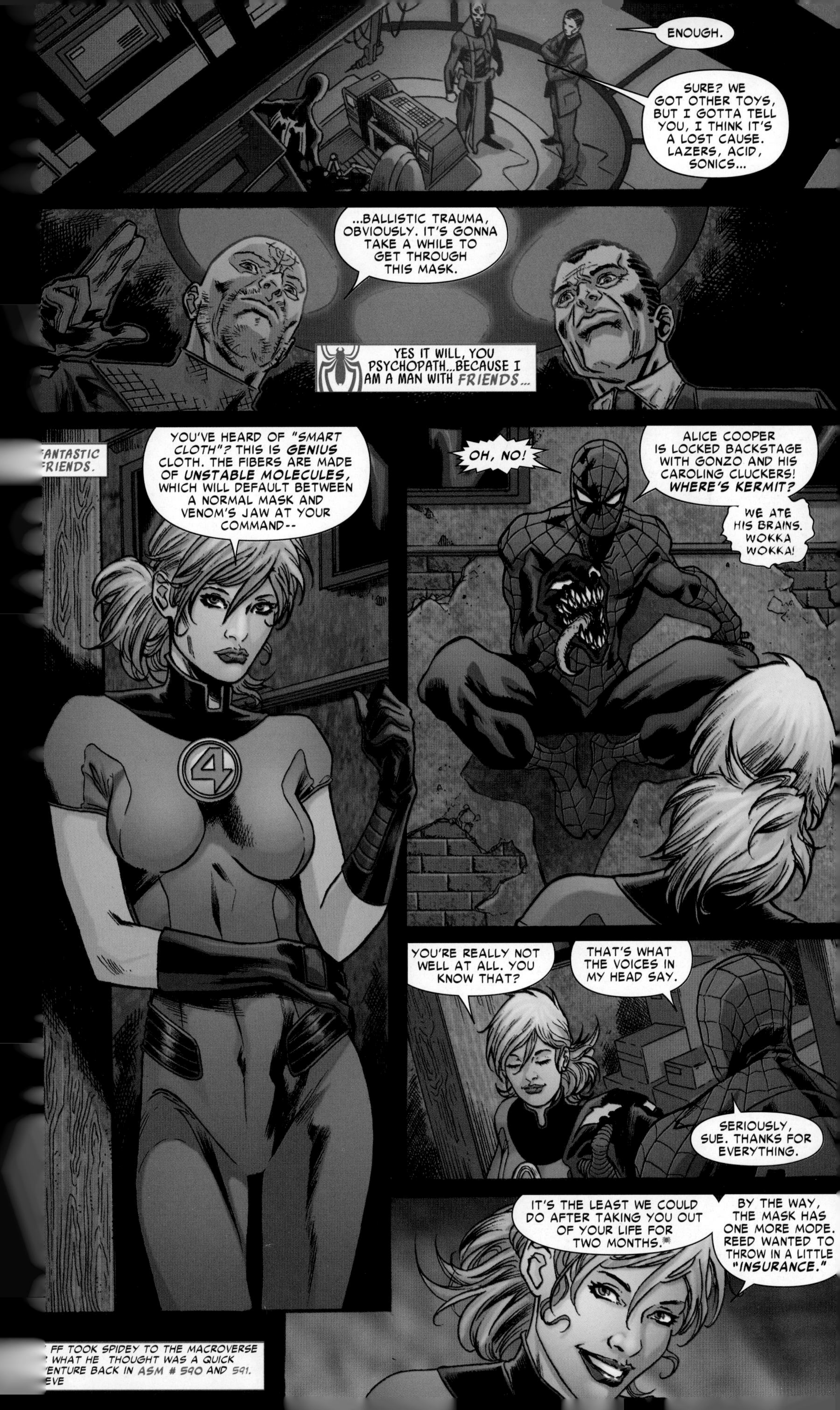
ENOUGH.
SURE? WE GOT OTHER TOYS, BUT I GOTTA TELL YOU, I THINK IT'S A LOST CAUSE. LAZERS, ACID, SONICS...
...BALLISTIC TRAUMA, OBVIOUSLY. IT'S GONNA TAKE A WHILE TO GET THROUGH THIS MASK.
YES IT WILL, YOU PSYCHOPATH...BECAUSE I AM A MAN WITH FRIENDS...
FANTASTIC FRIENDS.
YOU'VE HEARD OF "SMART CLOTH"? THIS IS GENIUS CLOTH. THE FIBERS ARE MADE OF UNSTABLE MOLECULES, WHICH WILL DEFAULT BETWEEN A NORMAL MASK AND VENOM'S JAW AT YOUR COMMAND--
OH, NO!
ALICE COOPER IS LOCKED BACKSTAGE WITH GONZO AND HIS CAROLING CLUCKERS! WHERE'S KERMIT?
WE ATE HIS BRAINS. WOKKA WOKKA!
YOU'RE REALLY NOT WELL AT ALL. YOU KNOW THAT?
THAT'S WHAT THE VOICES IN MY HEAD SAY.
SERIOUSLY, SUE. THANKS FOR EVERYTHING.
IT'S THE LEAST WE COULD DO AFTER TAKING YOU OUT OF YOUR LIFE FOR TWO MONTHS.
BY THE WAY, THE MASK HAS ONE MORE MODE. REED WANTED TO THROW IN A LITTLE "INSURANCE."
FF TOOK SPIDEY TO THE MACROVERSE WHAT HE THOUGHT WAS A QUICK ENTURE BACK IN ASM # 590 AND 591.
EVE

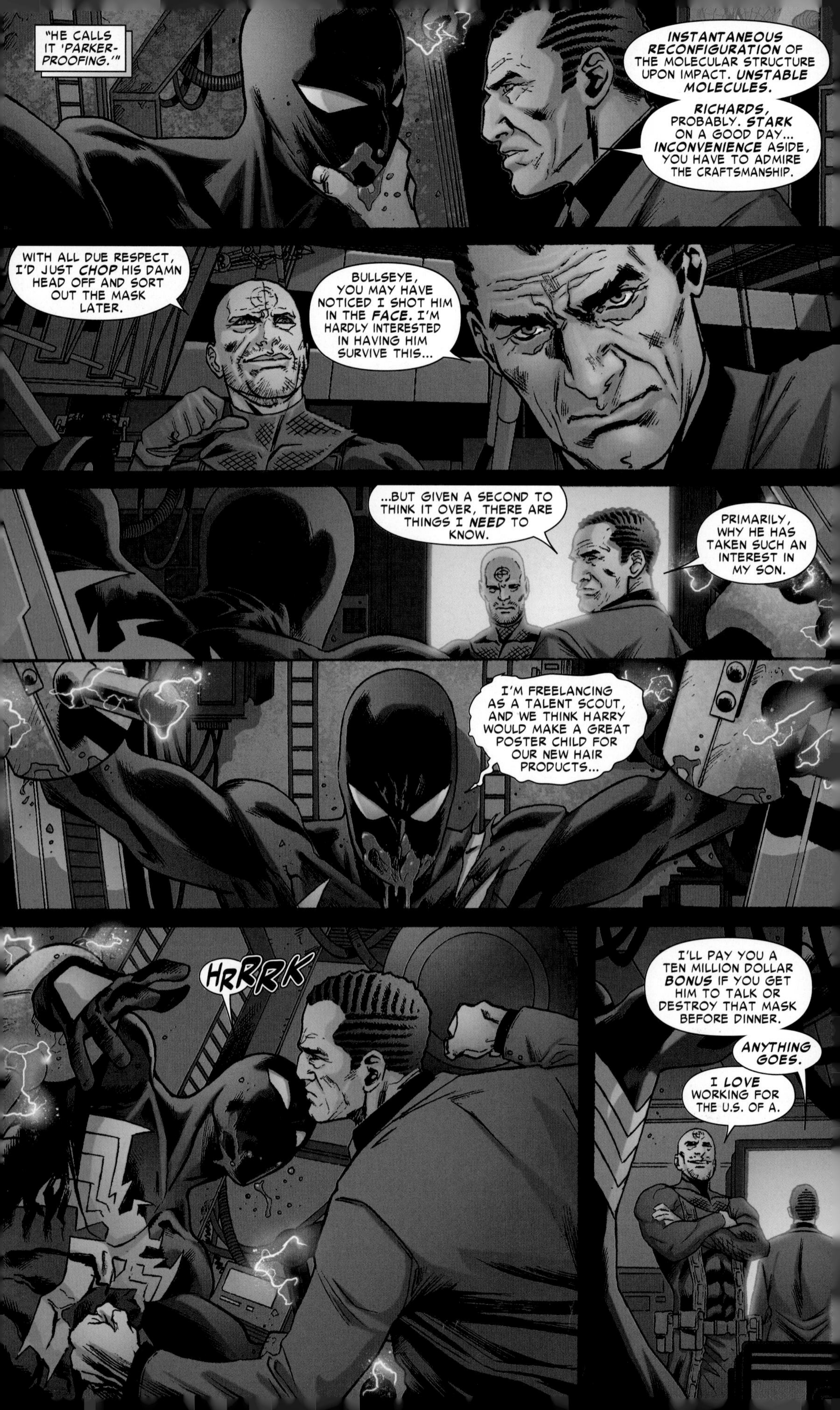

"HE CALLS IT 'PARKER-PROOFING.'"
INSTANTANEOUS RECONFIGURATION OF THE MOLECULAR STRUCTURE UPON IMPACT. UNSTABLE MOLECULES.
RICHARDS, PROBABLY. STARK ON A GOOD DAY... INCONVENIENCE ASIDE, YOU HAVE TO ADMIRE THE CRAFTSMANSHIP.
WITH ALL DUE RESPECT, I'D JUST CHOP HIS DAMN HEAD OFF AND SORT OUT THE MASK LATER.
BULLSEYE, YOU MAY HAVE NOTICED I SHOT HIM IN THE FACE. I'M HARDLY INTERESTED IN HAVING HIM SURVIVE THIS...
...BUT GIVEN A SECOND TO THINK IT OVER, THERE ARE THINGS I NEED TO KNOW.
PRIMARILY, WHY HE HAS TAKEN SUCH AN INTEREST IN MY SON.
I'M FREELANCING AS A TALENT SCOUT, AND WE THINK HARRY WOULD MAKE A GREAT POSTER CHILD FOR OUR NEW HAIR PRODUCTS...
HRRRK
I'LL PAY YOU A TEN MILLION DOLLAR BONUS IF YOU GET HIM TO TALK OR DESTROY THAT MASK BEFORE DINNER.
ANYTHING GOES.
I LOVE WORKING FOR THE U.S. OF A.

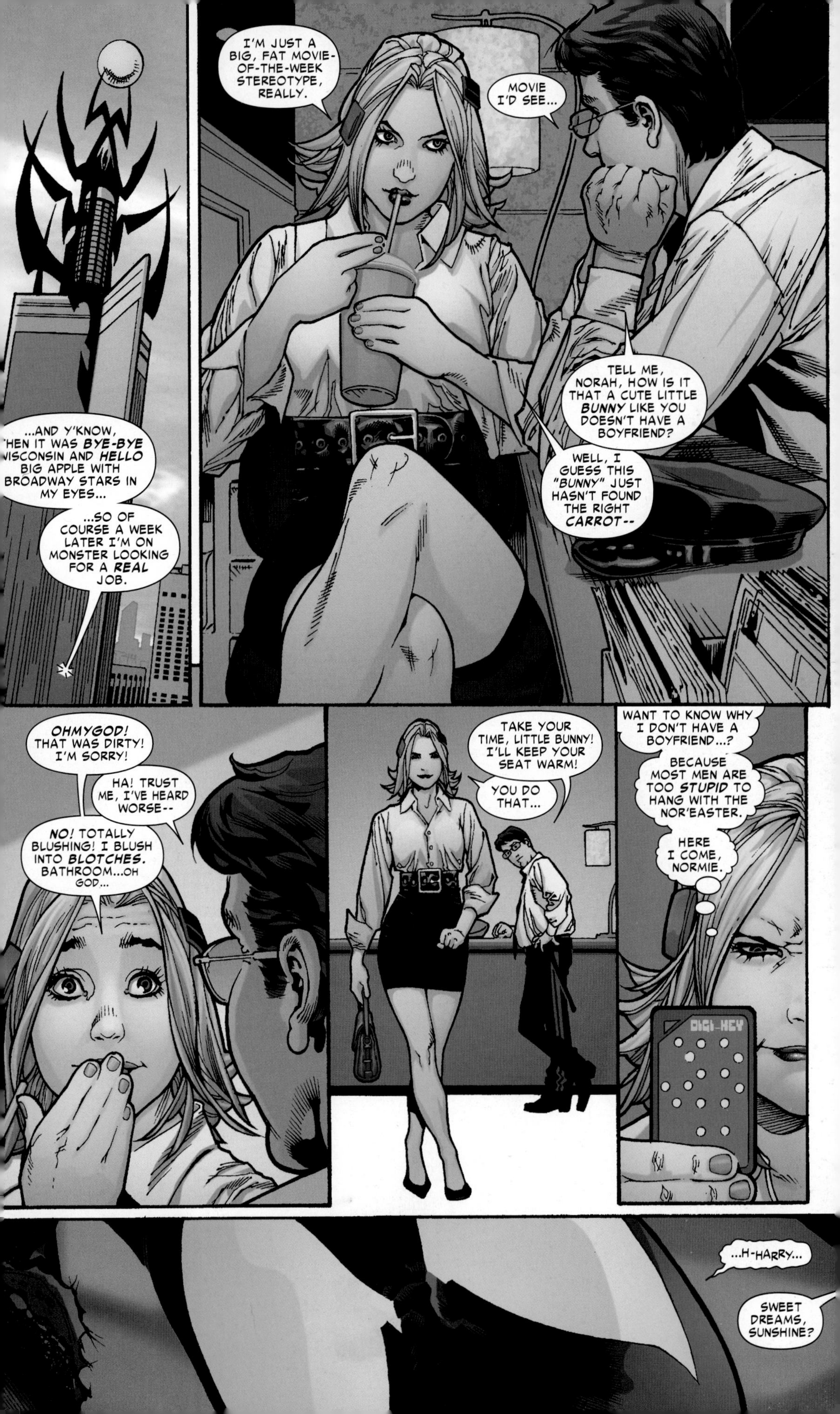
...AND Y'KNOW, THEN IT WAS BYE-BYE WISCONSIN AND HELLO BIG APPLE WITH BROADWAY STARS IN MY EYES...
...SO OF COURSE A WEEK LATER I'M ON MONSTER LOOKING FOR A REAL JOB.
I'M JUST A BIG, FAT MOVIE-OF-THE-WEEK STEREOTYPE, REALLY.
MOVIE I'D SEE...
TELL ME, NORAH, HOW IS IT THAT A CUTE LITTLE BUNNY LIKE YOU DOESN'T HAVE A BOYFRIEND?
WELL, I GUESS THIS "BUNNY" JUST HASN'T FOUND THE RIGHT CARROT--
OHMYGOD! THAT WAS DIRTY! I'M SORRY!
HA! TRUST ME, I'VE HEARD WORSE--
NO! TOTALLY BLUSHING! I BLUSH INTO BLOTCHES. BATHROOM...OH GOD...
TAKE YOUR TIME, LITTLE BUNNY! I'LL KEEP YOUR SEAT WARM!
YOU DO THAT...
WANT TO KNOW WHY I DON'T HAVE A BOYFRIEND...?
BECAUSE MOST MEN ARE TOO STUPID TO HANG WITH THE NOR'EASTER.
HERE I COME, NORMIE.
DIGI-KEY
...H-HARRY...
SWEET DREAMS, SUNSHINE?

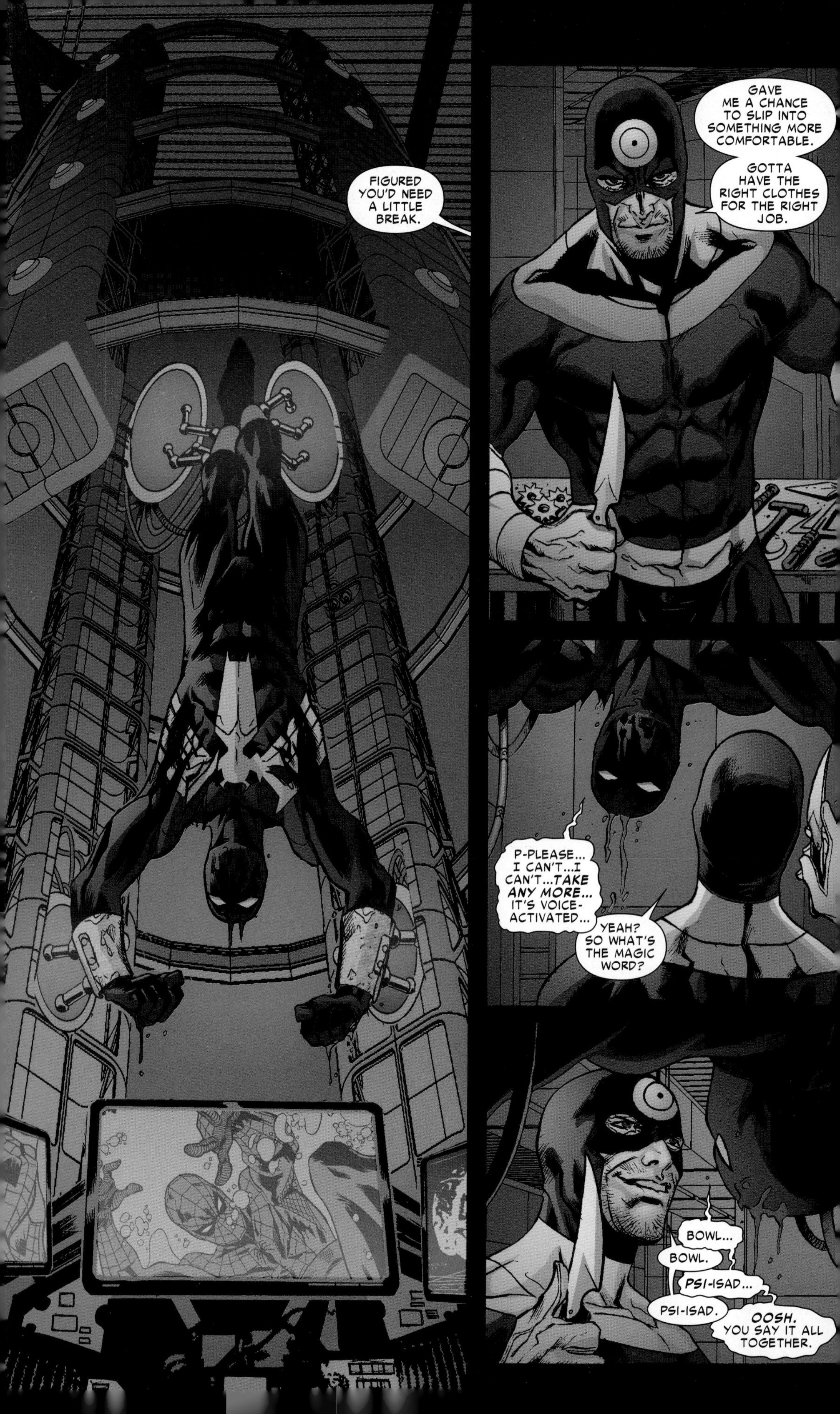
FIGURED YOU'D NEED A LITTLE BREAK.
GAVE ME A CHANCE TO SLIP INTO SOMETHING MORE COMFORTABLE.
GOTTA HAVE THE RIGHT CLOTHES FOR THE RIGHT JOB.
P-PLEASE... I CAN'T...I CAN'T...TAKE ANY MORE... IT'S VOICE-ACTIVATED...
YEAH? SO WHAT'S THE MAGIC WORD?
BOWL...
BOWL.
PSI-ISAD...
PSI-ISAD.
OOSH. YOU SAY IT ALL TOGETHER.

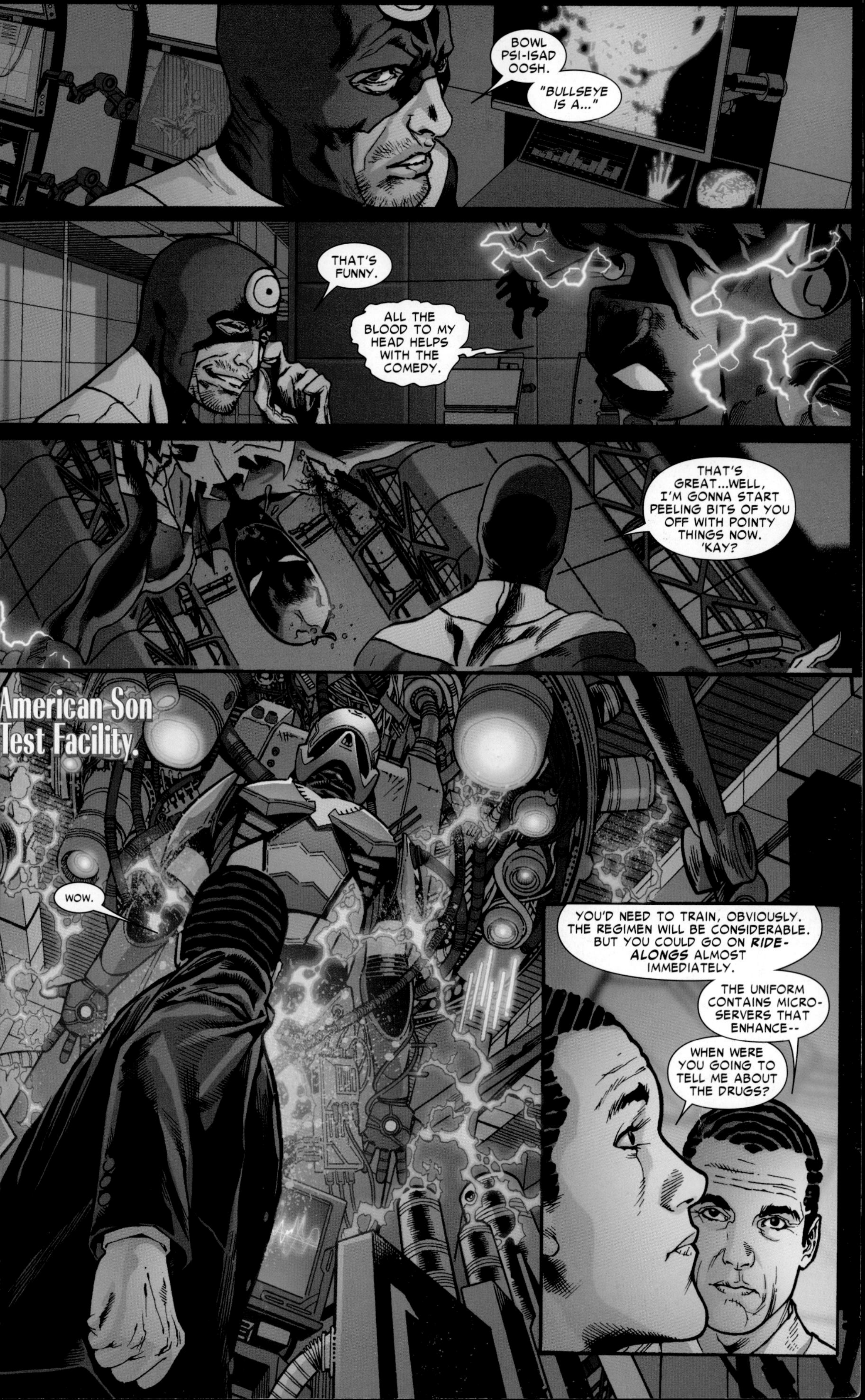
BOWL PSI-ISAD OOSH.
"BULLSEYE IS A..."
THAT'S FUNNY.
ALL THE BLOOD TO MY HEAD HELPS WITH THE COMEDY.
THAT'S GREAT...WELL, I'M GONNA START PEELING BITS OF YOU OFF WITH POINTY THINGS NOW. 'KAY?
American Son Test Facility.
WOW.
YOU'D NEED TO TRAIN, OBVIOUSLY. THE REGIMEN WILL BE CONSIDERABLE. BUT YOU COULD GO ON *RIDE-ALONGS* ALMOST IMMEDIATELY.
THE UNIFORM CONTAINS MICRO-SERVERS THAT ENHANCE--
WHEN WERE YOU GOING TO TELL ME ABOUT THE DRUGS?

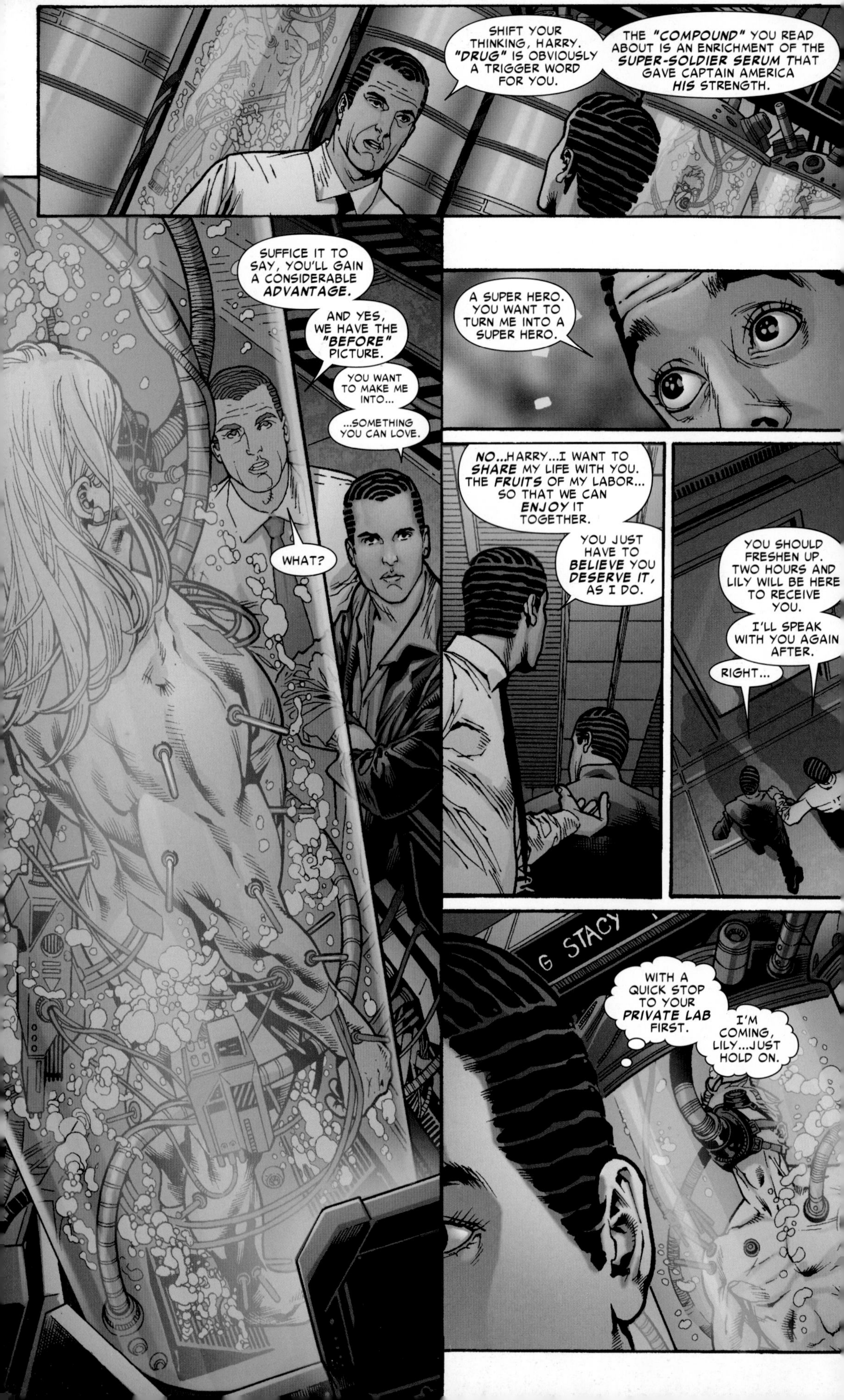

SHIFT YOUR THINKING, HARRY. "DRUG" IS OBVIOUSLY A TRIGGER WORD FOR YOU.
THE "COMPOUND" YOU READ ABOUT IS AN ENRICHMENT OF THE SUPER-SOLDIER SERUM THAT GAVE CAPTAIN AMERICA HIS STRENGTH.
SUFFICE IT TO SAY, YOU'LL GAIN A CONSIDERABLE ADVANTAGE.
AND YES, WE HAVE THE "BEFORE" PICTURE.
YOU WANT TO MAKE ME INTO...
...SOMETHING YOU CAN LOVE.
WHAT?
A SUPER HERO. YOU WANT TO TURN ME INTO A SUPER HERO.
NO...HARRY...I WANT TO SHARE MY LIFE WITH YOU. THE FRUITS OF MY LABOR... SO THAT WE CAN ENJOY IT TOGETHER.
YOU JUST HAVE TO BELIEVE YOU DESERVE IT, AS I DO.
YOU SHOULD FRESHEN UP. TWO HOURS AND LILY WILL BE HERE TO RECEIVE YOU.
I'LL SPEAK WITH YOU AGAIN AFTER.
RIGHT...
G STACY
WITH A QUICK STOP TO YOUR PRIVATE LAB FIRST.
I'M COMING, LILY...JUST HOLD ON.

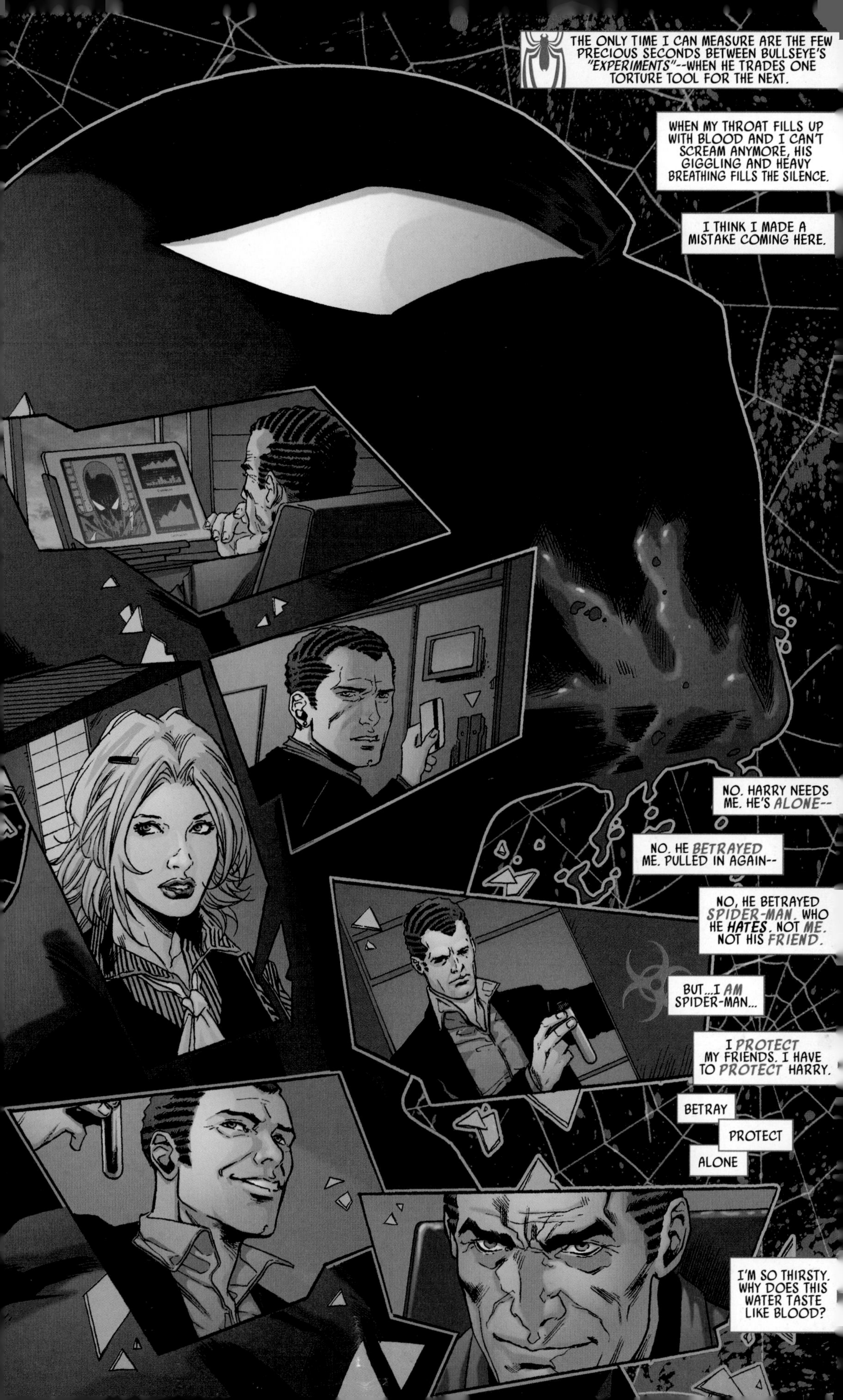

THE ONLY TIME I CAN MEASURE ARE THE FEW PRECIOUS SECONDS BETWEEN BULLSEYE'S "EXPERIMENTS"--WHEN HE TRADES ONE TORTURE TOOL FOR THE NEXT.
WHEN MY THROAT FILLS UP WITH BLOOD AND I CAN'T SCREAM ANYMORE, HIS GIGGLING AND HEAVY BREATHING FILLS THE SILENCE.
I THINK I MADE A MISTAKE COMING HERE.
NO. HARRY NEEDS ME. HE'S ALONE--
NO. HE BETRAYED ME. PULLED IN AGAIN--
NO, HE BETRAYED SPIDER-MAN. WHO HE HATES. NOT ME. NOT HIS FRIEND.
BUT...I AM SPIDER-MAN...
I PROTECT MY FRIENDS. I HAVE TO PROTECT HARRY.
BETRAY
PROTECT
ALONE
I'M SO THIRSTY. WHY DOES THIS WATER TASTE LIKE BLOOD?

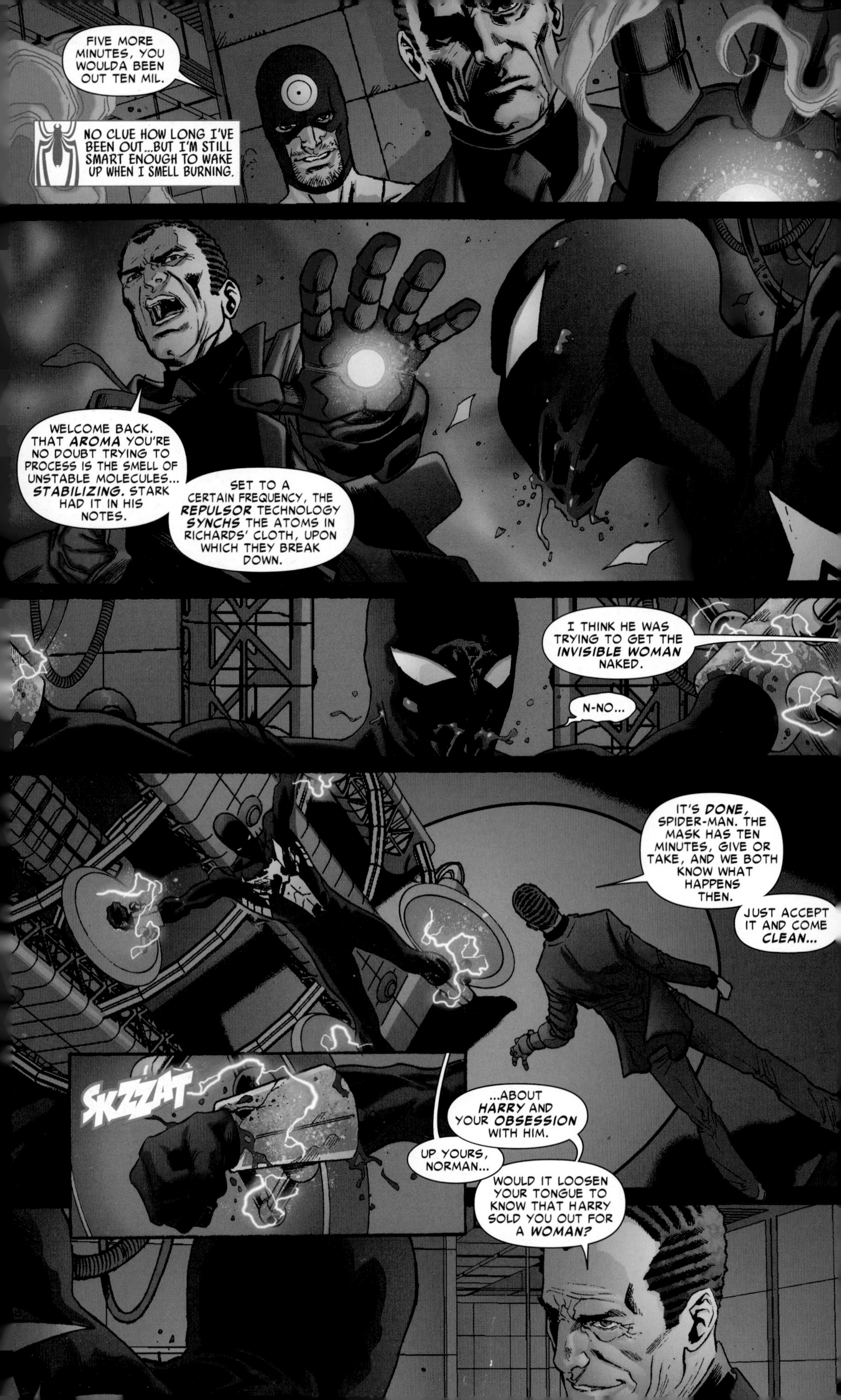

FIVE MORE MINUTES, YOU WOULDA BEEN OUT TEN MIL.
NO CLUE HOW LONG I'VE BEEN OUT...BUT I'M STILL SMART ENOUGH TO WAKE UP WHEN I SMELL BURNING.
WELCOME BACK. THAT AROMA YOU'RE NO DOUBT TRYING TO PROCESS IS THE SMELL OF UNSTABLE MOLECULES... STABILIZING. STARK HAD IT IN HIS NOTES.
SET TO A CERTAIN FREQUENCY, THE REPULSOR TECHNOLOGY SYNCHS THE ATOMS IN RICHARDS' CLOTH, UPON WHICH THEY BREAK DOWN.
I THINK HE WAS TRYING TO GET THE INVISIBLE WOMAN NAKED.
N-NO...
IT'S DONE, SPIDER-MAN. THE MASK HAS TEN MINUTES, GIVE OR TAKE, AND WE BOTH KNOW WHAT HAPPENS THEN.
JUST ACCEPT IT AND COME CLEAN...
SKZZZAT
...ABOUT HARRY AND YOUR OBSESSION WITH HIM.
UP YOURS, NORMAN...
WOULD IT LOOSEN YOUR TONGUE TO KNOW THAT HARRY SOLD YOU OUT FOR A WOMAN?

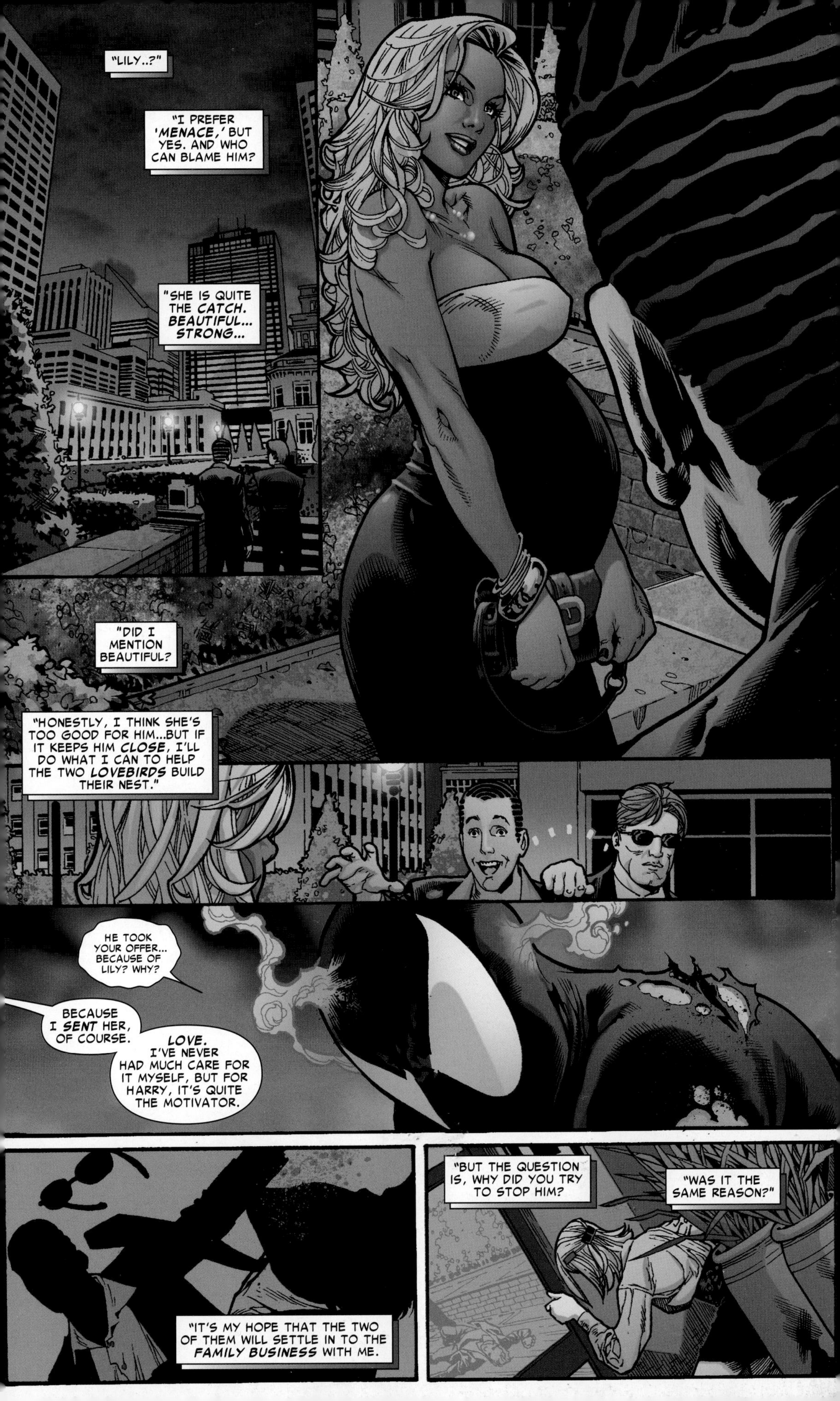
"LILY..?"
"I PREFER 'MENACE,' BUT YES. AND WHO CAN BLAME HIM?
"SHE IS QUITE THE CATCH. BEAUTIFUL... STRONG...
"DID I MENTION BEAUTIFUL?
"HONESTLY, I THINK SHE'S TOO GOOD FOR HIM...BUT IF IT KEEPS HIM CLOSE, I'LL DO WHAT I CAN TO HELP THE TWO LOVEBIRDS BUILD THEIR NEST."
HE TOOK YOUR OFFER... BECAUSE OF LILY? WHY?
BECAUSE I SENT HER, OF COURSE.
LOVE. I'VE NEVER HAD MUCH CARE FOR IT MYSELF, BUT FOR HARRY, IT'S QUITE THE MOTIVATOR.
"IT'S MY HOPE THAT THE TWO OF THEM WILL SETTLE IN TO THE FAMILY BUSINESS WITH ME.
"BUT THE QUESTION IS, WHY DID YOU TRY TO STOP HIM?
"WAS IT THE SAME REASON?"

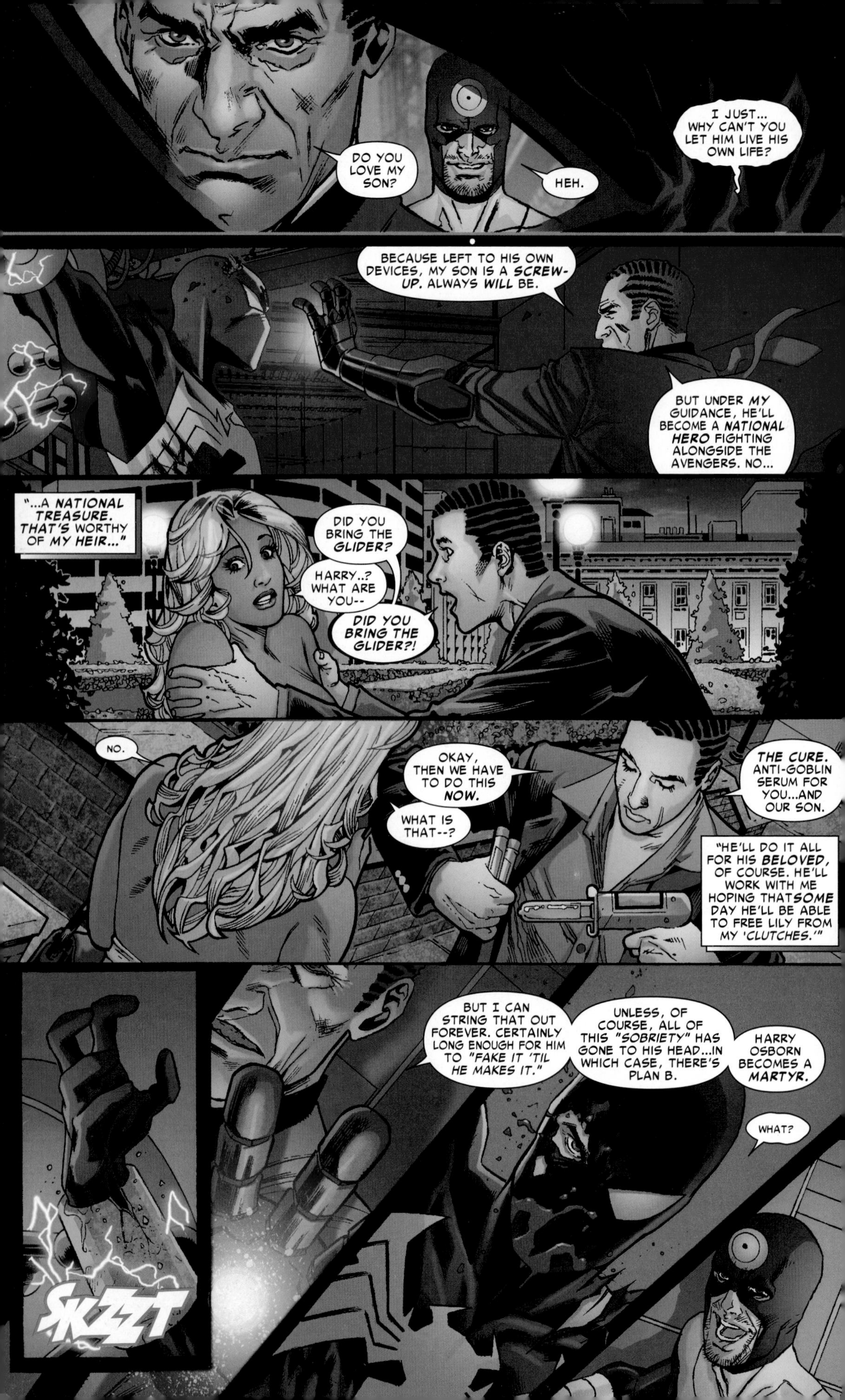
DO YOU LOVE MY SON?
HEH.
I JUST... WHY CAN'T YOU LET HIM LIVE HIS OWN LIFE?
BECAUSE LEFT TO HIS OWN DEVICES, MY SON IS A SCREW-UP. ALWAYS WILL BE.
BUT UNDER MY GUIDANCE, HE'LL BECOME A NATIONAL HERO FIGHTING ALONGSIDE THE AVENGERS. NO...
"...A NATIONAL TREASURE. THAT'S WORTHY OF MY HEIR..."
DID YOU BRING THE GLIDER?
HARRY..? WHAT ARE YOU--
DID YOU BRING THE GLIDER?!
NO.
OKAY, THEN WE HAVE TO DO THIS NOW.
WHAT IS THAT--?
THE CURE. ANTI-GOBLIN SERUM FOR YOU...AND OUR SON.
"HE'LL DO IT ALL FOR HIS BELOVED, OF COURSE. HE'LL WORK WITH ME HOPING THATSOME DAY HE'LL BE ABLE TO FREE LILY FROM MY 'CLUTCHES.'"
BUT I CAN STRING THAT OUT FOREVER. CERTAINLY LONG ENOUGH FOR HIM TO "FAKE IT 'TIL HE MAKES IT."
UNLESS, OF COURSE, ALL OF THIS "SOBRIETY" HAS GONE TO HIS HEAD...IN WHICH CASE, THERE'S PLAN B.
HARRY OSBORN BECOMES A MARTYR.
WHAT?
SKZZT

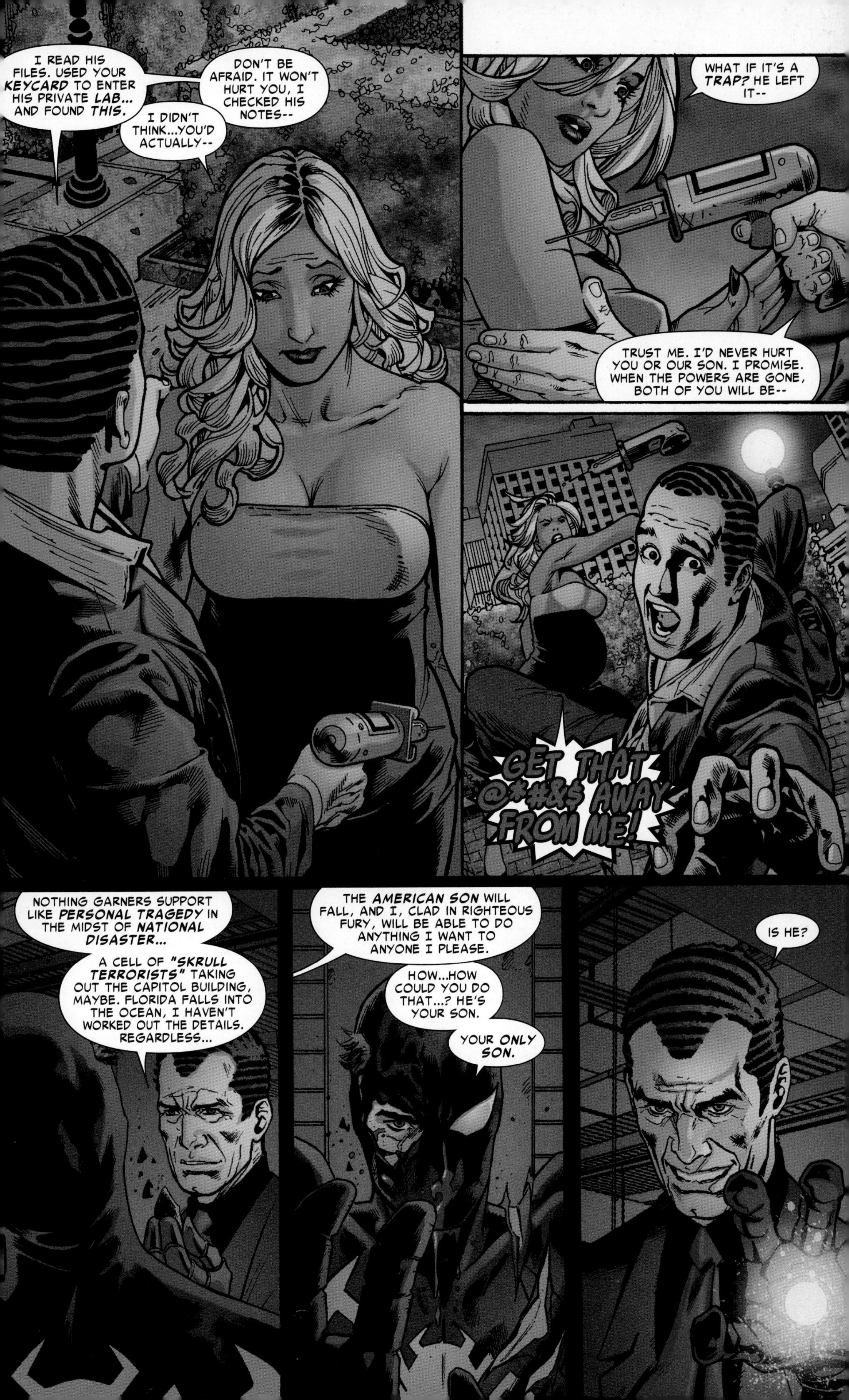
I READ HIS FILES. USED YOUR KEYCARD TO ENTER HIS PRIVATE LAB... AND FOUND THIS.
DON'T BE AFRAID. IT WON'T HURT YOU, I CHECKED HIS NOTES--
I DIDN'T THINK...YOU'D ACTUALLY--
WHAT IF IT'S A TRAP? HE LEFT IT--
TRUST ME. I'D NEVER HURT YOU OR OUR SON. I PROMISE. WHEN THE POWERS ARE GONE, BOTH OF YOU WILL BE--
GET THAT @*#&$ AWAY FROM ME!
NOTHING GARNERS SUPPORT LIKE PERSONAL TRAGEDY IN THE MIDST OF NATIONAL DISASTER...
A CELL OF "SKRULL TERRORISTS" TAKING OUT THE CAPITOL BUILDING, MAYBE. FLORIDA FALLS INTO THE OCEAN, I HAVEN'T WORKED OUT THE DETAILS. REGARDLESS...
THE AMERICAN SON WILL FALL, AND I, CLAD IN RIGHTEOUS FURY, WILL BE ABLE TO DO ANYTHING I WANT TO ANYONE I PLEASE.
HOW...HOW COULD YOU DO THAT...? HE'S YOUR SON.
YOUR ONLY SON.
IS HE?

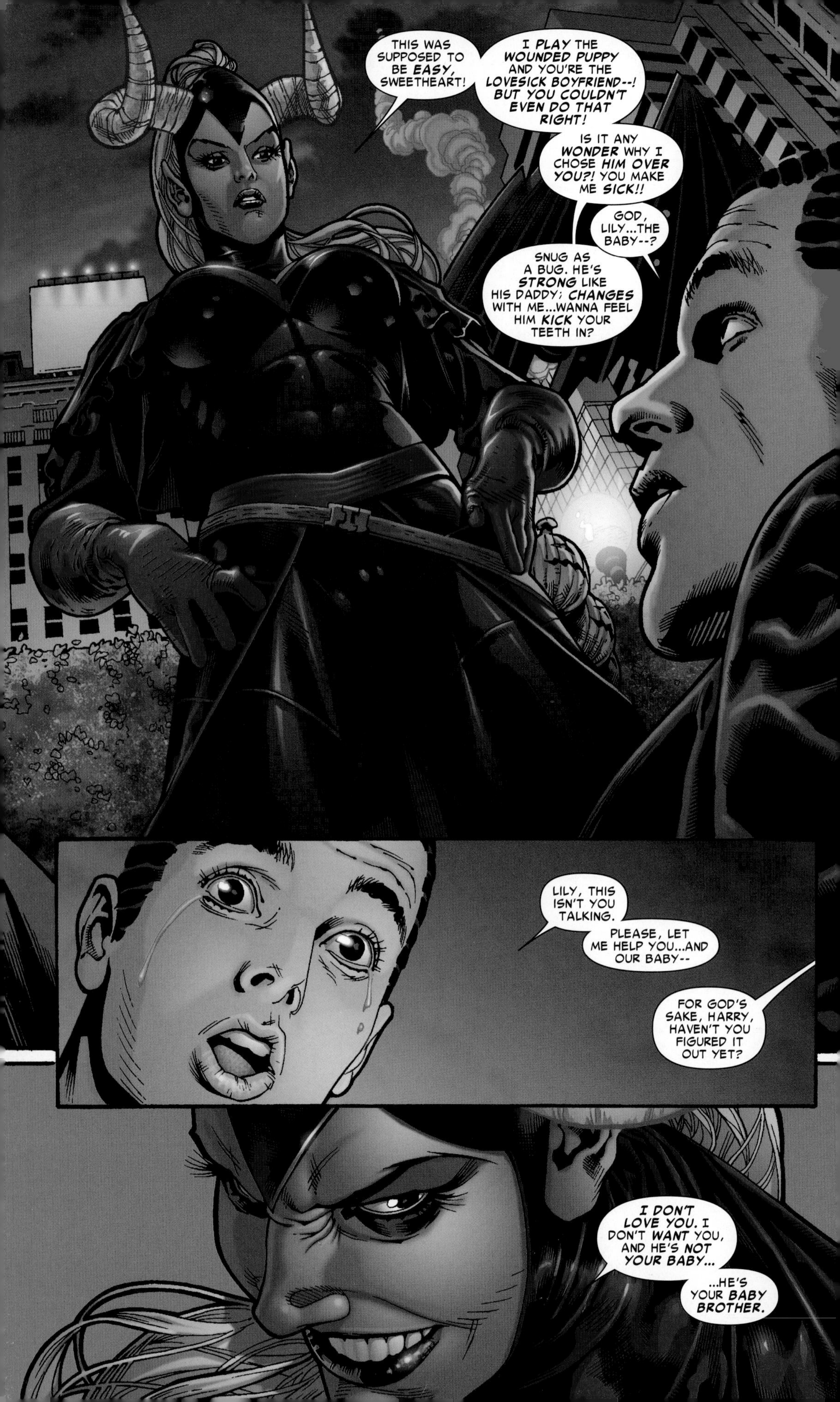
THIS WAS SUPPOSED TO BE EASY, SWEETHEART!
I PLAY THE WOUNDED PUPPY AND YOU'RE THE LOVESICK BOYFRIEND--! BUT YOU COULDN'T EVEN DO THAT RIGHT!
IS IT ANY WONDER WHY I CHOSE HIM OVER YOU?! YOU MAKE ME SICK!!
GOD, LILY...THE BABY--?
SNUG AS A BUG. HE'S STRONG LIKE HIS DADDY; CHANGES WITH ME...WANNA FEEL HIM KICK YOUR TEETH IN?
LILY, THIS ISN'T YOU TALKING.
PLEASE, LET ME HELP YOU...AND OUR BABY--
FOR GOD'S SAKE, HARRY, HAVEN'T YOU FIGURED IT OUT YET?
I DON'T LOVE YOU. I DON'T WANT YOU, AND HE'S NOT YOUR BABY...
...HE'S YOUR BABY BROTHER.

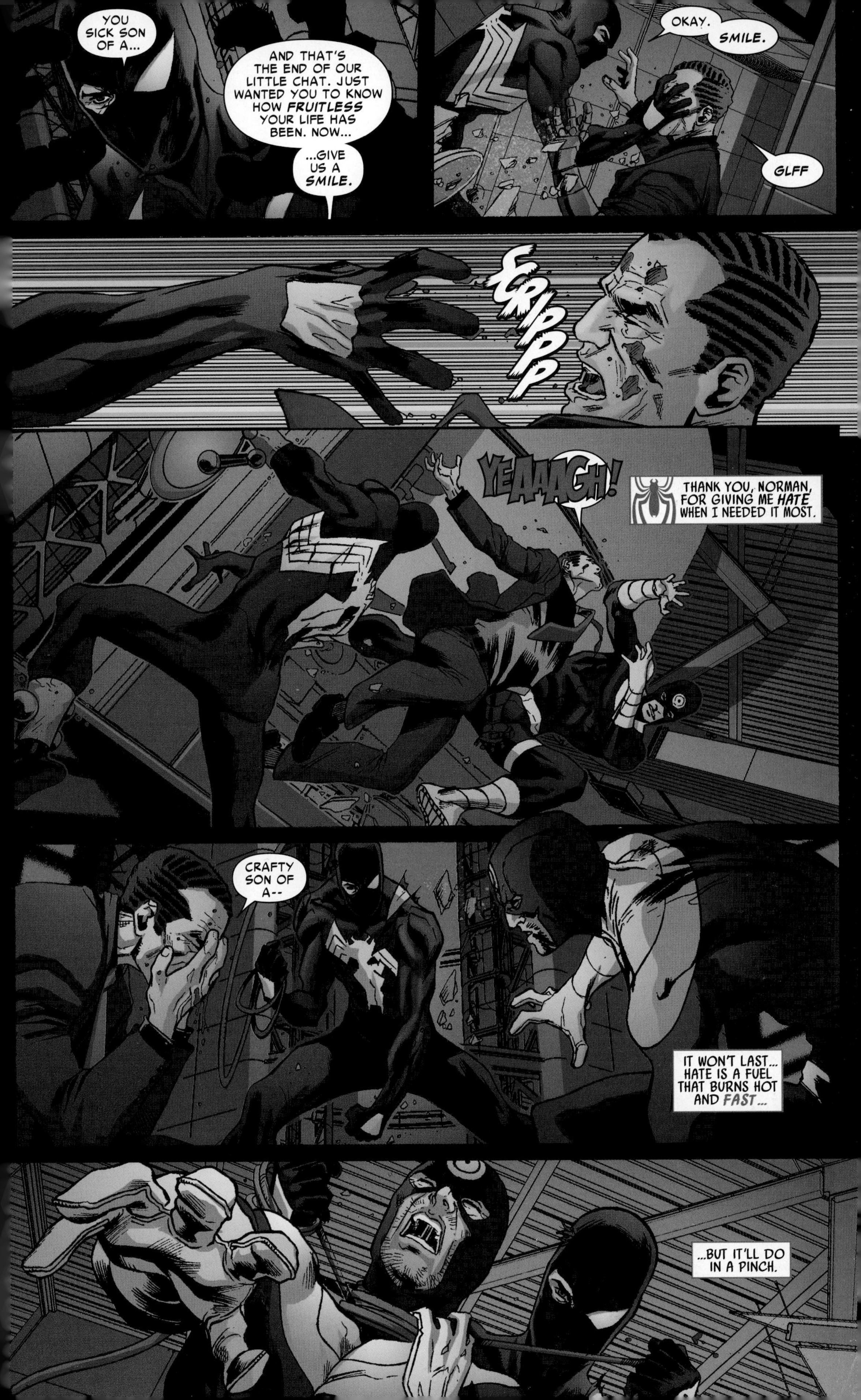
YOU SICK SON OF A...
AND THAT'S THE END OF OUR LITTLE CHAT. JUST WANTED YOU TO KNOW HOW FRUITLESS YOUR LIFE HAS BEEN. NOW...
...GIVE US A SMILE.
OKAY.
SMILE.
GLFF
SKRIPPP
YEAAAGH!
THANK YOU, NORMAN, FOR GIVING ME HATE WHEN I NEEDED IT MOST.
CRAFTY SON OF A--
IT WON'T LAST... HATE IS A FUEL THAT BURNS HOT AND FAST...
...BUT IT'LL DO IN A PINCH.

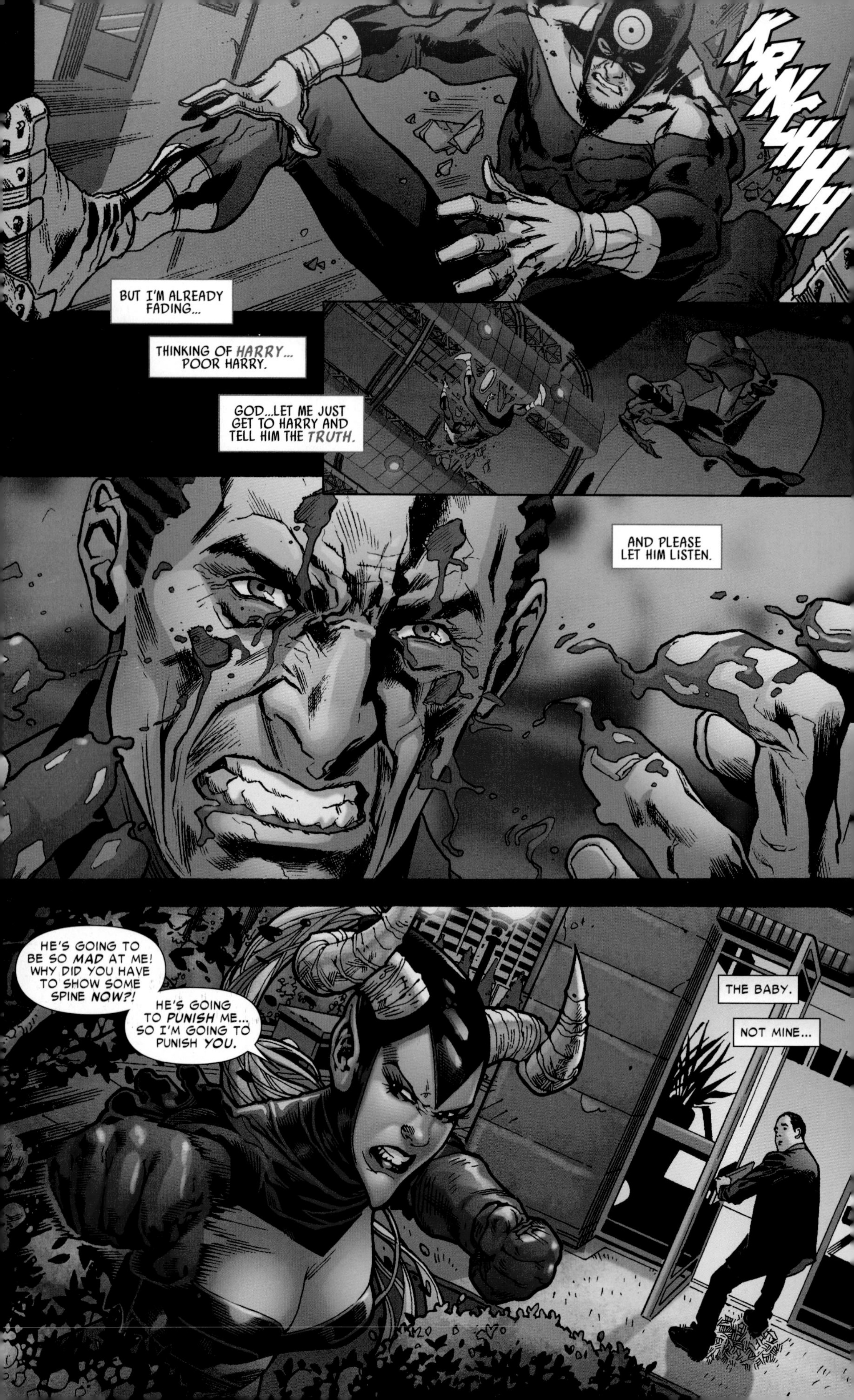
KRNCHHHH
BUT I'M ALREADY FADING...
THINKING OF HARRY... POOR HARRY.
GOD...LET ME JUST GET TO HARRY AND TELL HIM THE TRUTH.
AND PLEASE LET HIM LISTEN.
HE'S GOING TO BE SO MAD AT ME! WHY DID YOU HAVE TO SHOW SOME SPINE NOW?!
HE'S GOING TO PUNISH ME... SO I'M GOING TO PUNISH YOU.
THE BABY.
NOT MINE...

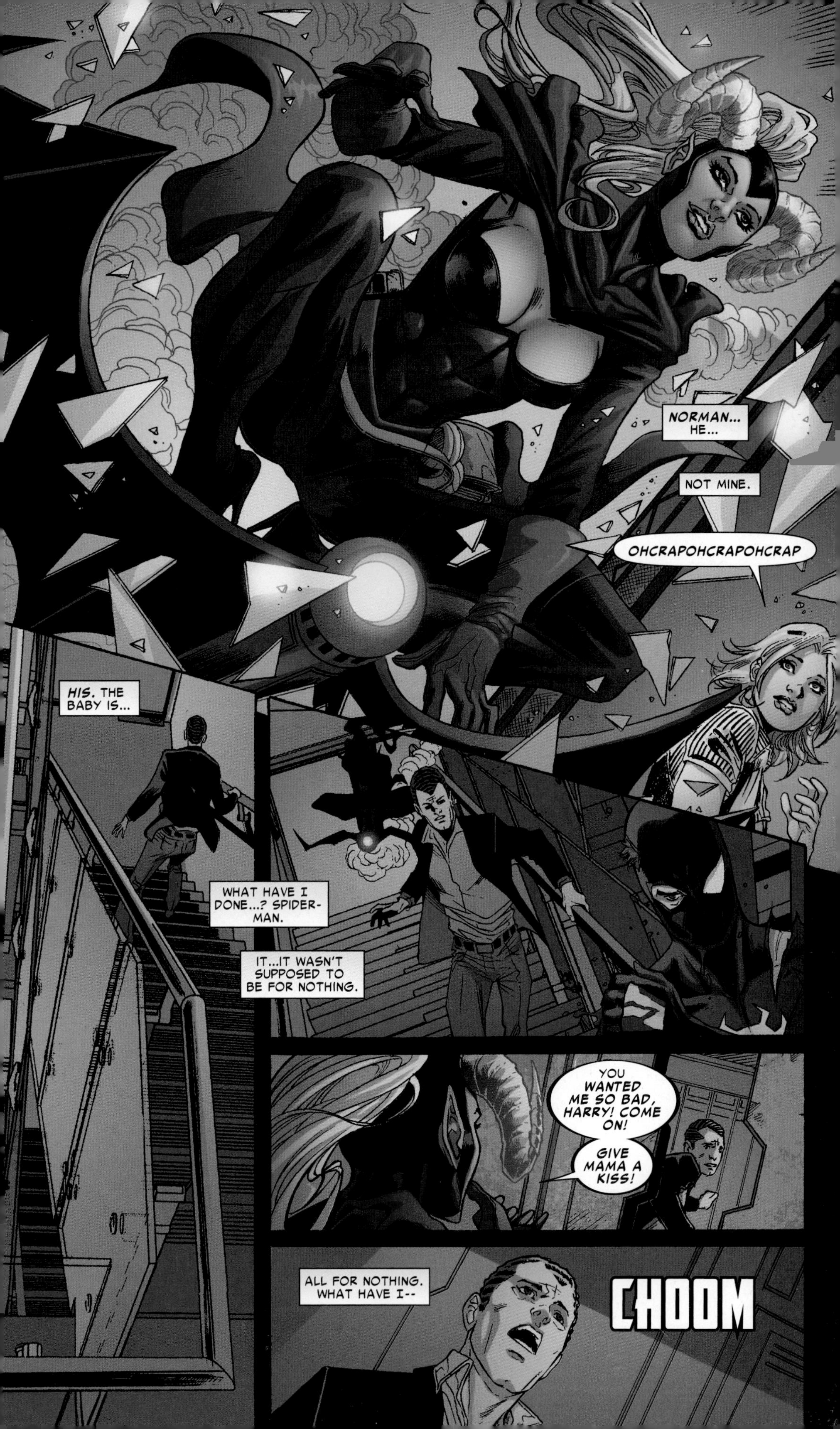
NORMAN... HE...
NOT MINE.
OHCRAPOHCRAPOHCRAP
HIS. THE BABY IS...
WHAT HAVE I DONE...? SPIDER-MAN.
IT...IT WASN'T SUPPOSED TO BE FOR NOTHING.
YOU WANTED ME SO BAD, HARRY! COME ON!
GIVE MAMA A KISS!
ALL FOR NOTHING. WHAT HAVE I--
CHOOM

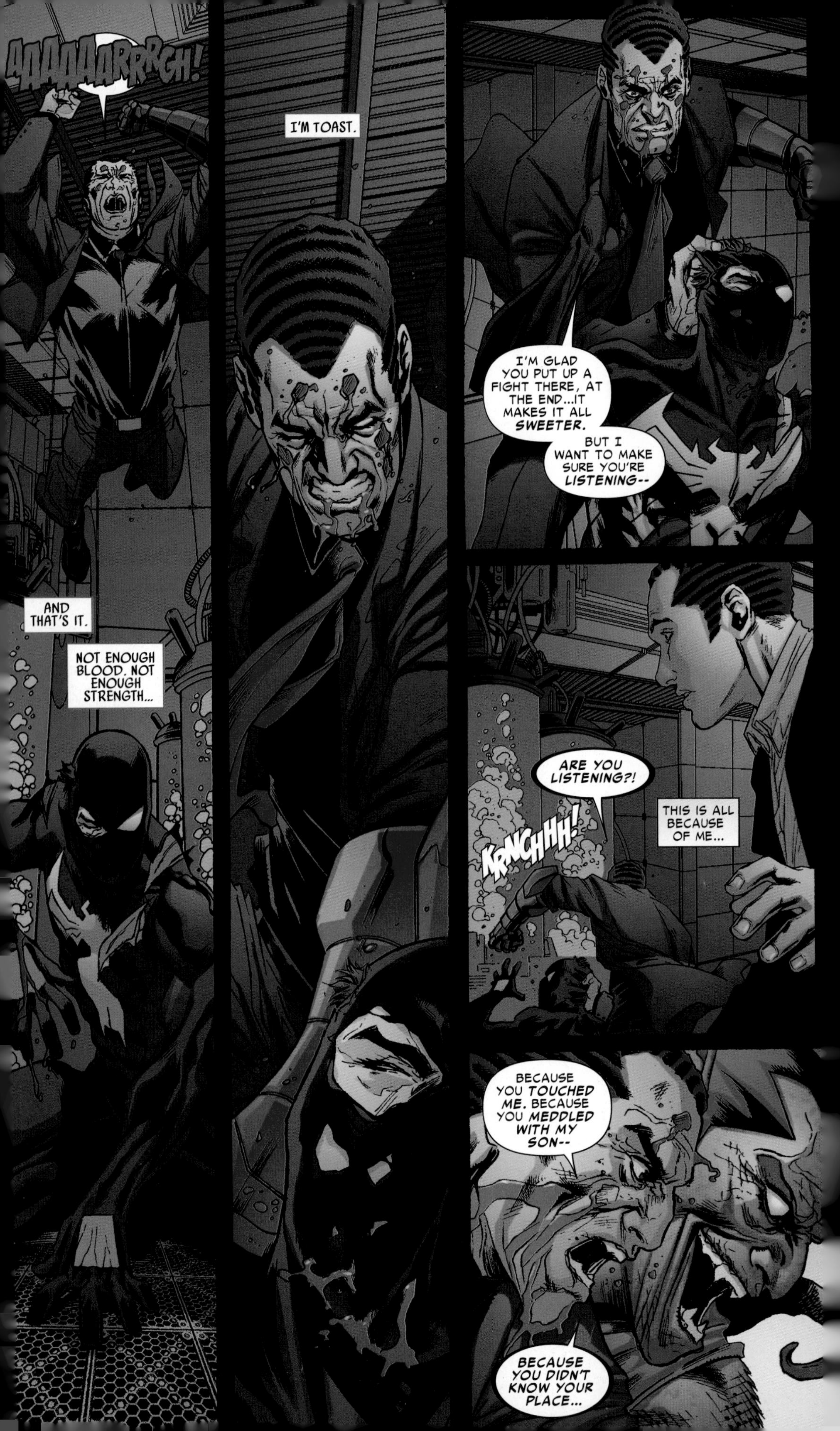
AAAAAARRRGH!
I'M TOAST.
I'M GLAD YOU PUT UP A FIGHT THERE, AT THE END...IT MAKES IT ALL SWEETER.
BUT I WANT TO MAKE SURE YOU'RE LISTENING--
AND THAT'S IT.
NOT ENOUGH BLOOD. NOT ENOUGH STRENGTH...
ARE YOU LISTENING?!
KRNCHHH!
THIS IS ALL BECAUSE OF ME...
BECAUSE YOU TOUCHED ME. BECAUSE YOU MEDDLED WITH MY SON--
BECAUSE YOU DIDN'T KNOW YOUR PLACE...

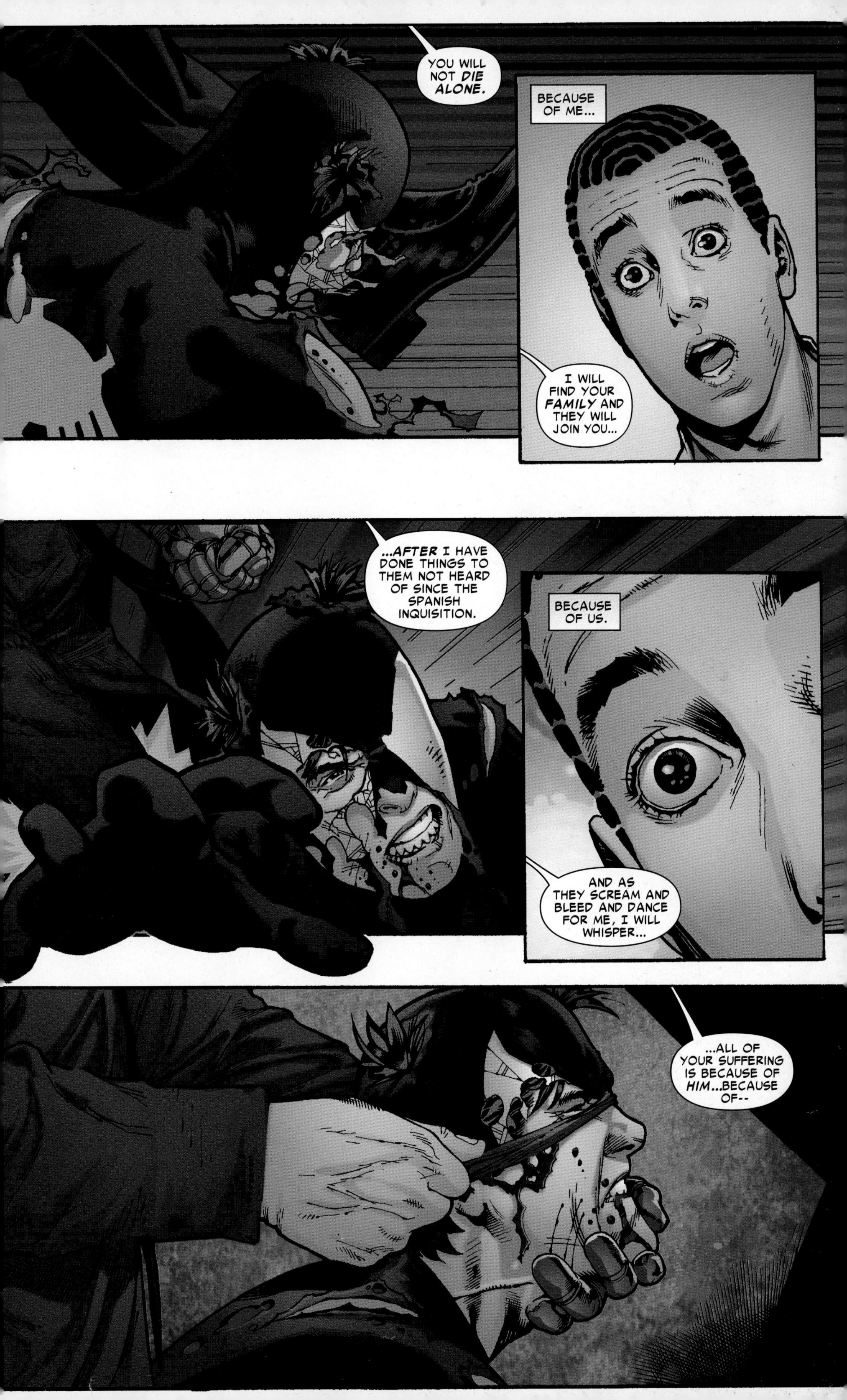
YOU WILL NOT DIE ALONE.
BECAUSE OF ME...
I WILL FIND YOUR FAMILY AND THEY WILL JOIN YOU...
...AFTER I HAVE DONE THINGS TO THEM NOT HEARD OF SINCE THE SPANISH INQUISITION.
BECAUSE OF US.
AND AS THEY SCREAM AND BLEED AND DANCE FOR ME, I WILL WHISPER...
...ALL OF YOUR SUFFERING IS BECAUSE OF HIM...BECAUSE OF--

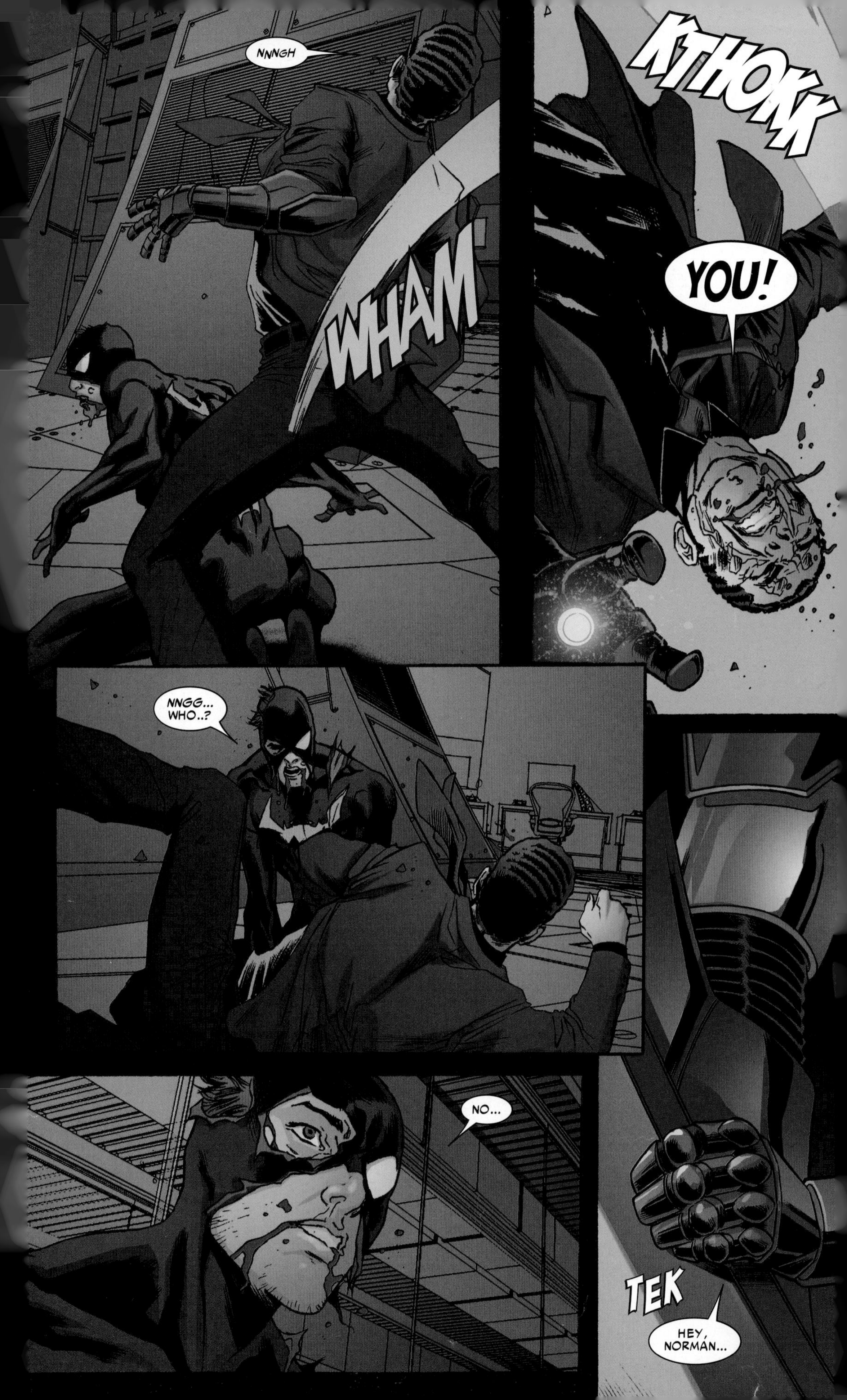
NNNGH
WHAM
KTHOKK
YOU!
NNGG... WHO..?
NO...
TEK
HEY, NORMAN...

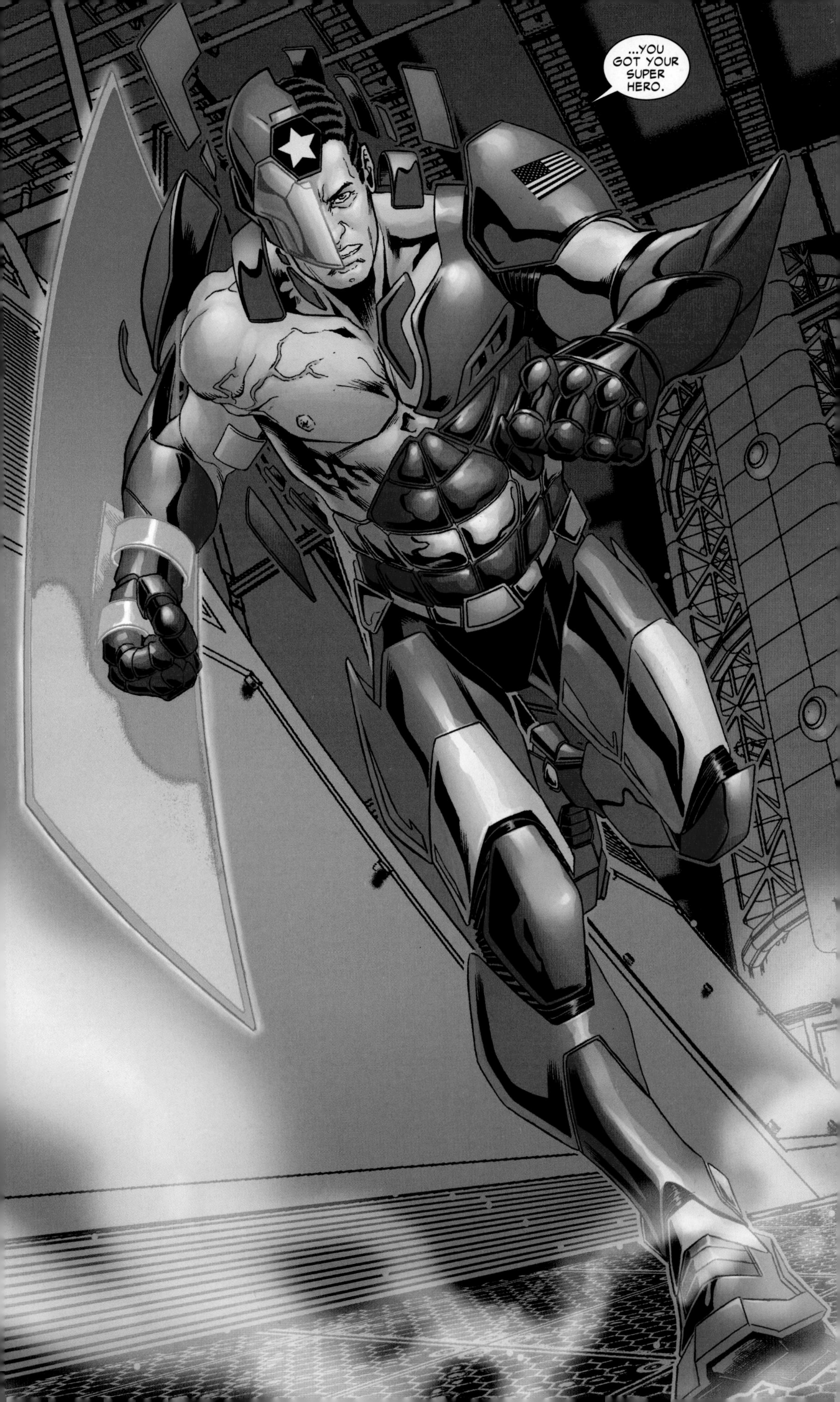
...YOU GOT YOUR SUPER HERO.

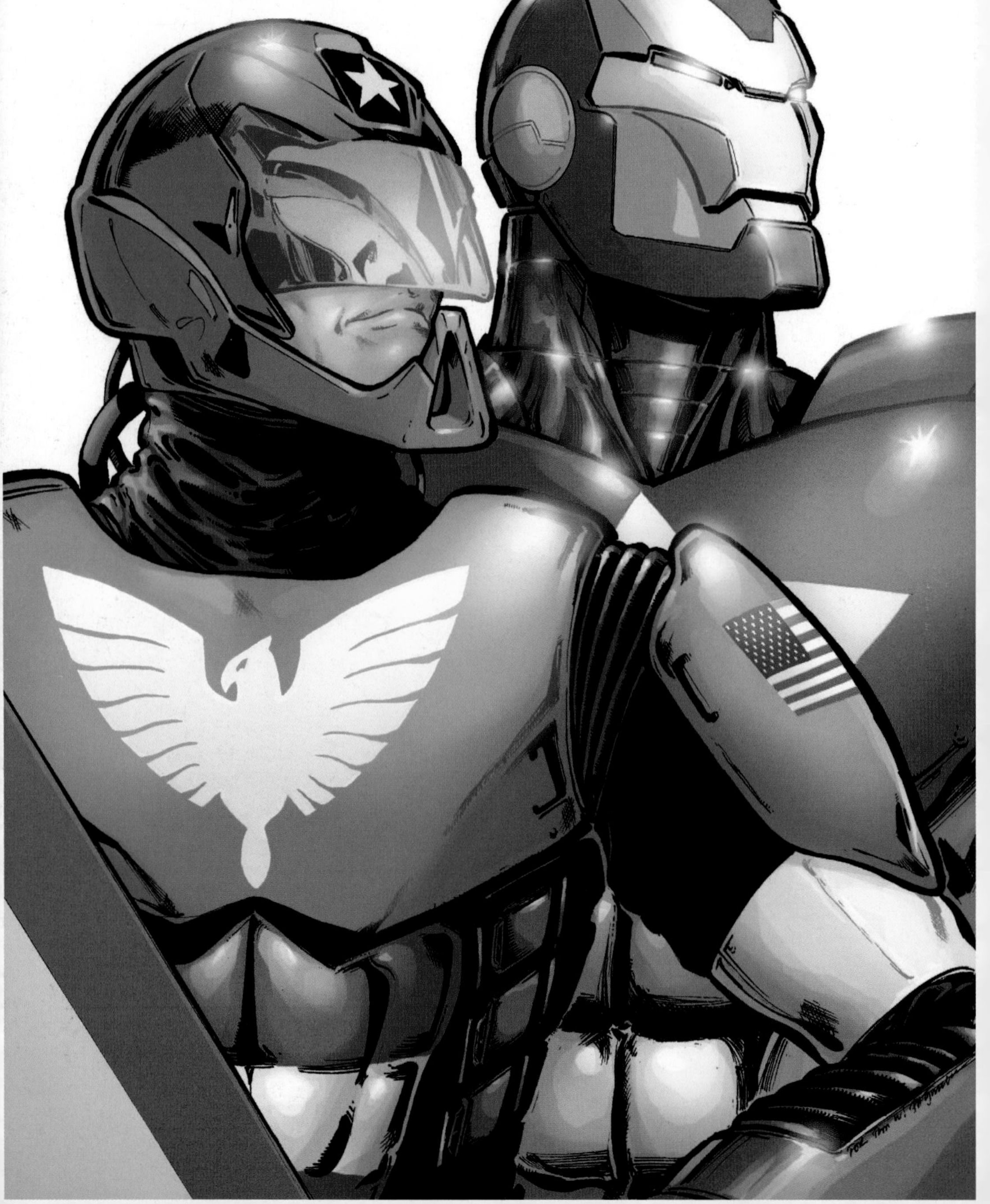

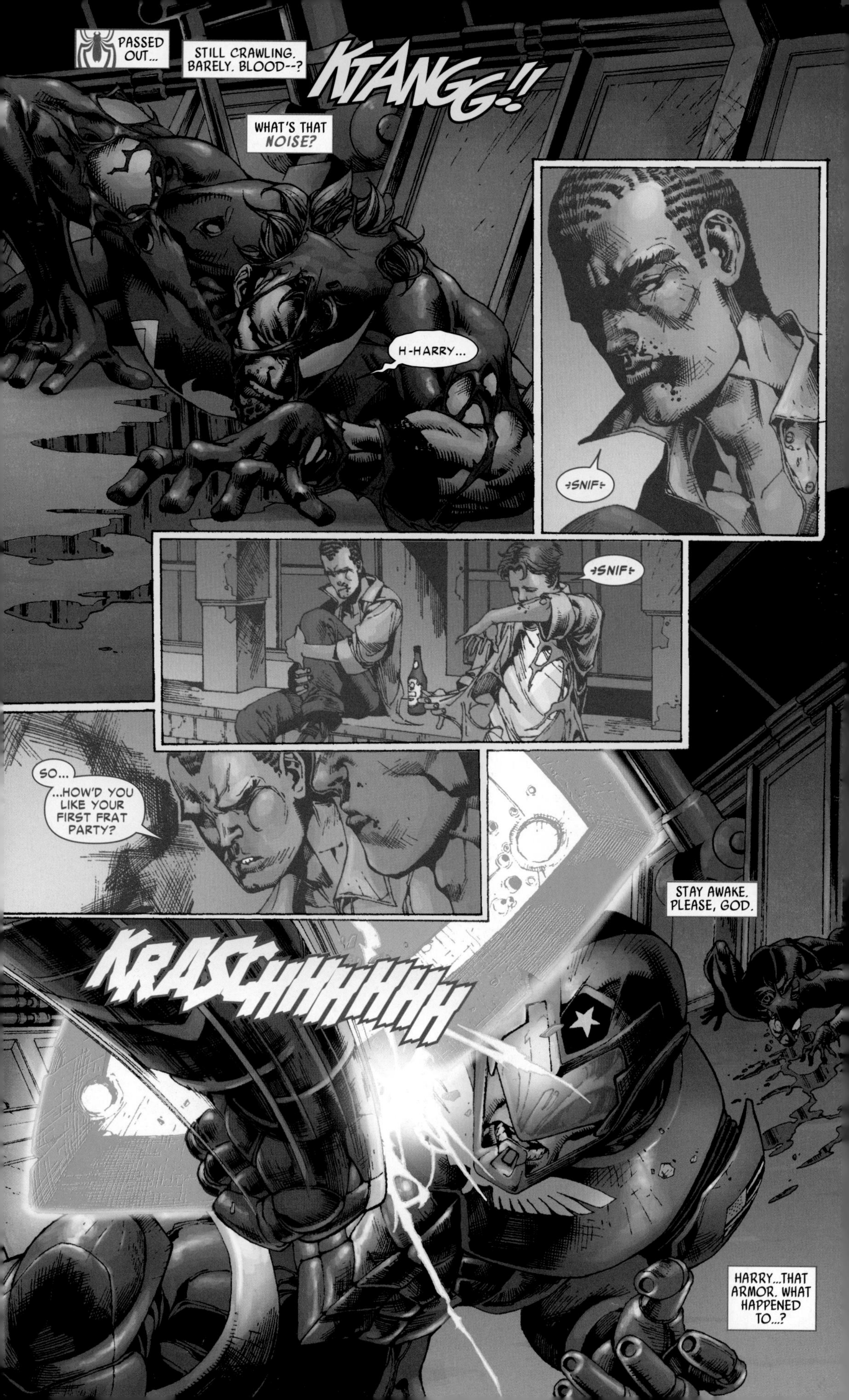
PASSED OUT...
STILL CRAWLING. BARELY. BLOOD--?
KTANGG!!
WHAT'S THAT NOISE?
H-HARRY...
SNIF
SNIF
SO... ...HOW'D YOU LIKE YOUR FIRST FRAT PARTY?
STAY AWAKE. PLEASE, GOD.
KRASCHHHHHHH
HARRY...THAT ARMOR. WHAT HAPPENED TO...?

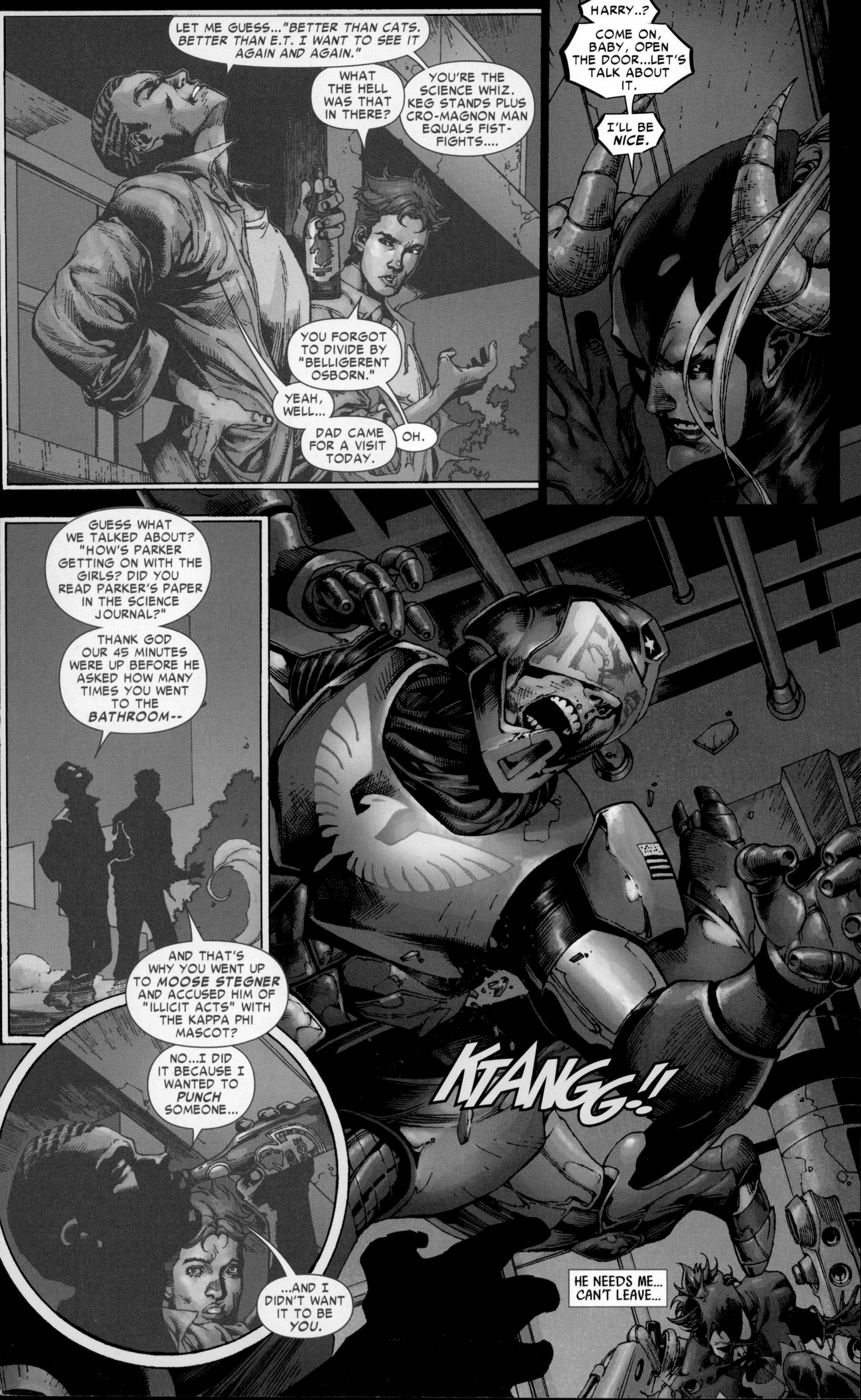

LET ME GUESS..."BETTER THAN CATS. BETTER THAN E.T. I WANT TO SEE IT AGAIN AND AGAIN."
WHAT THE HELL WAS THAT IN THERE?
YOU'RE THE SCIENCE WHIZ. KEG STANDS PLUS CRO-MAGNON MAN EQUALS FIST-FIGHTS....
YOU FORGOT TO DIVIDE BY "BELLIGERENT OSBORN."
YEAH, WELL...
DAD CAME FOR A VISIT TODAY.
OH.
HARRY..?
COME ON, BABY, OPEN THE DOOR...LET'S TALK ABOUT IT.
I'LL BE NICE.
GUESS WHAT WE TALKED ABOUT? "HOW'S PARKER GETTING ON WITH THE GIRLS? DID YOU READ PARKER'S PAPER IN THE SCIENCE JOURNAL?"
THANK GOD OUR 45 MINUTES WERE UP BEFORE HE ASKED HOW MANY TIMES YOU WENT TO THE BATHROOM--
AND THAT'S WHY YOU WENT UP TO MOOSE STEGNER AND ACCUSED HIM OF "ILLICIT ACTS" WITH THE KAPPA PHI MASCOT?
NO...I DID IT BECAUSE I WANTED TO PUNCH SOMEONE...
...AND I DIDN'T WANT IT TO BE YOU.
KTANGG!!
HE NEEDS ME... CAN'T LEAVE...

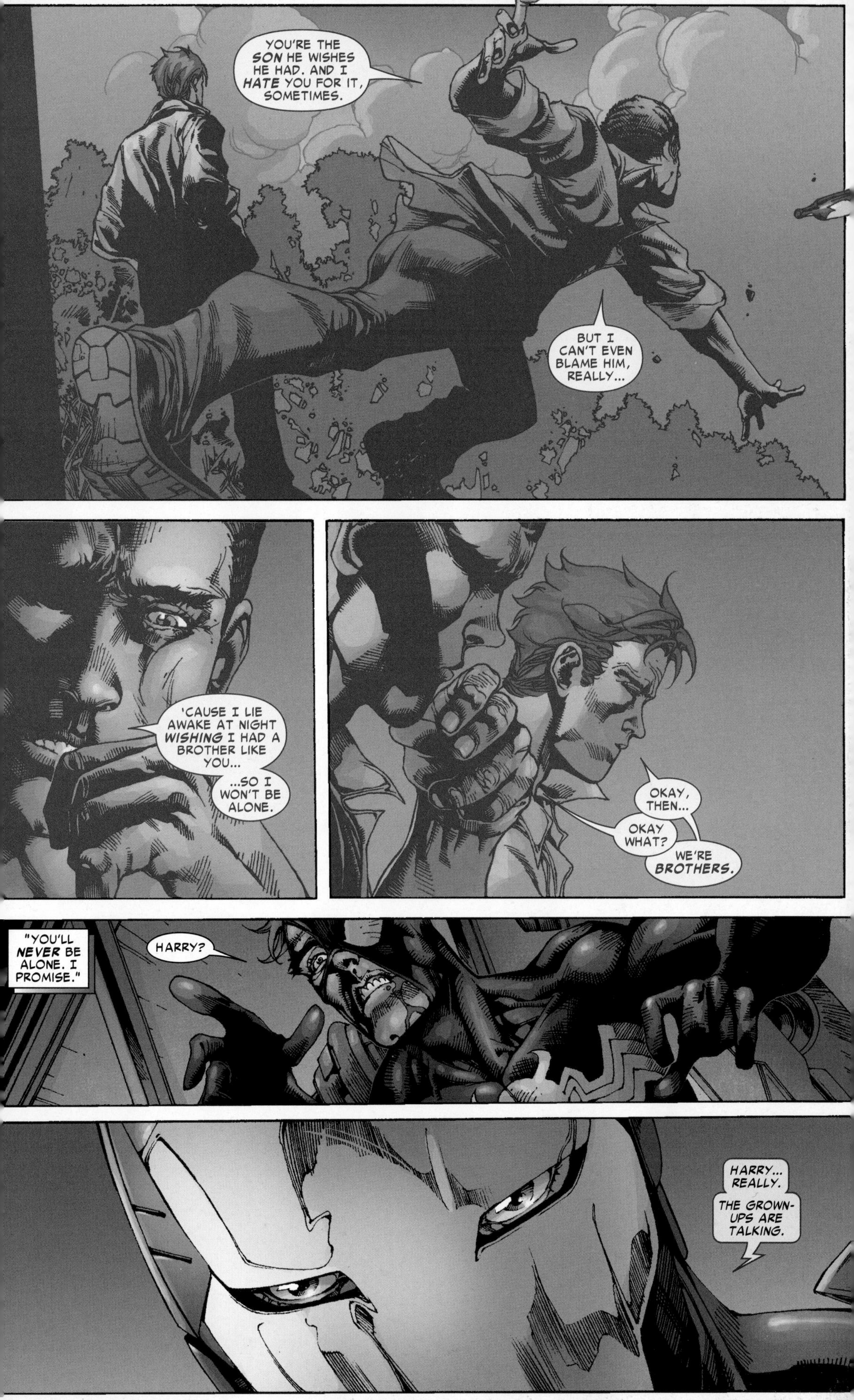
YOU'RE THE SON HE WISHES HE HAD. AND I HATE YOU FOR IT, SOMETIMES.
BUT I CAN'T EVEN BLAME HIM, REALLY...
'CAUSE I LIE AWAKE AT NIGHT WISHING I HAD A BROTHER LIKE YOU...
...SO I WON'T BE ALONE.
OKAY, THEN...
OKAY WHAT?
WE'RE BROTHERS.
"YOU'LL NEVER BE ALONE. I PROMISE."
HARRY?
HARRY... REALLY.
THE GROWN-UPS ARE TALKING.

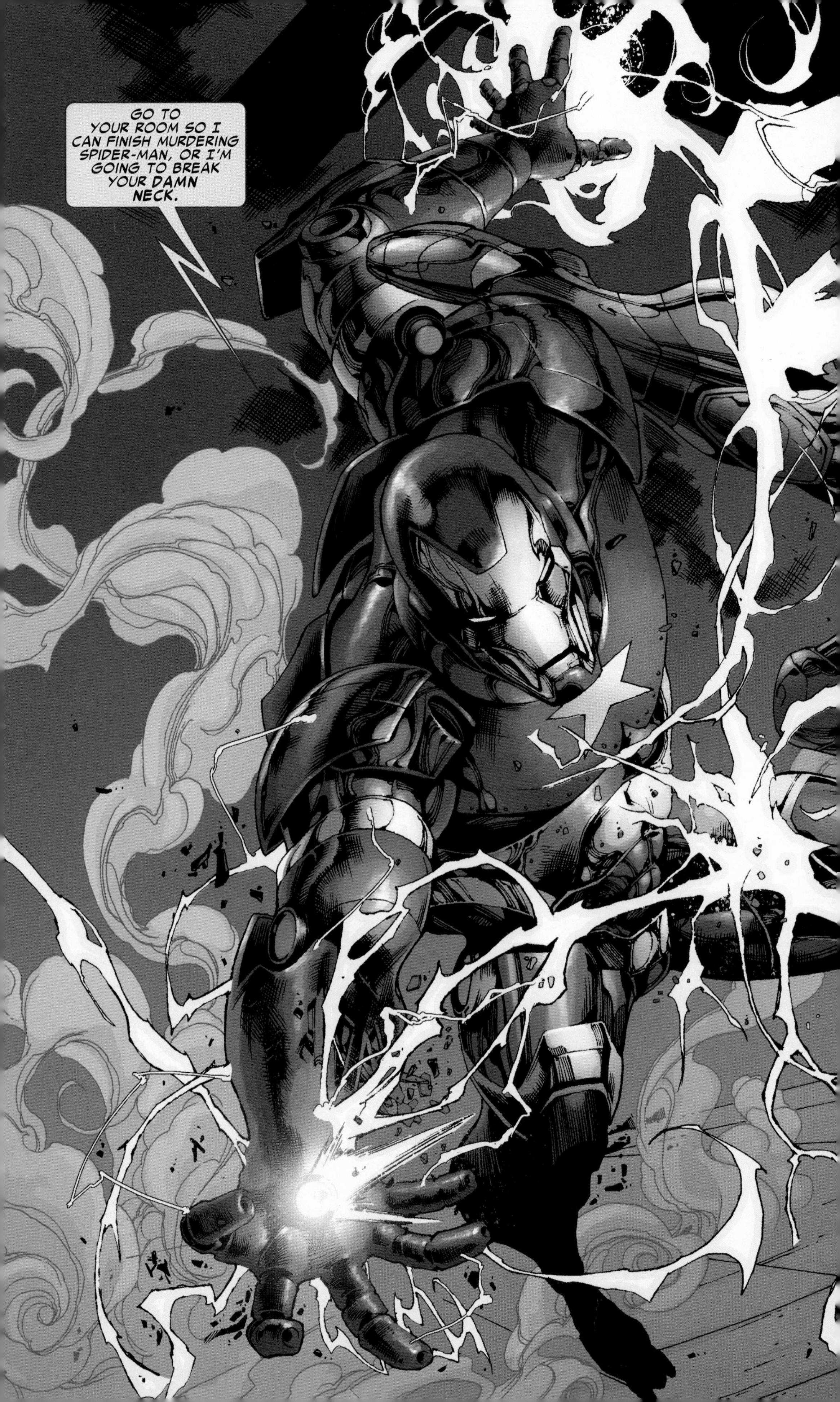
GO TO YOUR ROOM SO I CAN FINISH MURDERING SPIDER-MAN, OR I'M GOING TO BREAK YOUR DAMN NECK.

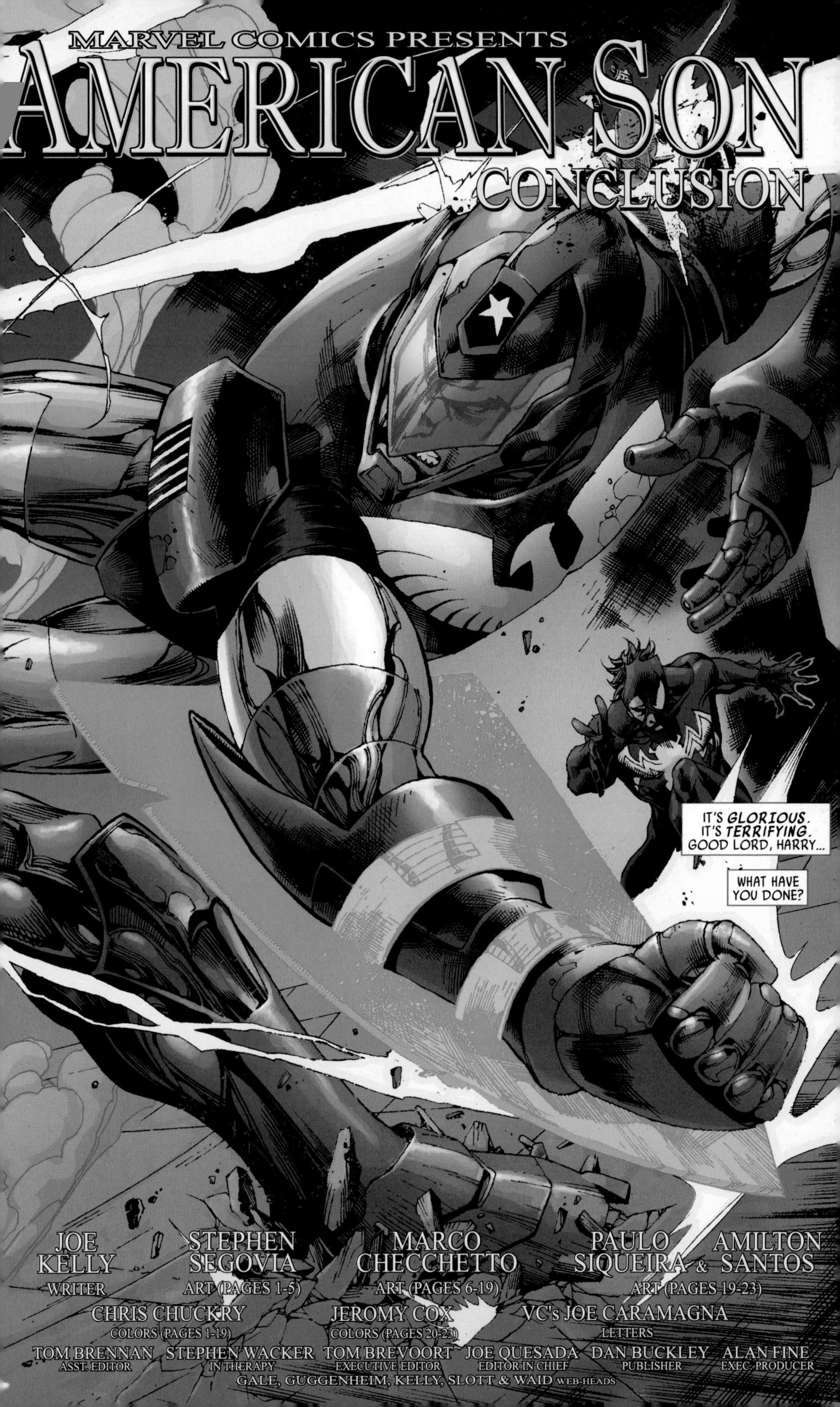
MARVEL COMICS PRESENTS
AMERICAN SON
CONCLUSION
IT'S GLORIOUS. IT'S TERRIFYING. GOOD LORD, HARRY...
WHAT HAVE YOU DONE?
JOE KELLY WRITER
STEPHEN SEGOVIA ART (PAGES 1-5)
MARCO CHECCHETTO ART (PAGES 6-19)
PAULO SIQUEIRA & AMILTON SANTOS ART (PAGES 19-23)
CHRIS CHUCKRY COLORS (PAGES 1-19)
JEROMY COX COLORS (PAGES 20-23)
VC's JOE CARAMAGNA LETTERS
TOM BRENNAN ASST. EDITOR
STEPHEN WACKER IN THERAPY
TOM BREVOORT EXECUTIVE EDITOR
JOE QUESADA EDITOR IN CHIEF
DAN BUCKLEY PUBLISHER
ALAN FINE EXEC. PRODUCER
GALE, GUGGENHEIM, KELLY, SLOTT & WAID WEB-HEADS

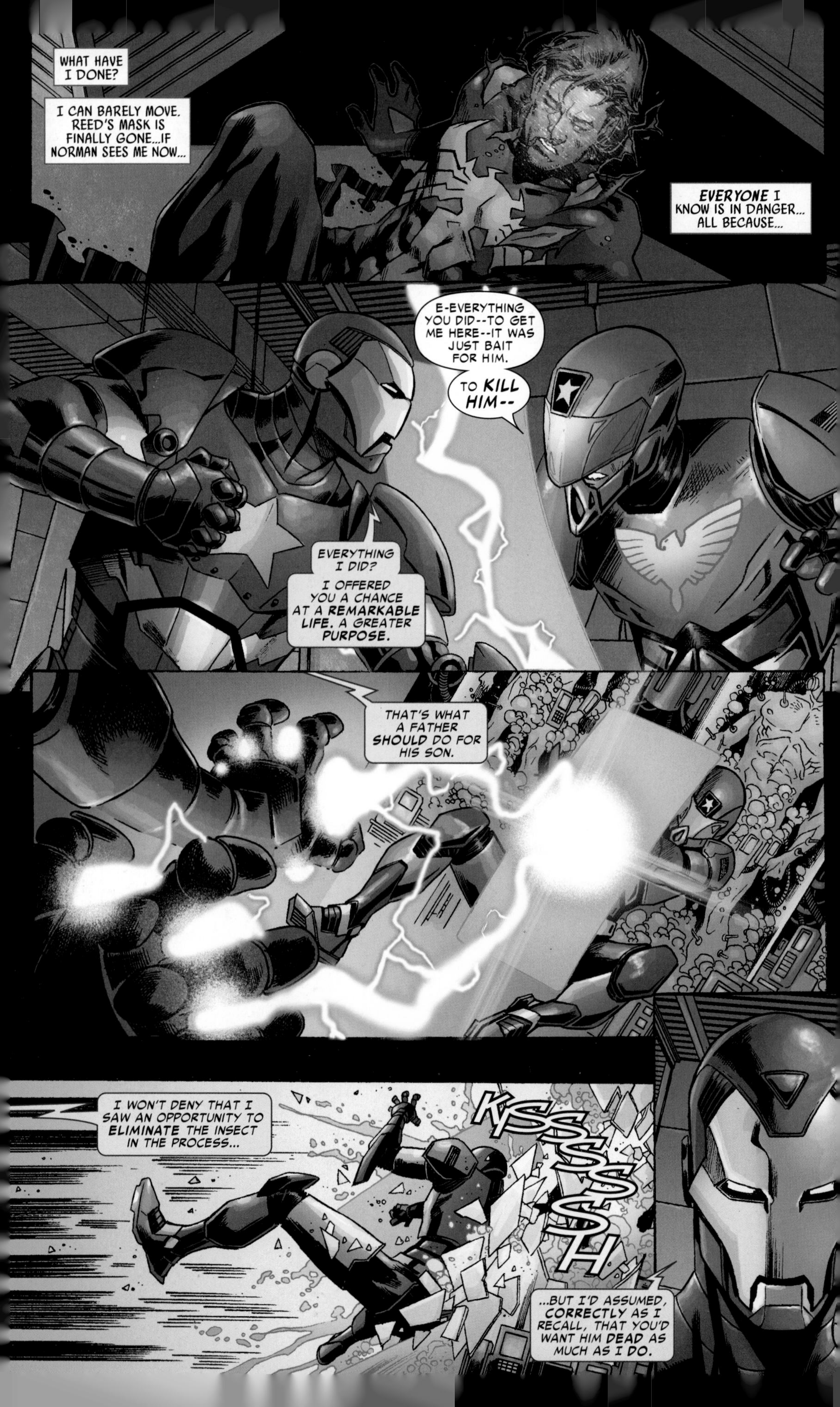
WHAT HAVE I DONE?
I CAN BARELY MOVE. REED'S MASK IS FINALLY GONE...IF NORMAN SEES ME NOW...
EVERYONE I KNOW IS IN DANGER... ALL BECAUSE...
E-EVERYTHING YOU DID--TO GET ME HERE--IT WAS JUST BAIT FOR HIM.
TO KILL HIM--
EVERYTHING I DID?
I OFFERED YOU A CHANCE AT A REMARKABLE LIFE. A GREATER PURPOSE.
THAT'S WHAT A FATHER SHOULD DO FOR HIS SON.
I WON'T DENY THAT I SAW AN OPPORTUNITY TO ELIMINATE THE INSECT IN THE PROCESS...
KSSSSSH
...BUT I'D ASSUMED, CORRECTLY AS I RECALL, THAT YOU'D WANT HIM DEAD AS MUCH AS I DO.

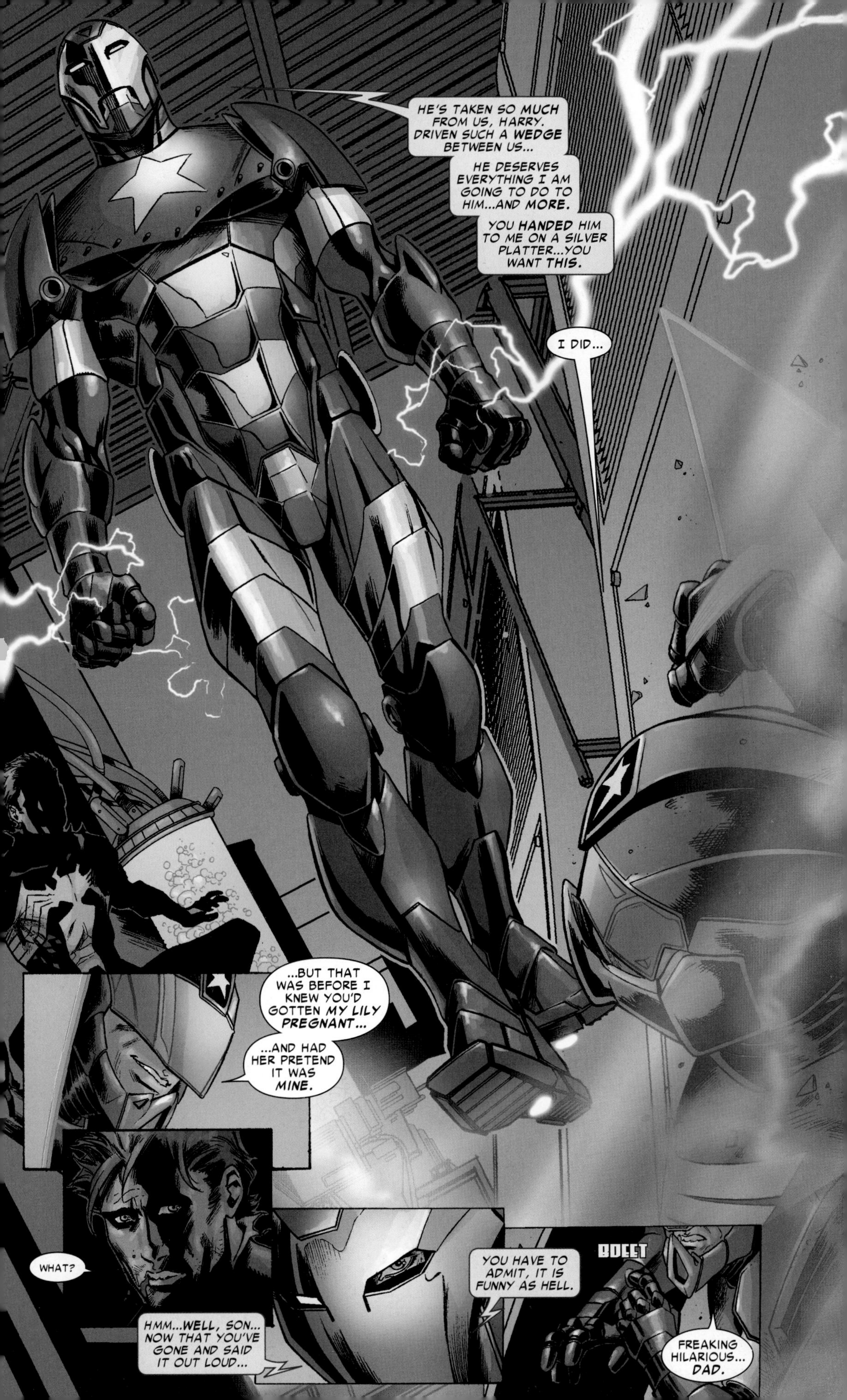
HE'S TAKEN SO MUCH FROM US, HARRY. DRIVEN SUCH A WEDGE BETWEEN US...
HE DESERVES EVERYTHING I AM GOING TO DO TO HIM...AND MORE.
YOU HANDED HIM TO ME ON A SILVER PLATTER...YOU WANT THIS.
I DID...
...BUT THAT WAS BEFORE I KNEW YOU'D GOTTEN MY LILY PREGNANT...
...AND HAD HER PRETEND IT WAS MINE.
WHAT?
HMM...WELL, SON... NOW THAT YOU'VE GONE AND SAID IT OUT LOUD...
YOU HAVE TO ADMIT, IT IS FUNNY AS HELL.
BDEET
FREAKING HILARIOUS... DAD.

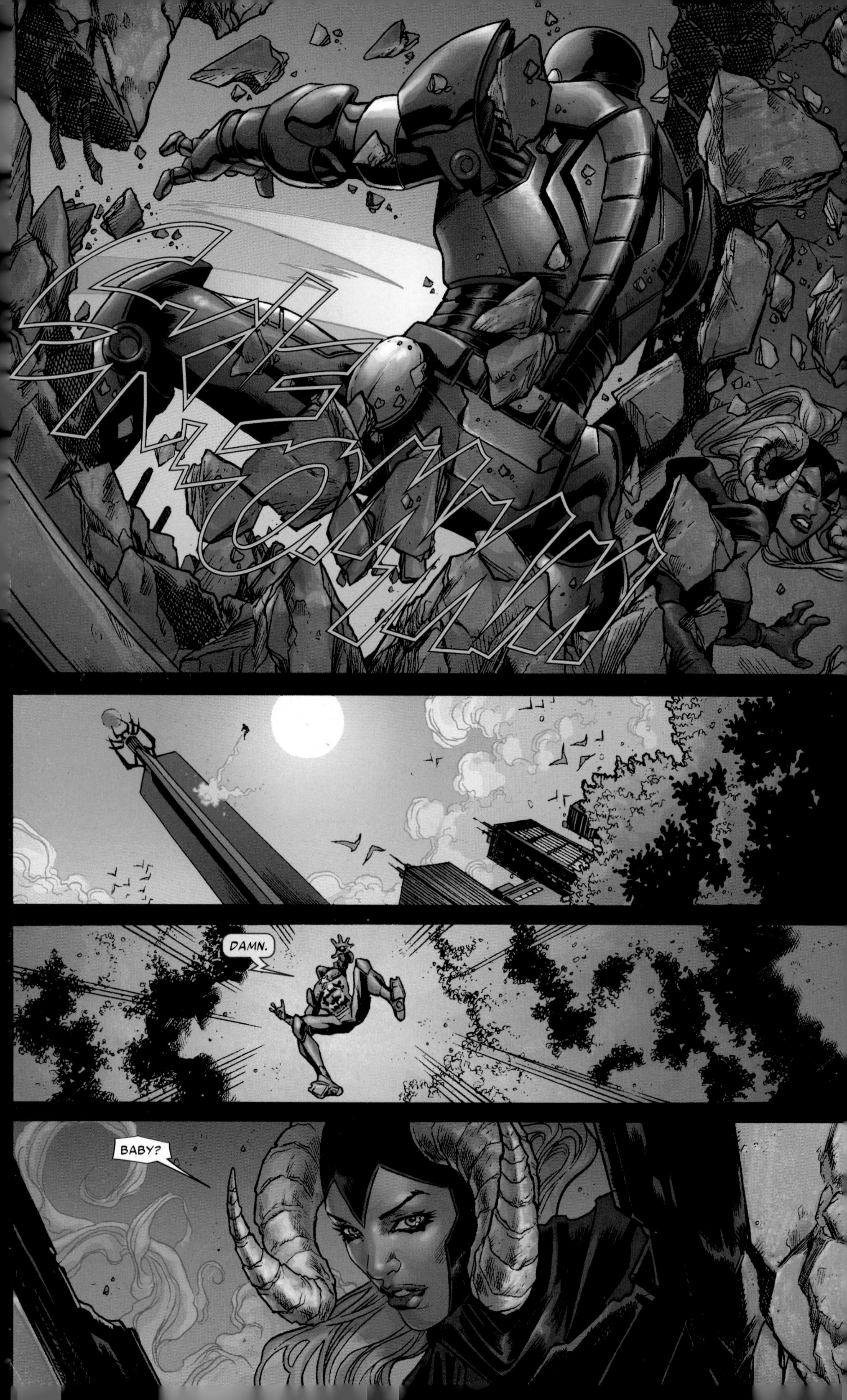
DAMN.
BABY?

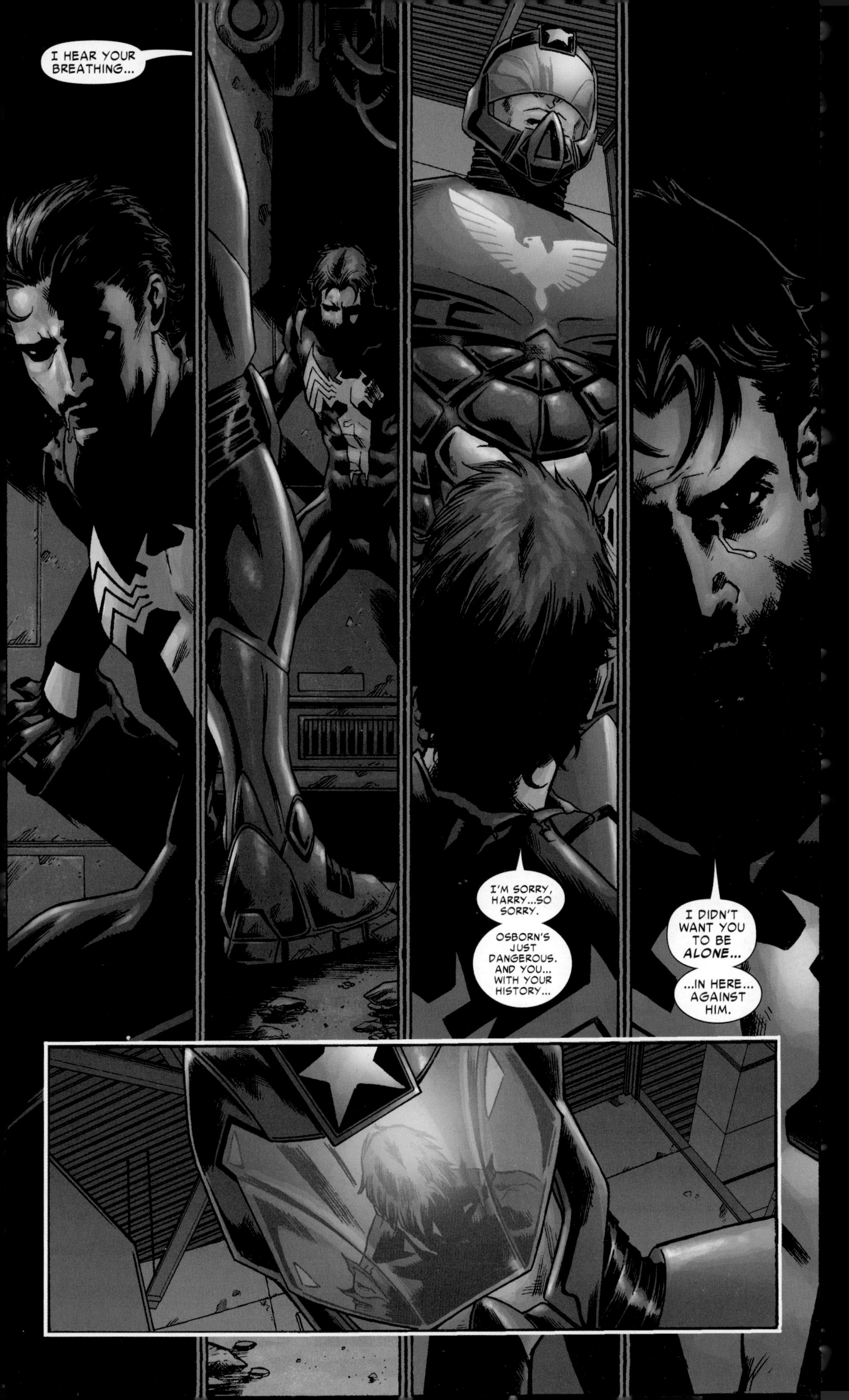

I HEAR YOUR BREATHING...
I'M SORRY, HARRY...SO SORRY.
OSBORN'S JUST DANGEROUS. AND YOU... WITH YOUR HISTORY...
I DIDN'T WANT YOU TO BE ALONE...
...IN HERE... AGAINST HIM.

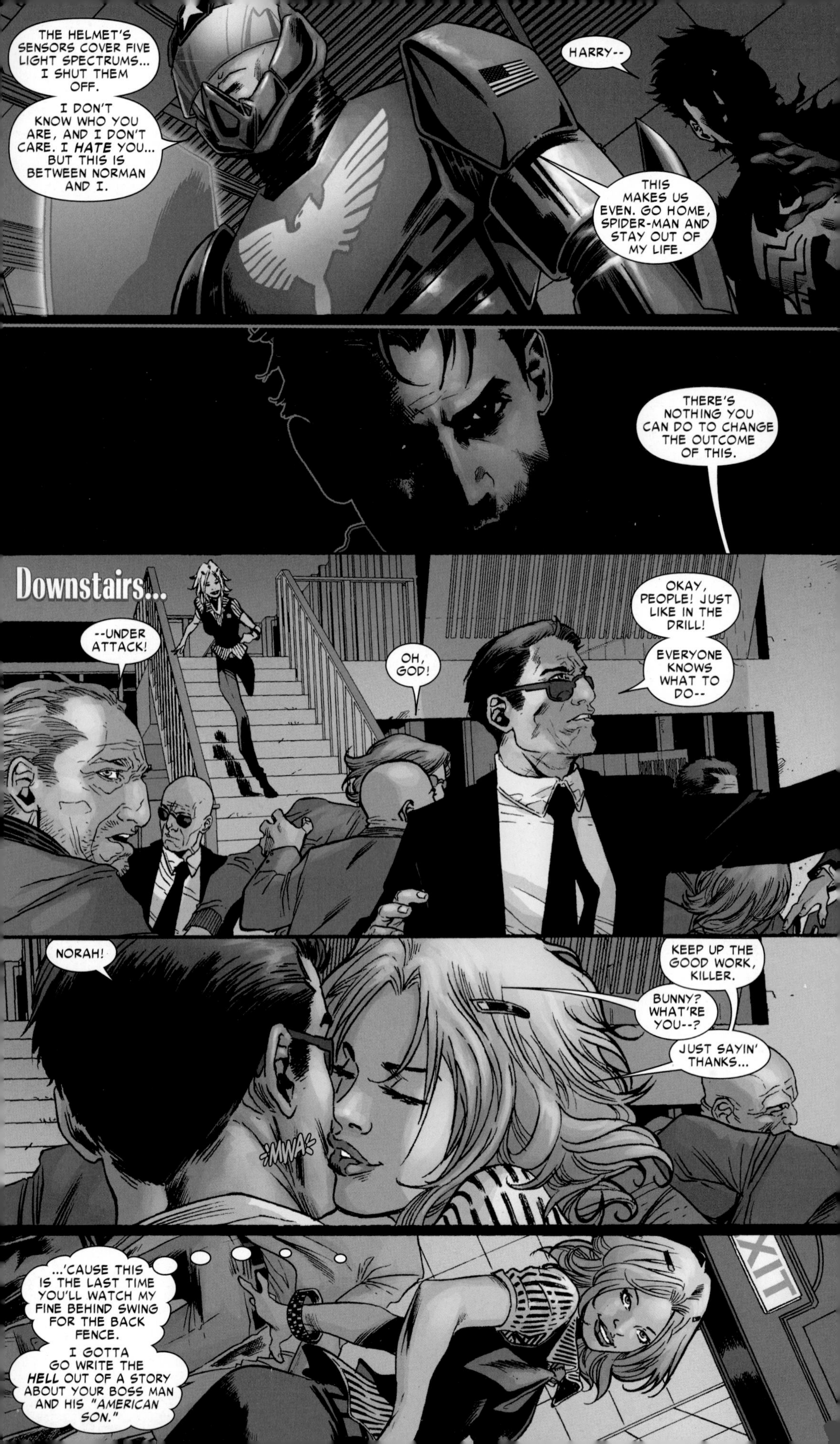
THE HELMET'S SENSORS COVER FIVE LIGHT SPECTRUMS... I SHUT THEM OFF.
I DON'T KNOW WHO YOU ARE, AND I DON'T CARE. I HATE YOU... BUT THIS IS BETWEEN NORMAN AND I.
HARRY--
THIS MAKES US EVEN. GO HOME, SPIDER-MAN AND STAY OUT OF MY LIFE.
THERE'S NOTHING YOU CAN DO TO CHANGE THE OUTCOME OF THIS.
Downstairs...
--UNDER ATTACK!
OH, GOD!
OKAY, PEOPLE! JUST LIKE IN THE DRILL!
EVERYONE KNOWS WHAT TO DO--
NORAH!
KEEP UP THE GOOD WORK, KILLER.
BUNNY? WHAT'RE YOU--?
JUST SAYIN' THANKS...
MWA
...'CAUSE THIS IS THE LAST TIME YOU'LL WATCH MY FINE BEHIND SWING FOR THE BACK FENCE.
I GOTTA GO WRITE THE HELL OUT OF A STORY ABOUT YOUR BOSS MAN AND HIS "AMERICAN SON."
EXIT

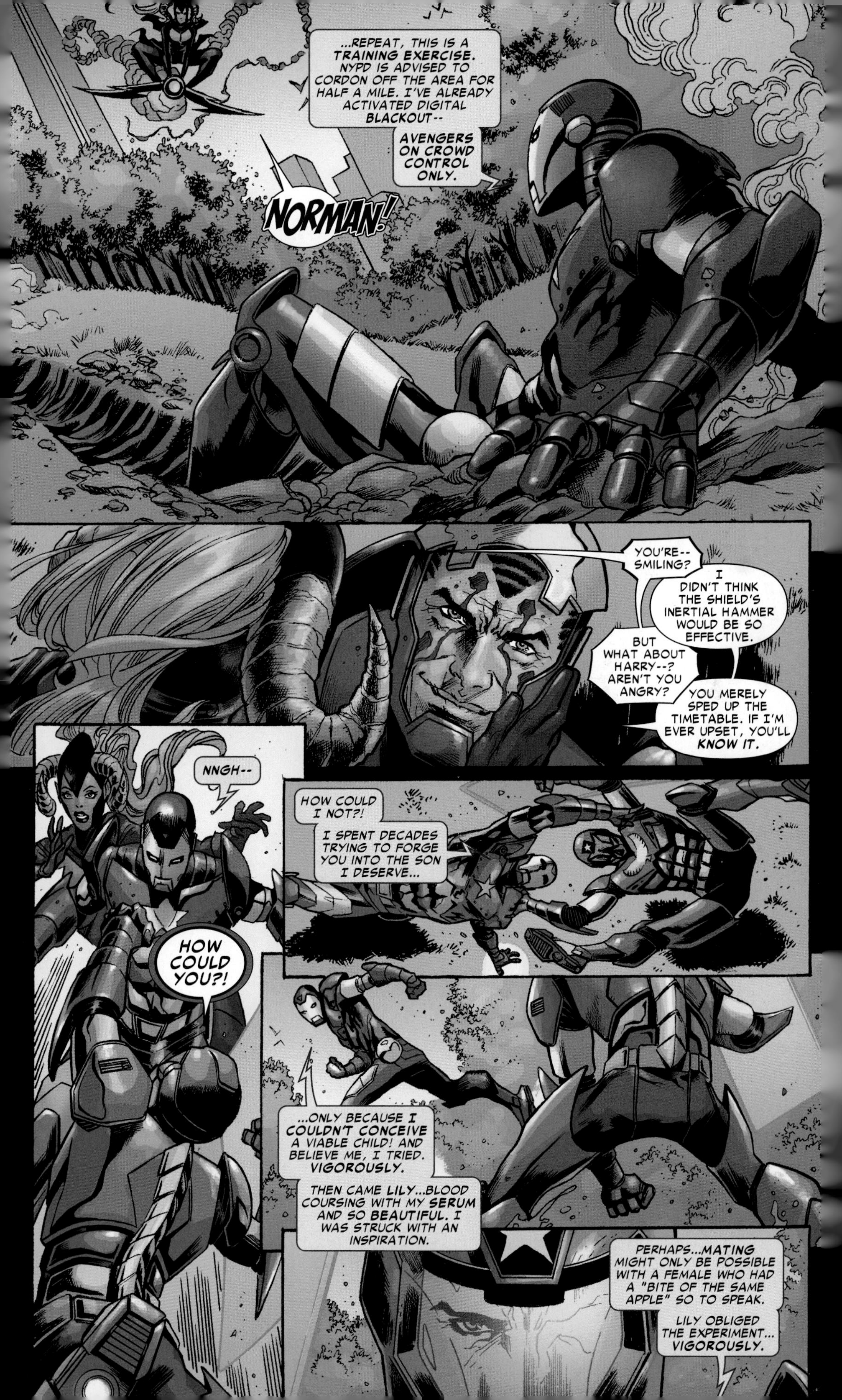
...REPEAT, THIS IS A TRAINING EXERCISE. NYPD IS ADVISED TO CORDON OFF THE AREA FOR HALF A MILE. I'VE ALREADY ACTIVATED DIGITAL BLACKOUT--
AVENGERS ON CROWD CONTROL ONLY.
NORMAN!
YOU'RE--SMILING?
I DIDN'T THINK THE SHIELD'S INERTIAL HAMMER WOULD BE SO EFFECTIVE.
BUT WHAT ABOUT HARRY--? AREN'T YOU ANGRY?
YOU MERELY SPED UP THE TIMETABLE. IF I'M EVER UPSET, YOU'LL KNOW IT.
NNGH--
HOW COULD YOU?!
HOW COULD I NOT?!
I SPENT DECADES TRYING TO FORGE YOU INTO THE SON I DESERVE...
...ONLY BECAUSE I COULDN'T CONCEIVE A VIABLE CHILD! AND BELIEVE ME, I TRIED. VIGOROUSLY.
THEN CAME LILY...BLOOD COURSING WITH MY SERUM AND SO BEAUTIFUL. I WAS STRUCK WITH AN INSPIRATION.
PERHAPS...MATING MIGHT ONLY BE POSSIBLE WITH A FEMALE WHO HAD A "BITE OF THE SAME APPLE" SO TO SPEAK.
LILY OBLIGED THE EXPERIMENT... VIGOROUSLY.

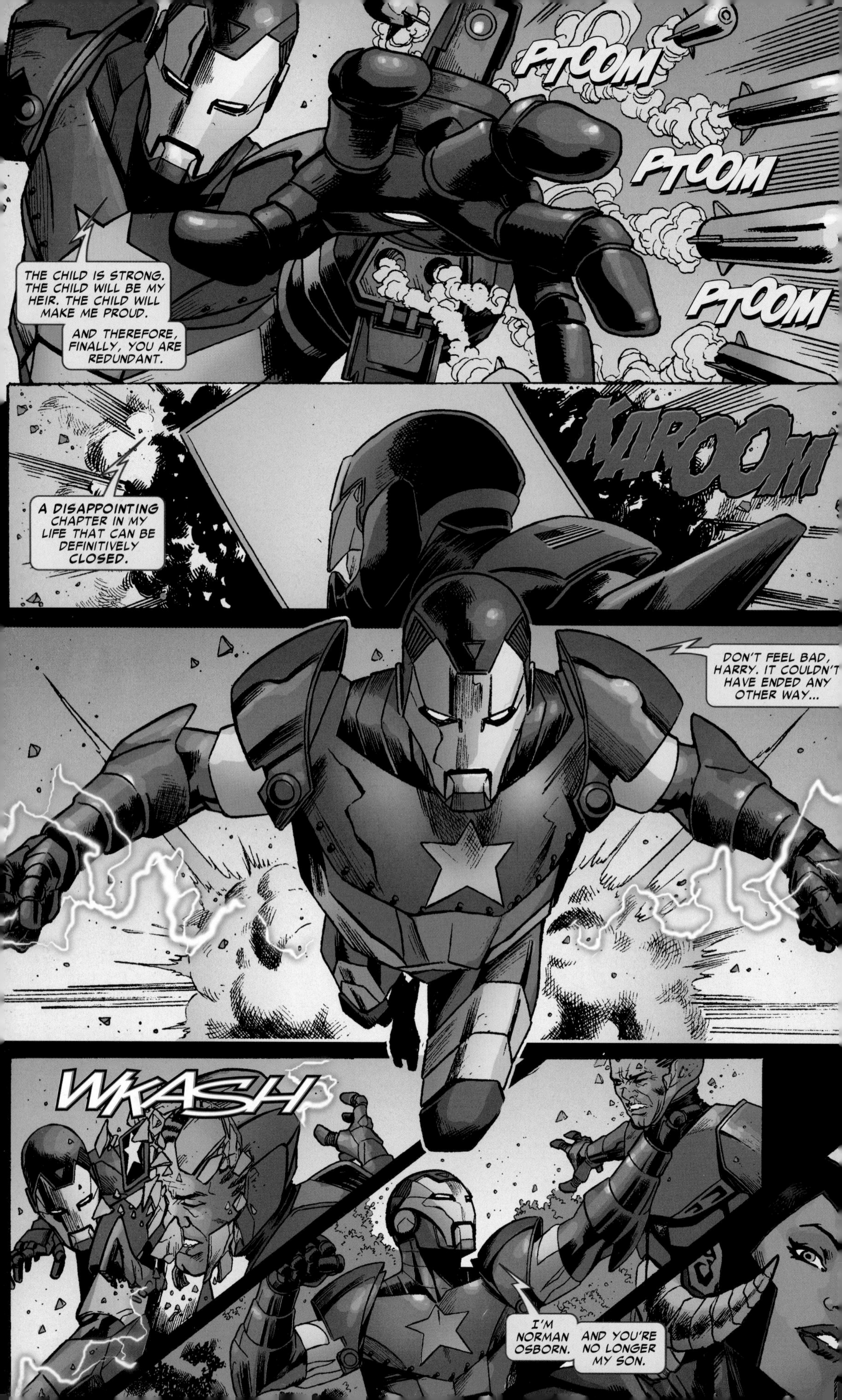
PTOOM
PTOOM
PTOOM
THE CHILD IS STRONG. THE CHILD WILL BE MY HEIR. THE CHILD WILL MAKE ME PROUD.
AND THEREFORE, FINALLY, YOU ARE REDUNDANT.
KAROOM
A DISAPPOINTING CHAPTER IN MY LIFE THAT CAN BE DEFINITIVELY CLOSED.
DON'T FEEL BAD, HARRY. IT COULDN'T HAVE ENDED ANY OTHER WAY...
WKASH
I'M NORMAN OSBORN.
AND YOU'RE NO LONGER MY SON.

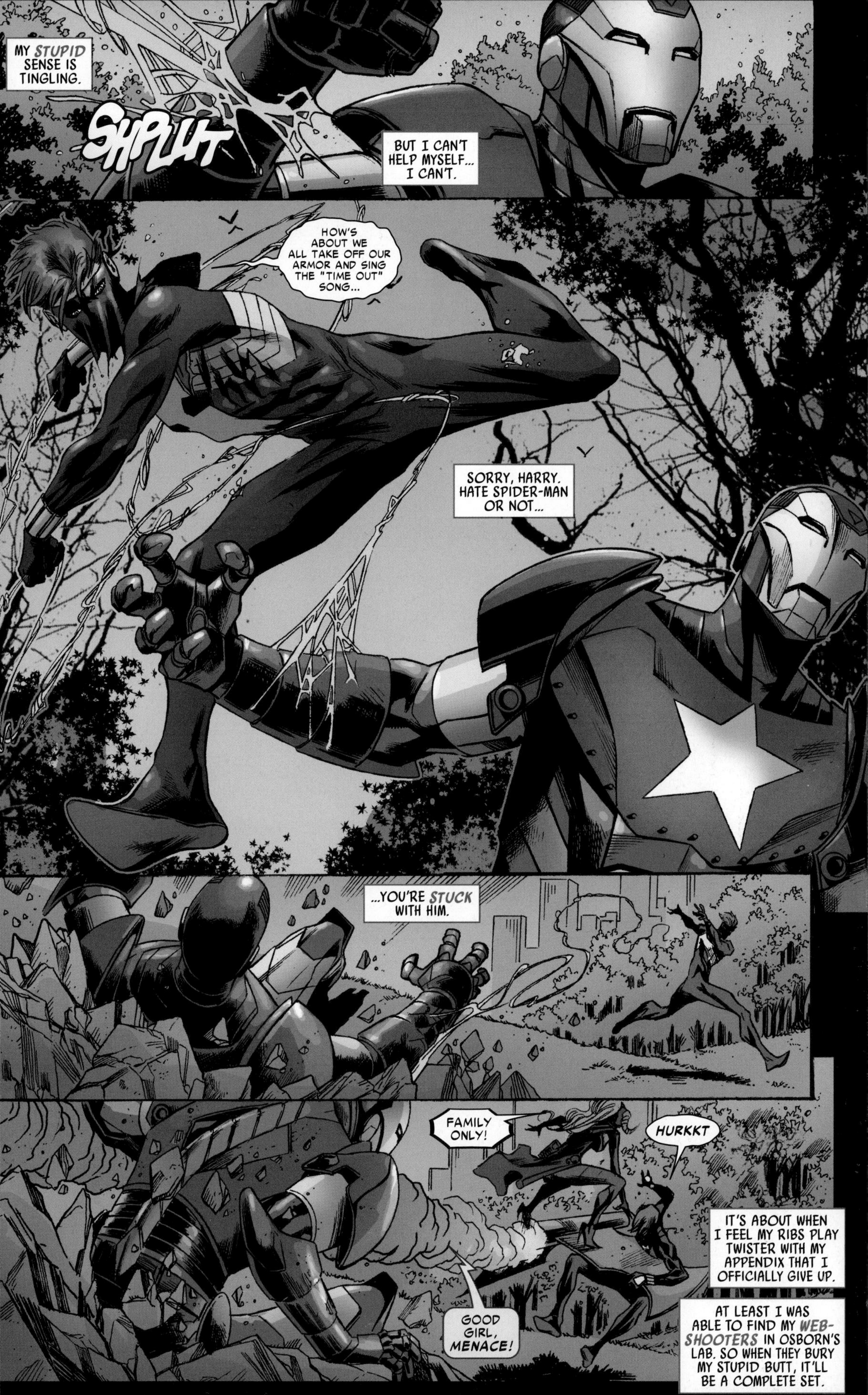

MY STUPID SENSE IS TINGLING.
SHPLUT
BUT I CAN'T HELP MYSELF... I CAN'T.
HOW'S ABOUT WE ALL TAKE OFF OUR ARMOR AND SING THE "TIME OUT" SONG...
SORRY, HARRY. HATE SPIDER-MAN OR NOT...
...YOU'RE STUCK WITH HIM.
FAMILY ONLY!
HURKKT
GOOD GIRL, MENACE!
IT'S ABOUT WHEN I FEEL MY RIBS PLAY TWISTER WITH MY APPENDIX THAT I OFFICIALLY GIVE UP.
AT LEAST I WAS ABLE TO FIND MY WEB-SHOOTERS IN OSBORN'S LAB. SO WHEN THEY BURY MY STUPID BUTT, IT'LL BE A COMPLETE SET.

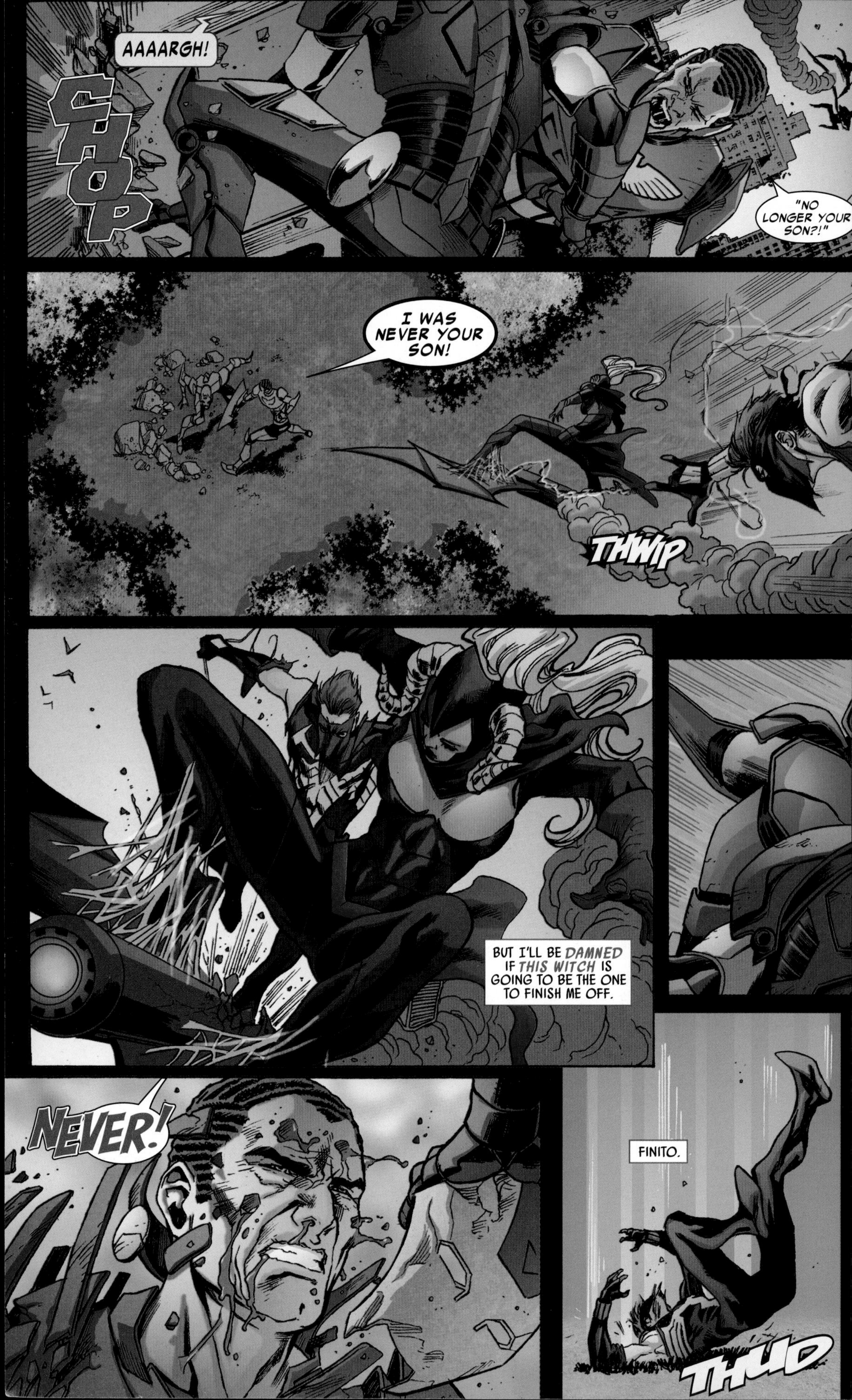
AAAARGH!
CHOP
"NO LONGER YOUR SON?!"
I WAS NEVER YOUR SON!
THWIP
BUT I'LL BE DAMNED IF THIS WITCH IS GOING TO BE THE ONE TO FINISH ME OFF.
NEVER!
FINITO.
THUD

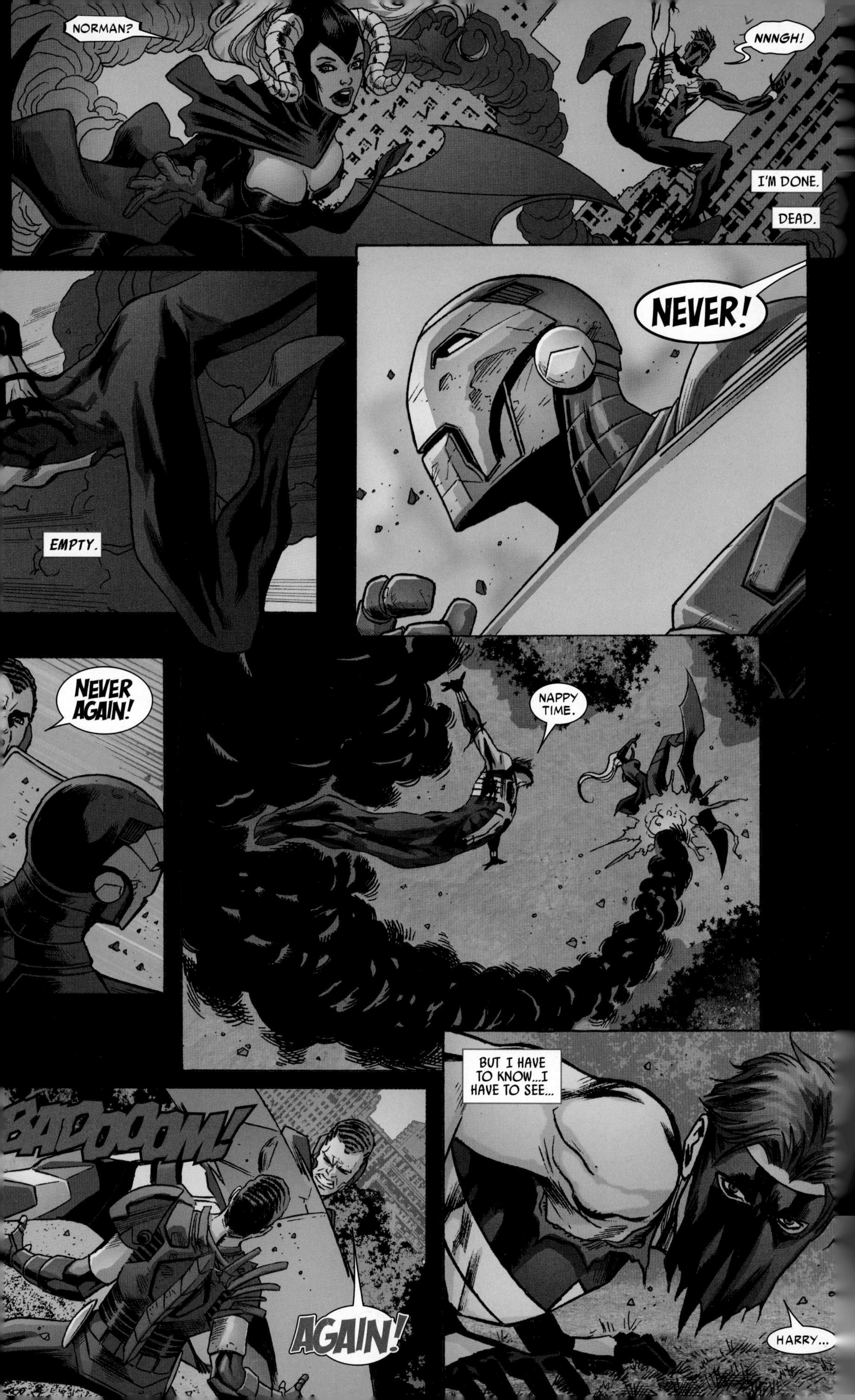
NORMAN?
NNNGH!
I'M DONE.
DEAD.
EMPTY.
NEVER!
NEVER AGAIN!
NAPPY TIME.
BADOOM!
AGAIN!
BUT I HAVE TO KNOW...I HAVE TO SEE...
HARRY...

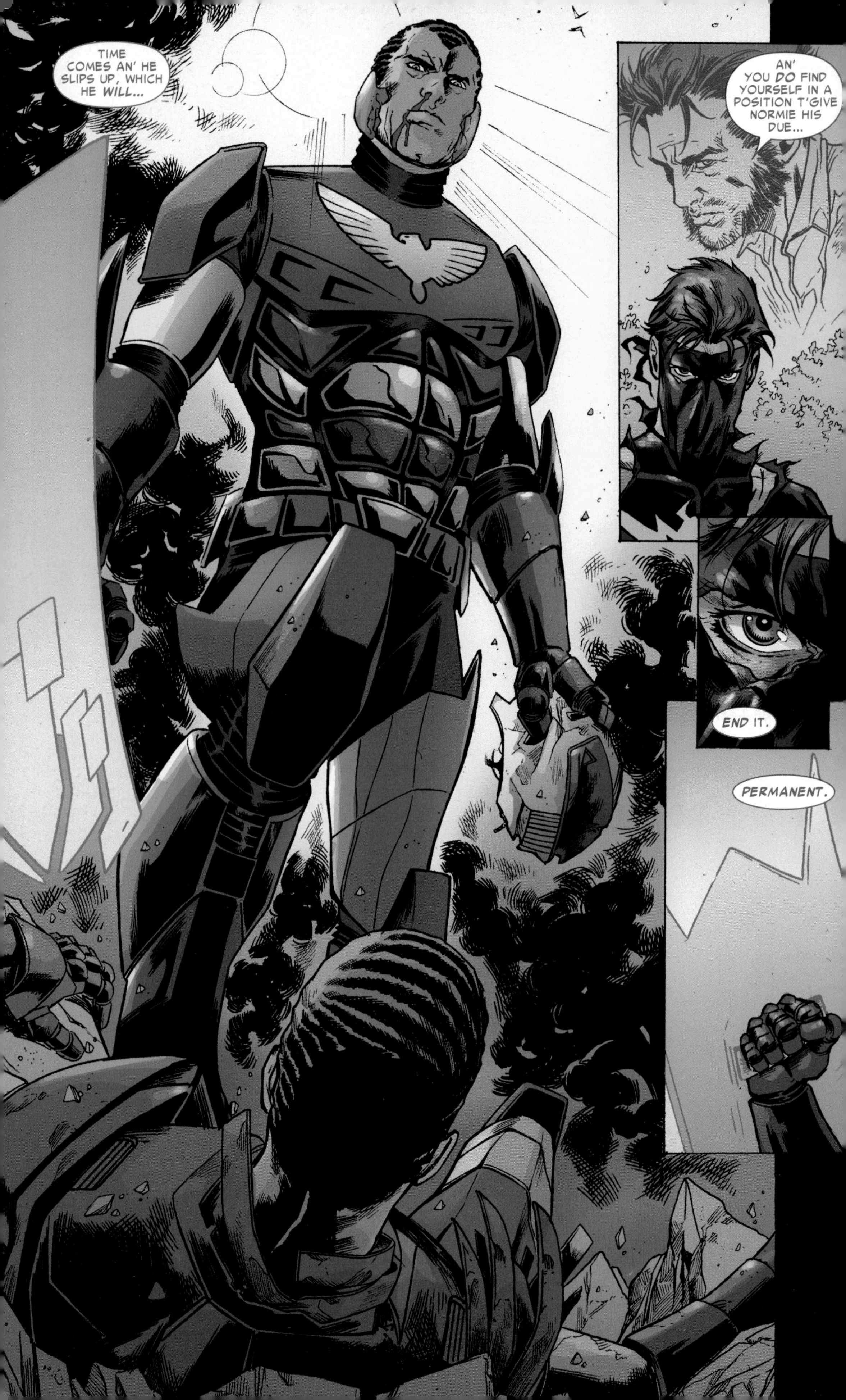
TIME COMES AN' HE SLIPS UP, WHICH HE WILL...
AN' YOU DO FIND YOURSELF IN A POSITION T'GIVE NORMIE HIS DUE...
END IT.
PERMANENT.

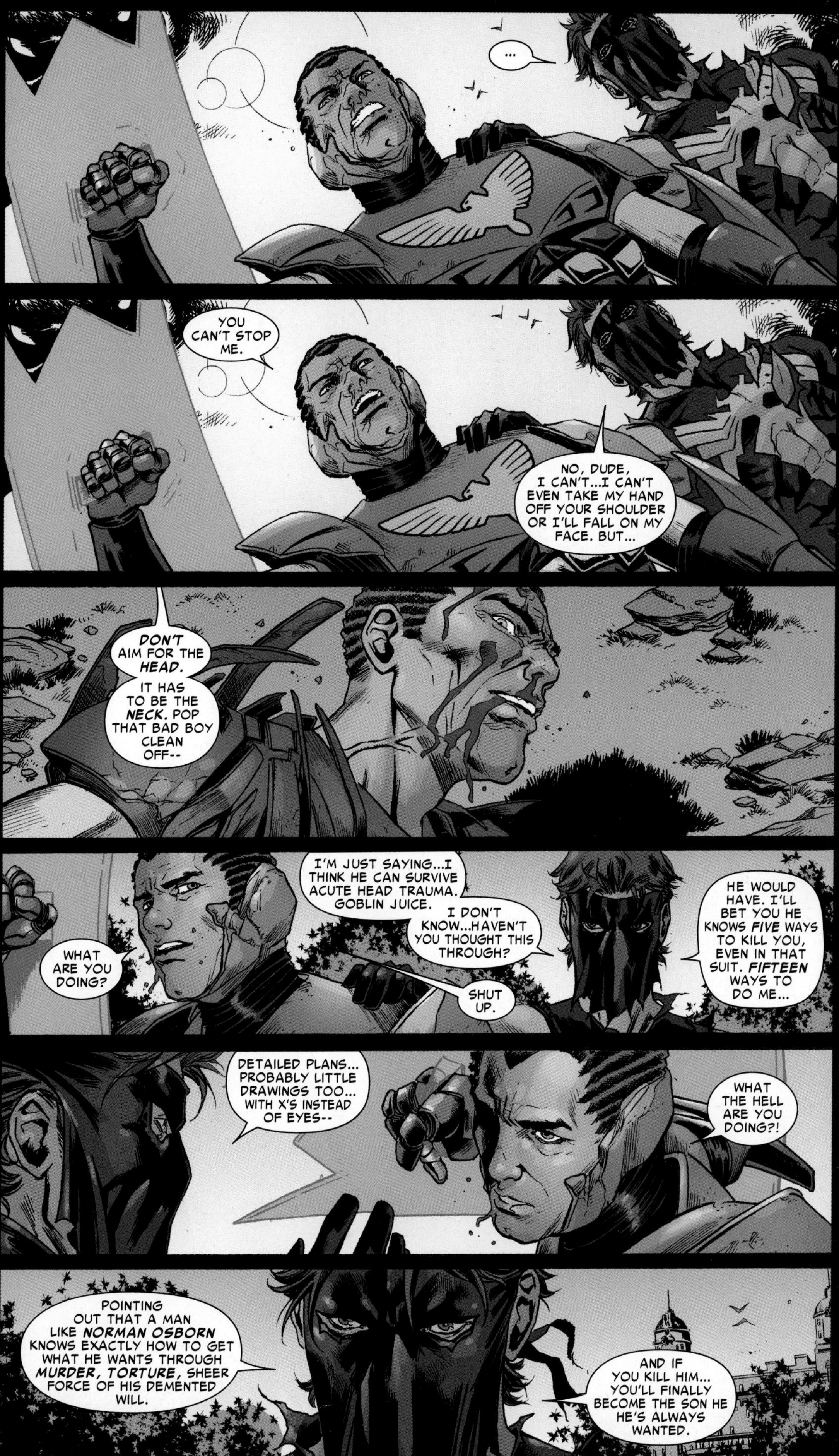
...
YOU CAN'T STOP ME.
NO, DUDE, I CAN'T...I CAN'T EVEN TAKE MY HAND OFF YOUR SHOULDER OR I'LL FALL ON MY FACE. BUT...
DON'T AIM FOR THE HEAD.
IT HAS TO BE THE NECK. POP THAT BAD BOY CLEAN OFF--
WHAT ARE YOU DOING?
I'M JUST SAYING...I THINK HE CAN SURVIVE ACUTE HEAD TRAUMA. GOBLIN JUICE.
I DON'T KNOW...HAVEN'T YOU THOUGHT THIS THROUGH?
SHUT UP.
HE WOULD HAVE. I'LL BET YOU HE KNOWS FIVE WAYS TO KILL YOU, EVEN IN THAT SUIT. FIFTEEN WAYS TO DO ME...
DETAILED PLANS... PROBABLY LITTLE DRAWINGS TOO... WITH X'S INSTEAD OF EYES--
WHAT THE HELL ARE YOU DOING?!
POINTING OUT THAT A MAN LIKE NORMAN OSBORN KNOWS EXACTLY HOW TO GET WHAT HE WANTS THROUGH MURDER, TORTURE, SHEER FORCE OF HIS DEMENTED WILL.
AND IF YOU KILL HIM... YOU'LL FINALLY BECOME THE SON HE HE'S ALWAYS WANTED.

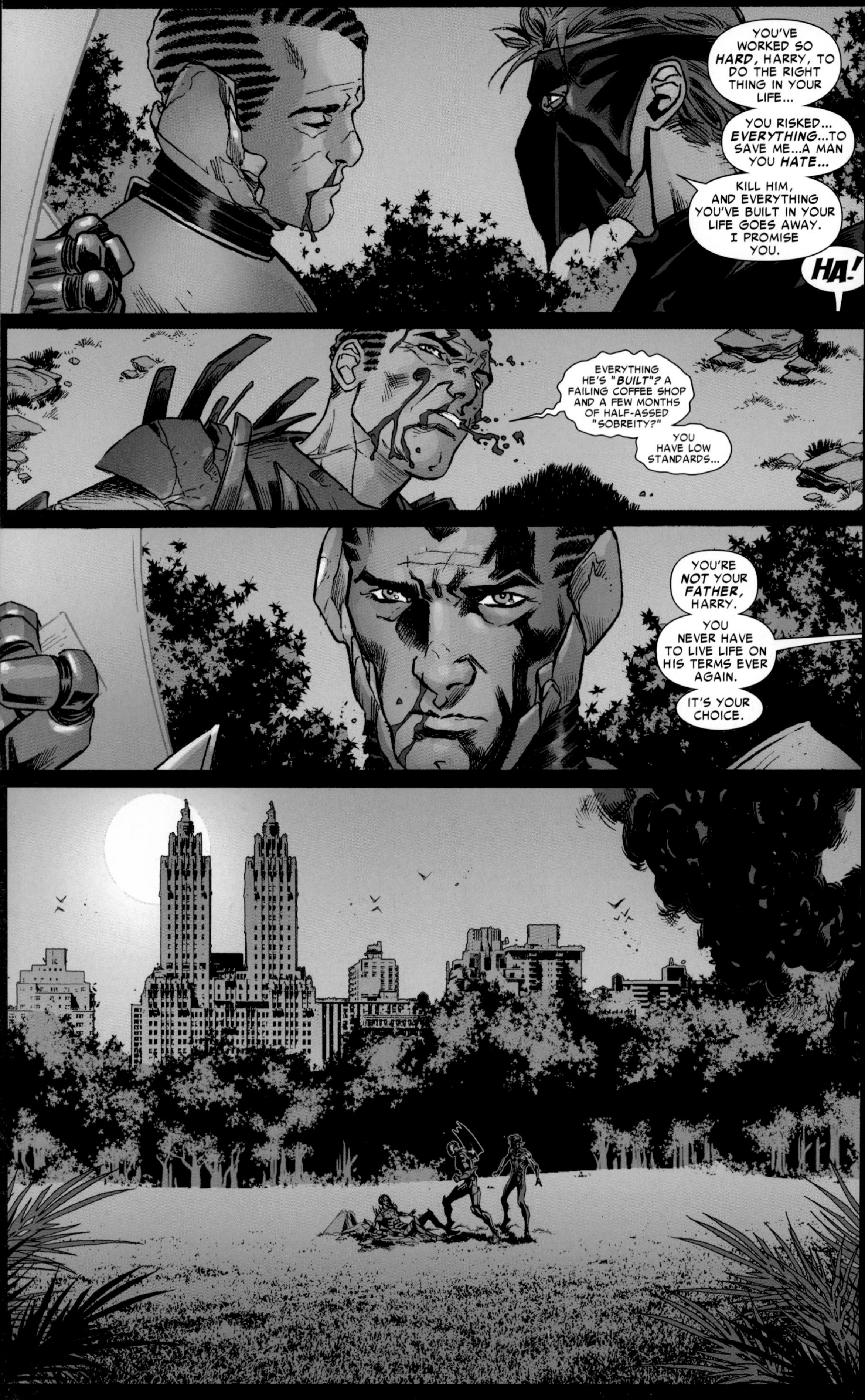
YOU'VE WORKED SO HARD, HARRY, TO DO THE RIGHT THING IN YOUR LIFE...
YOU RISKED... EVERYTHING...TO SAVE ME...A MAN YOU HATE...
KILL HIM, AND EVERYTHING YOU'VE BUILT IN YOUR LIFE GOES AWAY. I PROMISE YOU.
HA!
EVERYTHING HE'S "BUILT"? A FAILING COFFEE SHOP AND A FEW MONTHS OF HALF-ASSED "SOBREITY?"
YOU HAVE LOW STANDARDS...
YOU'RE NOT YOUR FATHER, HARRY.
YOU NEVER HAVE TO LIVE LIFE ON HIS TERMS EVER AGAIN.
IT'S YOUR CHOICE.

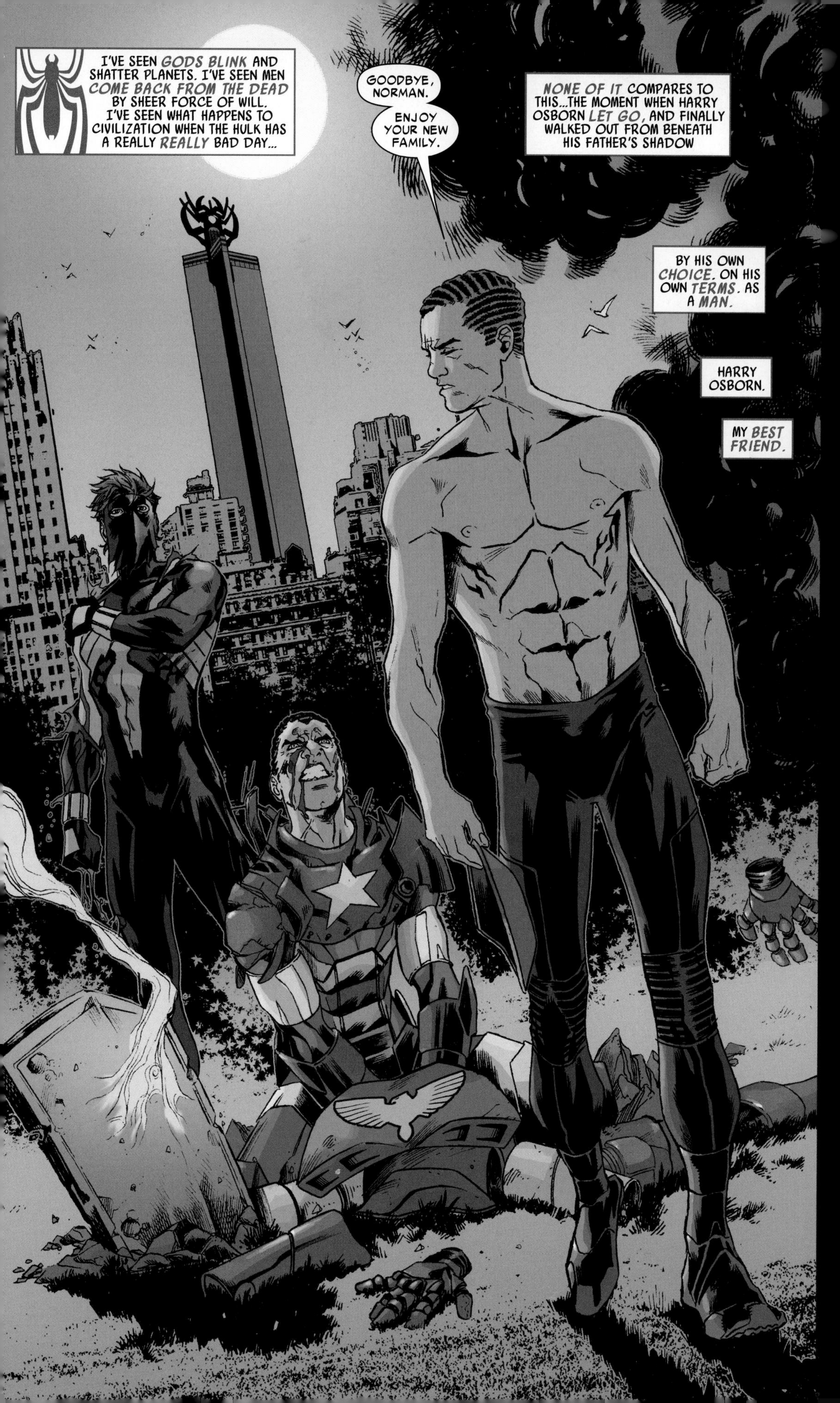
I'VE SEEN GODS BLINK AND SHATTER PLANETS. I'VE SEEN MEN COME BACK FROM THE DEAD BY SHEER FORCE OF WILL. I'VE SEEN WHAT HAPPENS TO CIVILIZATION WHEN THE HULK HAS A REALLY REALLY BAD DAY...
GOODBYE, NORMAN.
ENJOY YOUR NEW FAMILY.
NONE OF IT COMPARES TO THIS...THE MOMENT WHEN HARRY OSBORN LET GO, AND FINALLY WALKED OUT FROM BENEATH HIS FATHER'S SHADOW
BY HIS OWN CHOICE. ON HIS OWN TERMS. AS A MAN.
HARRY OSBORN.
MY BEST FRIEND.

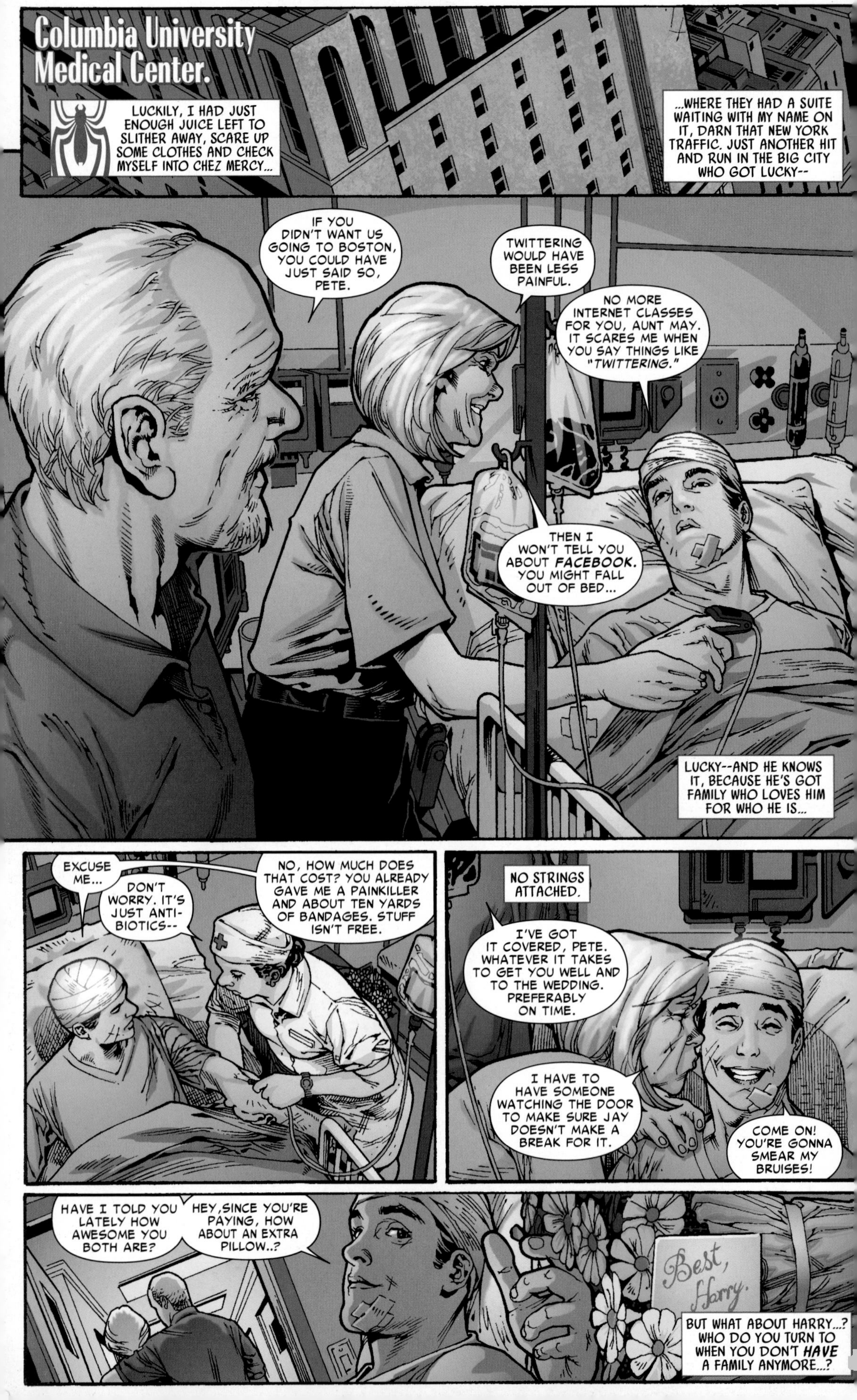
Columbia University Medical Center.
LUCKILY, I HAD JUST ENOUGH JUICE LEFT TO SLITHER AWAY, SCARE UP SOME CLOTHES AND CHECK MYSELF INTO CHEZ MERCY...
...WHERE THEY HAD A SUITE WAITING WITH MY NAME ON IT, DARN THAT NEW YORK TRAFFIC. JUST ANOTHER HIT AND RUN IN THE BIG CITY WHO GOT LUCKY--
IF YOU DIDN'T WANT US GOING TO BOSTON, YOU COULD HAVE JUST SAID SO, PETE.
TWITTERING WOULD HAVE BEEN LESS PAINFUL.
NO MORE INTERNET CLASSES FOR YOU, AUNT MAY. IT SCARES ME WHEN YOU SAY THINGS LIKE "TWITTERING."
THEN I WON'T TELL YOU ABOUT FACEBOOK. YOU MIGHT FALL OUT OF BED...
LUCKY--AND HE KNOWS IT, BECAUSE HE'S GOT FAMILY WHO LOVES HIM FOR WHO HE IS...
EXCUSE ME...
DON'T WORRY. IT'S JUST ANTI-BIOTICS--
NO, HOW MUCH DOES THAT COST? YOU ALREADY GAVE ME A PAINKILLER AND ABOUT TEN YARDS OF BANDAGES. STUFF ISN'T FREE.
NO STRINGS ATTACHED.
I'VE GOT IT COVERED, PETE. WHATEVER IT TAKES TO GET YOU WELL AND TO THE WEDDING. PREFERABLY ON TIME.
I HAVE TO HAVE SOMEONE WATCHING THE DOOR TO MAKE SURE JAY DOESN'T MAKE A BREAK FOR IT.
COME ON! YOU'RE GONNA SMEAR MY BRUISES!
HAVE I TOLD YOU LATELY HOW AWESOME YOU BOTH ARE?
HEY, SINCE YOU'RE PAYING, HOW ABOUT AN EXTRA PILLOW..?
Best, Harry.
BUT WHAT ABOUT HARRY...? WHO DO YOU TURN TO WHEN YOU DON'T HAVE A FAMILY ANYMORE...?

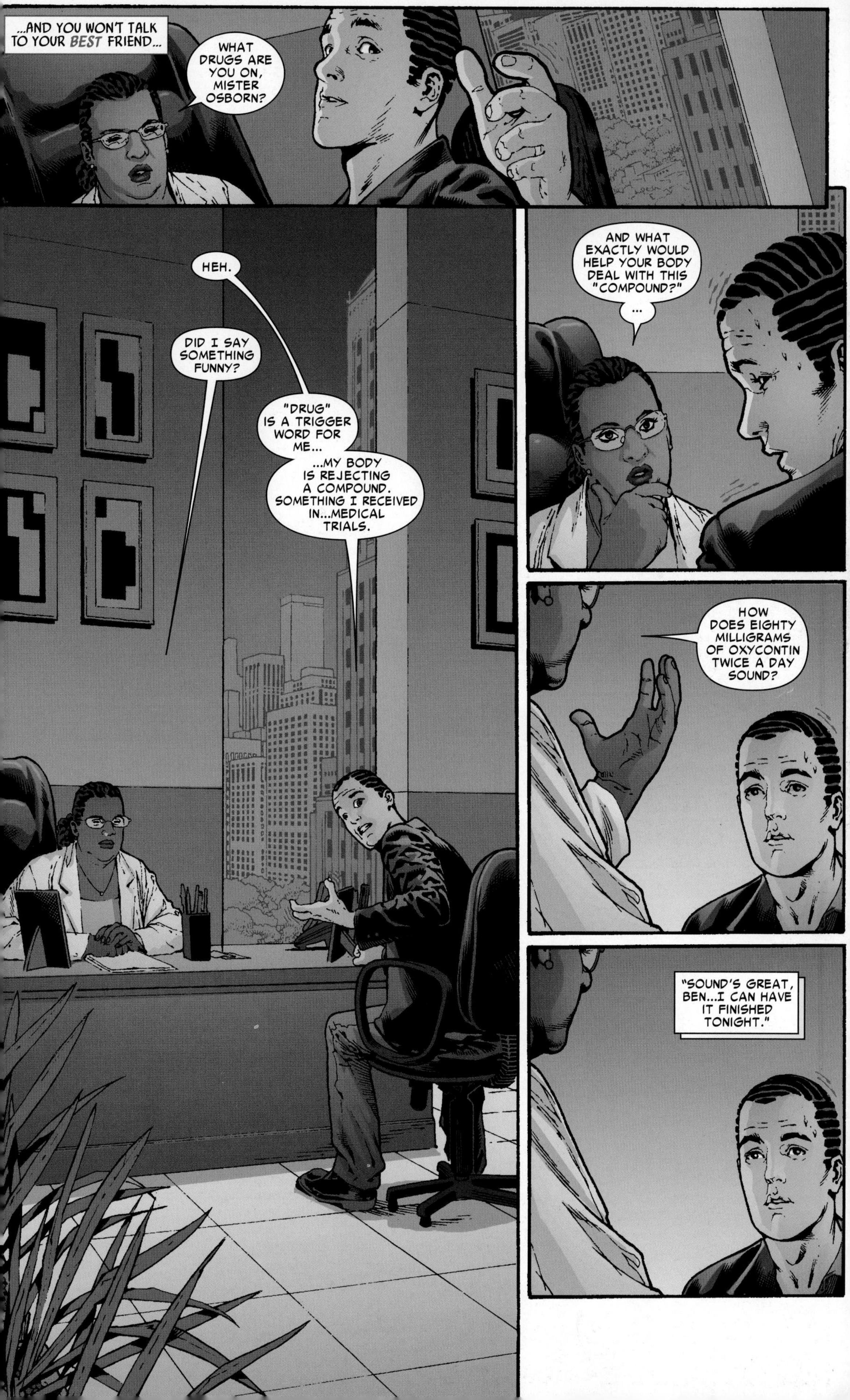
...AND YOU WON'T TALK TO YOUR BEST FRIEND...
WHAT DRUGS ARE YOU ON, MISTER OSBORN?
HEH.
DID I SAY SOMETHING FUNNY?
"DRUG" IS A TRIGGER WORD FOR ME...
...MY BODY IS REJECTING A COMPOUND. SOMETHING I RECEIVED IN...MEDICAL TRIALS.
AND WHAT EXACTLY WOULD HELP YOUR BODY DEAL WITH THIS "COMPOUND?"
...
HOW DOES EIGHTY MILLIGRAMS OF OXYCONTIN TWICE A DAY SOUND?
"SOUND'S GREAT, BEN...I CAN HAVE IT FINISHED TONIGHT."

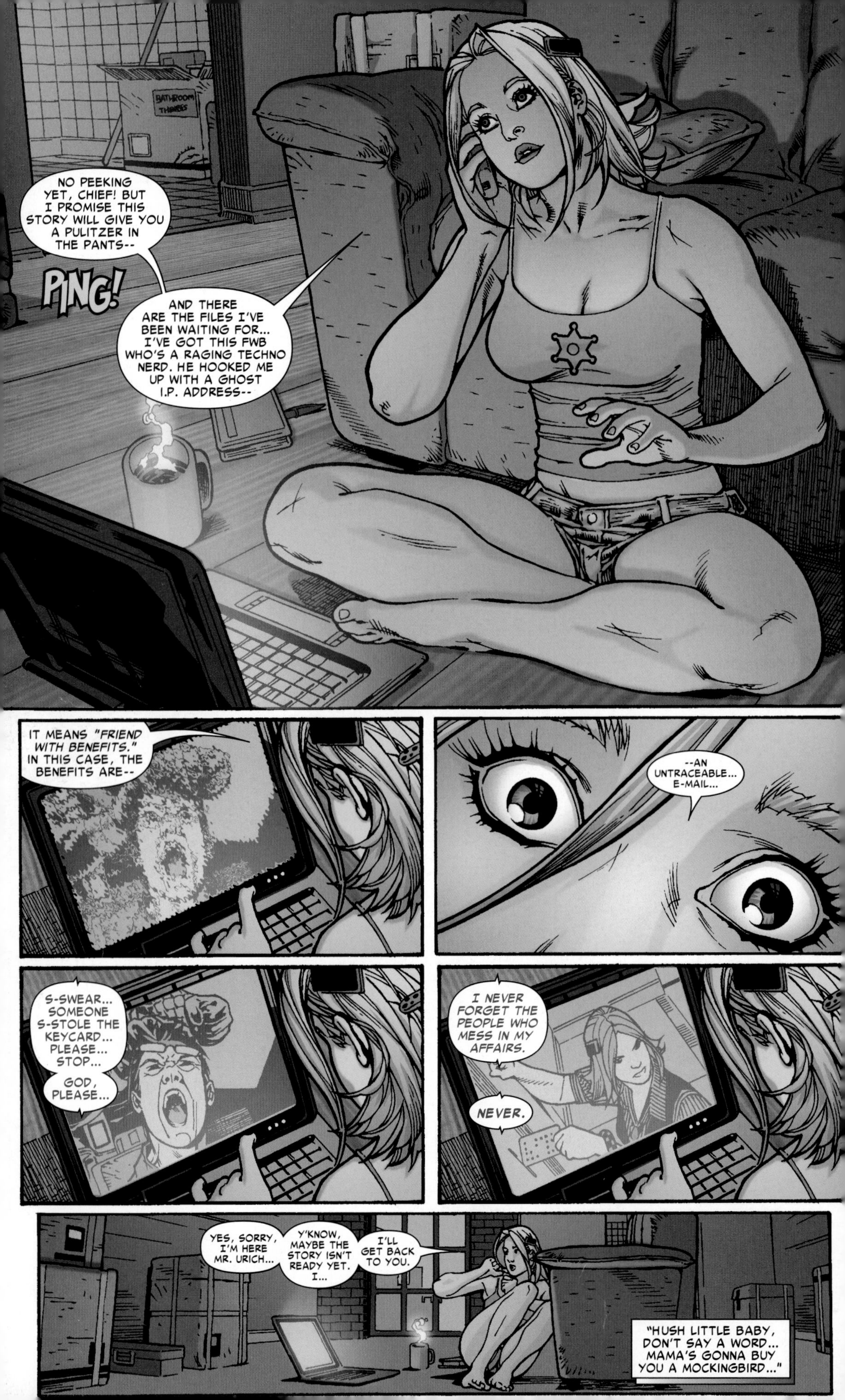

NO PEEKING YET, CHIEF! BUT I PROMISE THIS STORY WILL GIVE YOU A PULITZER IN THE PANTS--
PING!
AND THERE ARE THE FILES I'VE BEEN WAITING FOR... I'VE GOT THIS FWB WHO'S A RAGING TECHNO NERD. HE HOOKED ME UP WITH A GHOST I.P. ADDRESS--
BATHROOM THINGS
IT MEANS "FRIEND WITH BENEFITS." IN THIS CASE, THE BENEFITS ARE--
--AN UNTRACEABLE... E-MAIL...
S-SWEAR... SOMEONE S-STOLE THE KEYCARD... PLEASE... STOP...
GOD, PLEASE...
I NEVER FORGET THE PEOPLE WHO MESS IN MY AFFAIRS.
NEVER.
YES, SORRY, I'M HERE MR. URICH...
Y'KNOW, MAYBE THE STORY ISN'T READY YET. I...
I'LL GET BACK TO YOU.
"HUSH LITTLE BABY, DON'T SAY A WORD... MAMA'S GONNA BUY YOU A MOCKINGBIRD..."

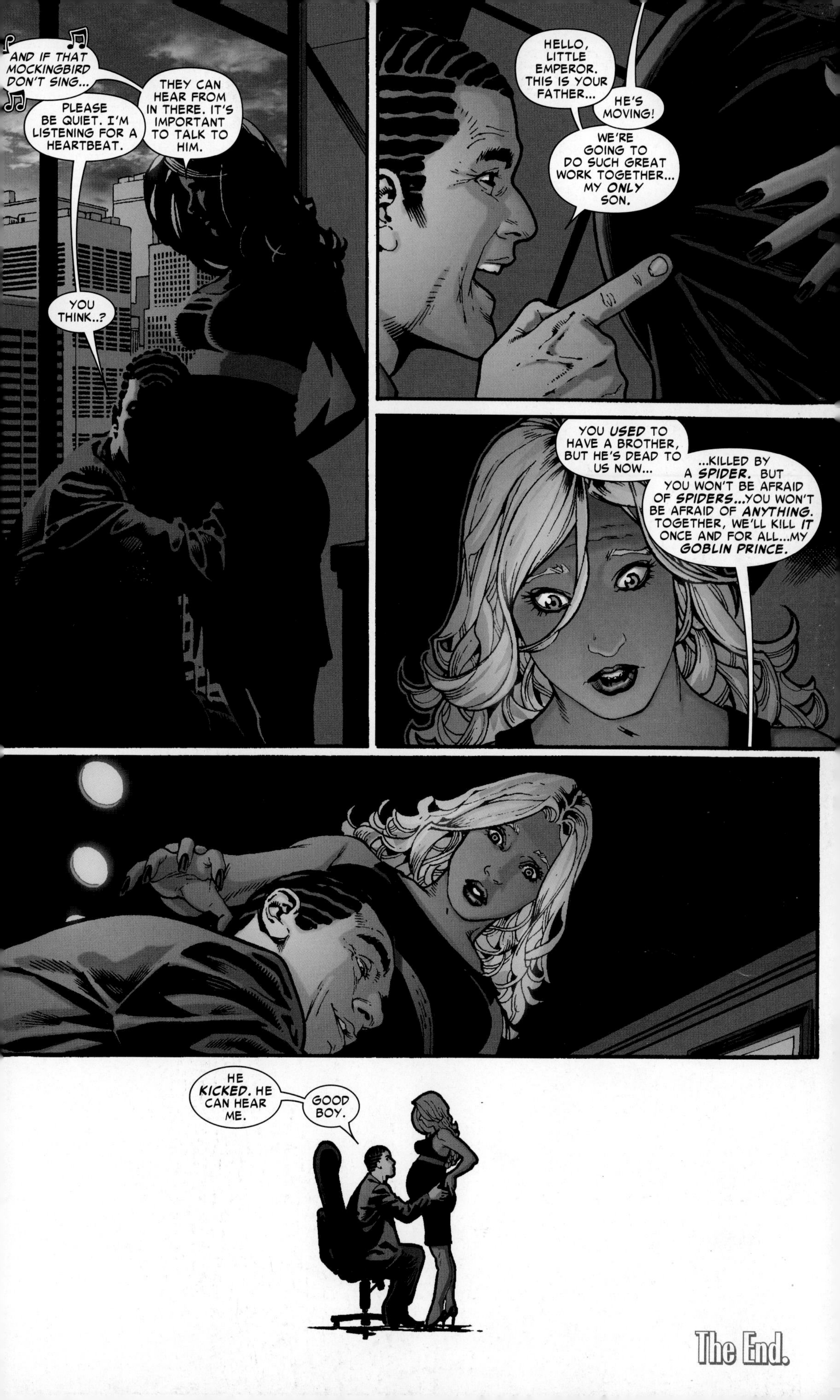
AND IF THAT MOCKINGBIRD DON'T SING...
THEY CAN HEAR FROM IN THERE. IT'S IMPORTANT TO TALK TO HIM.
PLEASE BE QUIET. I'M LISTENING FOR A HEARTBEAT.
YOU THINK..?
HELLO, LITTLE EMPEROR. THIS IS YOUR FATHER...
HE'S MOVING!
WE'RE GOING TO DO SUCH GREAT WORK TOGETHER... MY ONLY SON.
YOU USED TO HAVE A BROTHER, BUT HE'S DEAD TO US NOW...
...KILLED BY A SPIDER. BUT YOU WON'T BE AFRAID OF SPIDERS...YOU WON'T BE AFRAID OF ANYTHING. TOGETHER, WE'LL KILL IT ONCE AND FOR ALL...MY GOBLIN PRINCE.
HE KICKED. HE CAN HEAR ME.
GOOD BOY.
The End.

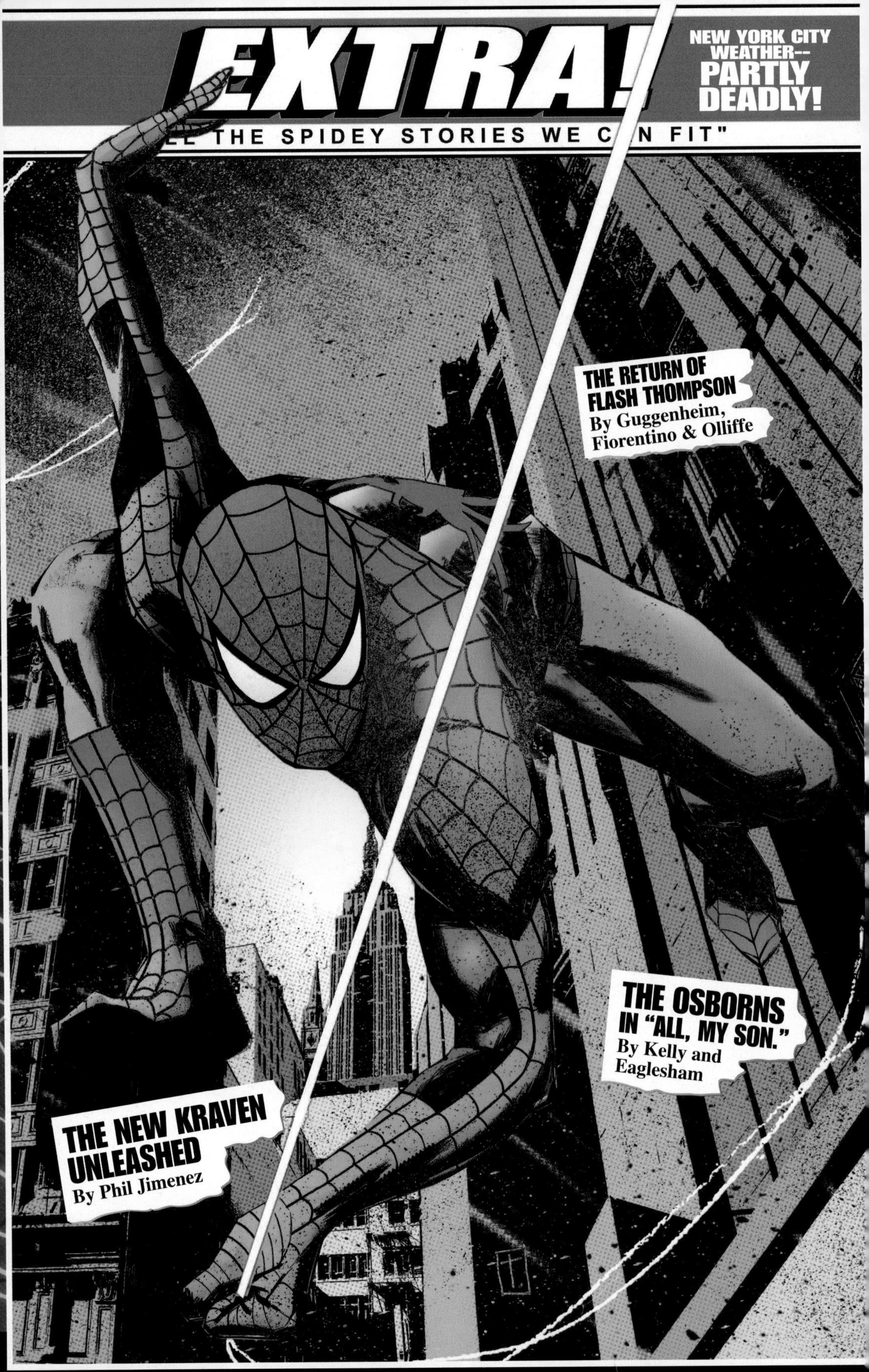

EXTRA!
NEW YORK CITY WEATHER-- PARTLY DEADLY!
"...LL THE SPIDEY STORIES WE C...N FIT"
THE RETURN OF FLASH THOMPSON
By Guggenheim, Fiorentino & Olliffe
THE OSBORNS IN "ALL, MY SON."
By Kelly and Eaglesham
THE NEW KRAVEN UNLEASHED
By Phil Jimenez

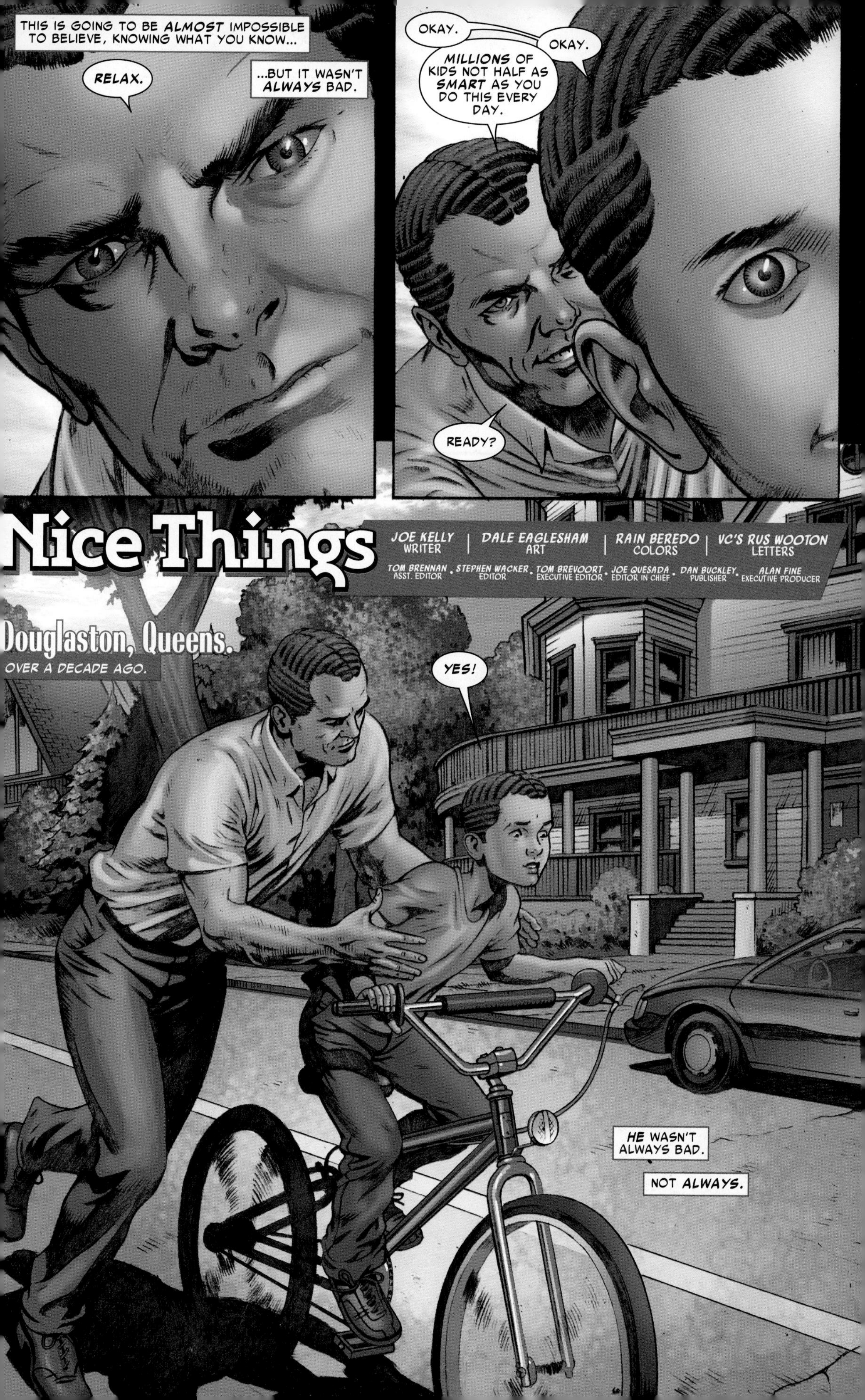
THIS IS GOING TO BE ALMOST IMPOSSIBLE TO BELIEVE, KNOWING WHAT YOU KNOW...
RELAX.
...BUT IT WASN'T ALWAYS BAD.
OKAY.
OKAY.
MILLIONS OF KIDS NOT HALF AS SMART AS YOU DO THIS EVERY DAY.
READY?
Nice Things
JOE KELLY WRITER | DALE EAGLESHAM ART | RAIN BEREDO COLORS | VC'S RUS WOOTON LETTERS
TOM BRENNAN ASST. EDITOR • STEPHEN WACKER EDITOR • TOM BREVOORT EXECUTIVE EDITOR • JOE QUESADA EDITOR IN CHIEF • DAN BUCKLEY PUBLISHER • ALAN FINE EXECUTIVE PRODUCER
Douglaston, Queens.
OVER A DECADE AGO.
YES!
HE WASN'T ALWAYS BAD.
NOT ALWAYS.

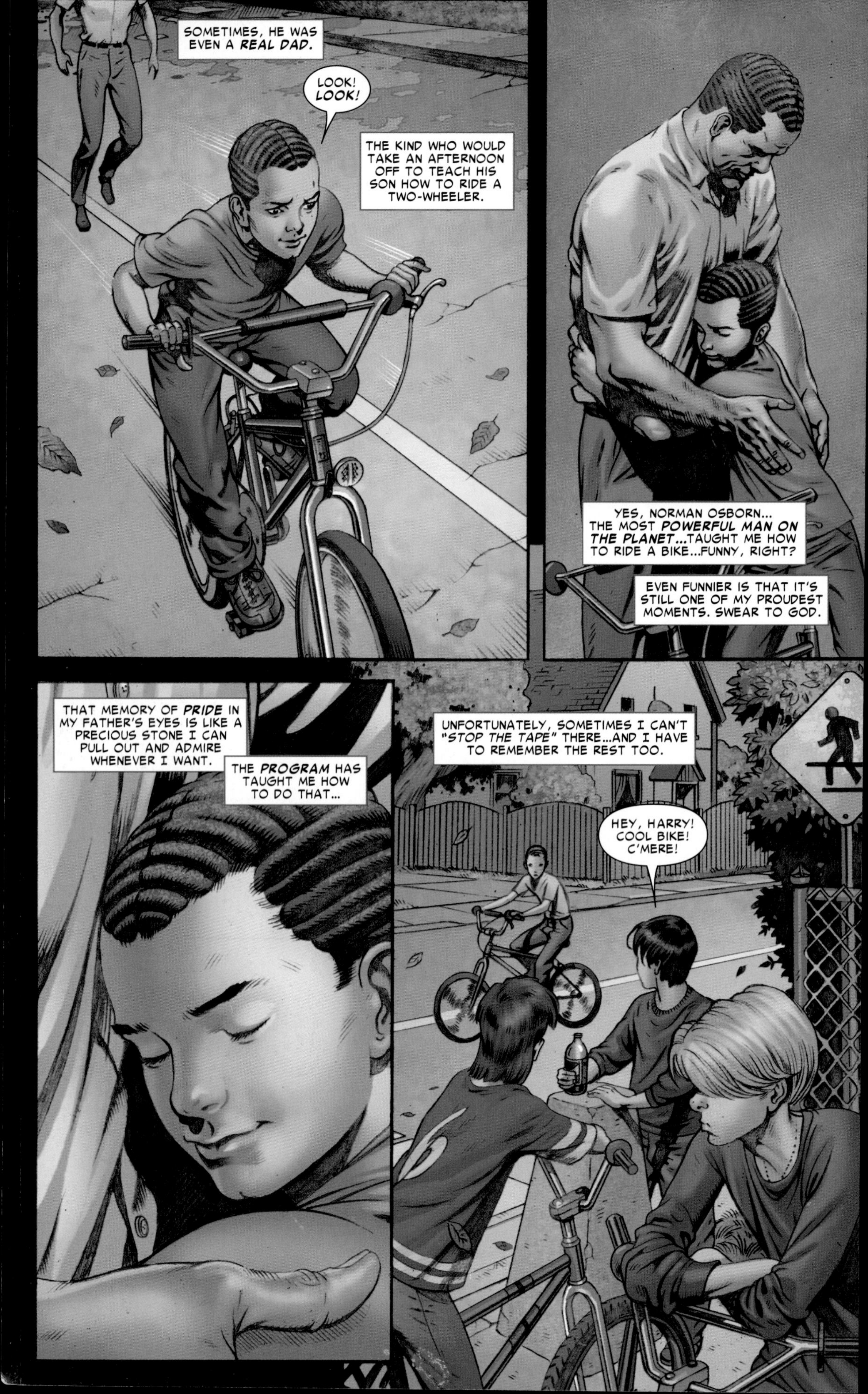

SOMETIMES, HE WAS EVEN A *REAL DAD*.
LOOK! *LOOK!*
THE KIND WHO WOULD TAKE AN AFTERNOON OFF TO TEACH HIS SON HOW TO RIDE A TWO-WHEELER.
YES, NORMAN OSBORN... THE MOST *POWERFUL MAN ON THE PLANET*...TAUGHT ME HOW TO RIDE A BIKE...FUNNY, RIGHT?
EVEN FUNNIER IS THAT IT'S STILL ONE OF MY PROUDEST MOMENTS. SWEAR TO GOD.
THAT MEMORY OF *PRIDE* IN MY FATHER'S EYES IS LIKE A PRECIOUS STONE I CAN PULL OUT AND ADMIRE WHENEVER I WANT.
THE *PROGRAM* HAS TAUGHT ME HOW TO DO THAT...
UNFORTUNATELY, SOMETIMES I CAN'T "*STOP THE TAPE*" THERE...AND I HAVE TO REMEMBER THE REST TOO.
HEY, HARRY! COOL BIKE! C'MERE!

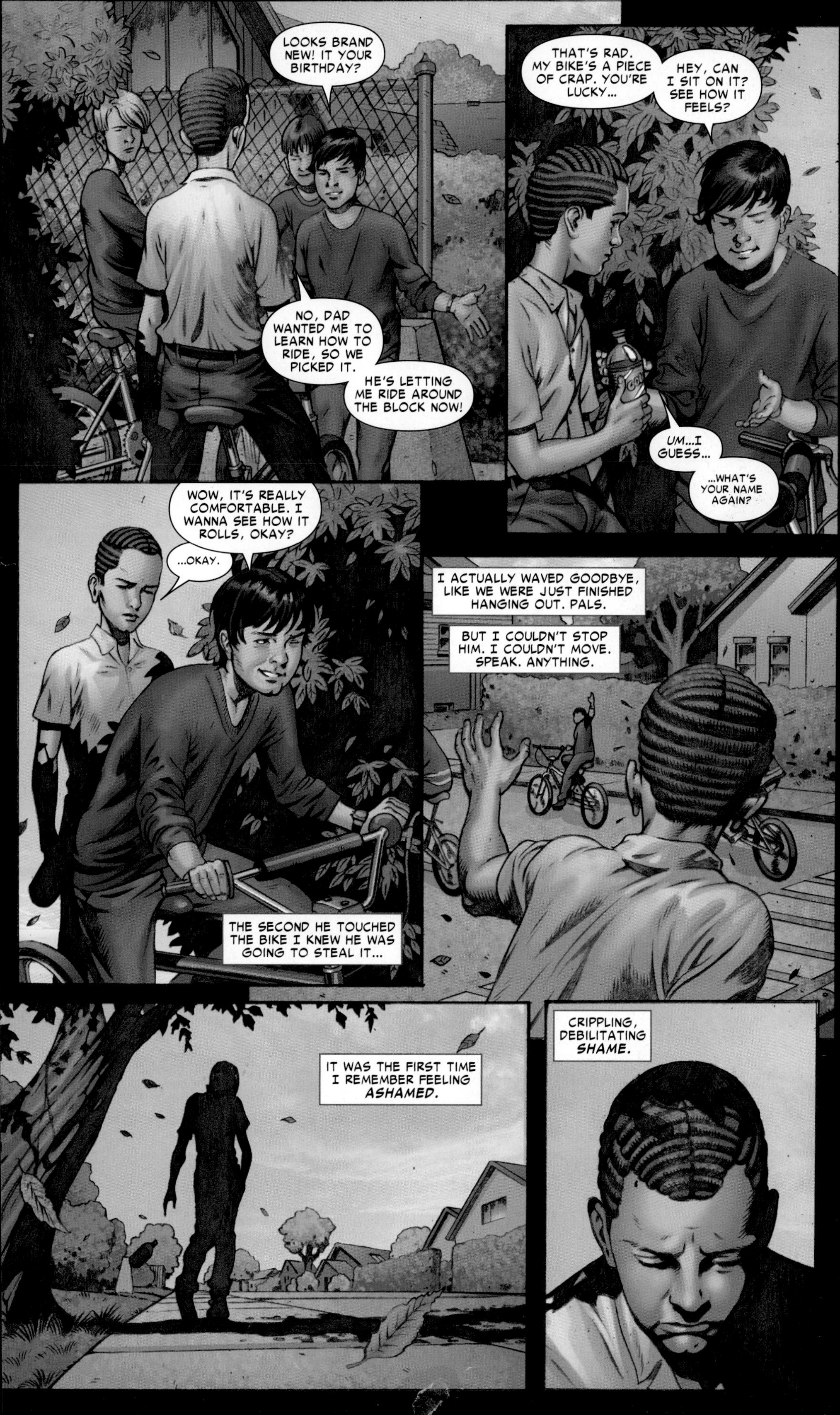
LOOKS BRAND NEW! IT YOUR BIRTHDAY?
NO, DAD WANTED ME TO LEARN HOW TO RIDE, SO WE PICKED IT.
HE'S LETTING ME RIDE AROUND THE BLOCK NOW!
THAT'S RAD. MY BIKE'S A PIECE OF CRAP. YOU'RE LUCKY...
HEY, CAN I SIT ON IT? SEE HOW IT FEELS?
UM...I GUESS...
...WHAT'S YOUR NAME AGAIN?
WOW, IT'S REALLY COMFORTABLE. I WANNA SEE HOW IT ROLLS, OKAY?
...OKAY.
THE SECOND HE TOUCHED THE BIKE I KNEW HE WAS GOING TO STEAL IT...
I ACTUALLY WAVED GOODBYE, LIKE WE WERE JUST FINISHED HANGING OUT. PALS.
BUT I COULDN'T STOP HIM. I COULDN'T MOVE. SPEAK. ANYTHING.
IT WAS THE FIRST TIME I REMEMBER FEELING *ASHAMED*.
CRIPPLING, DEBILITATING *SHAME*.

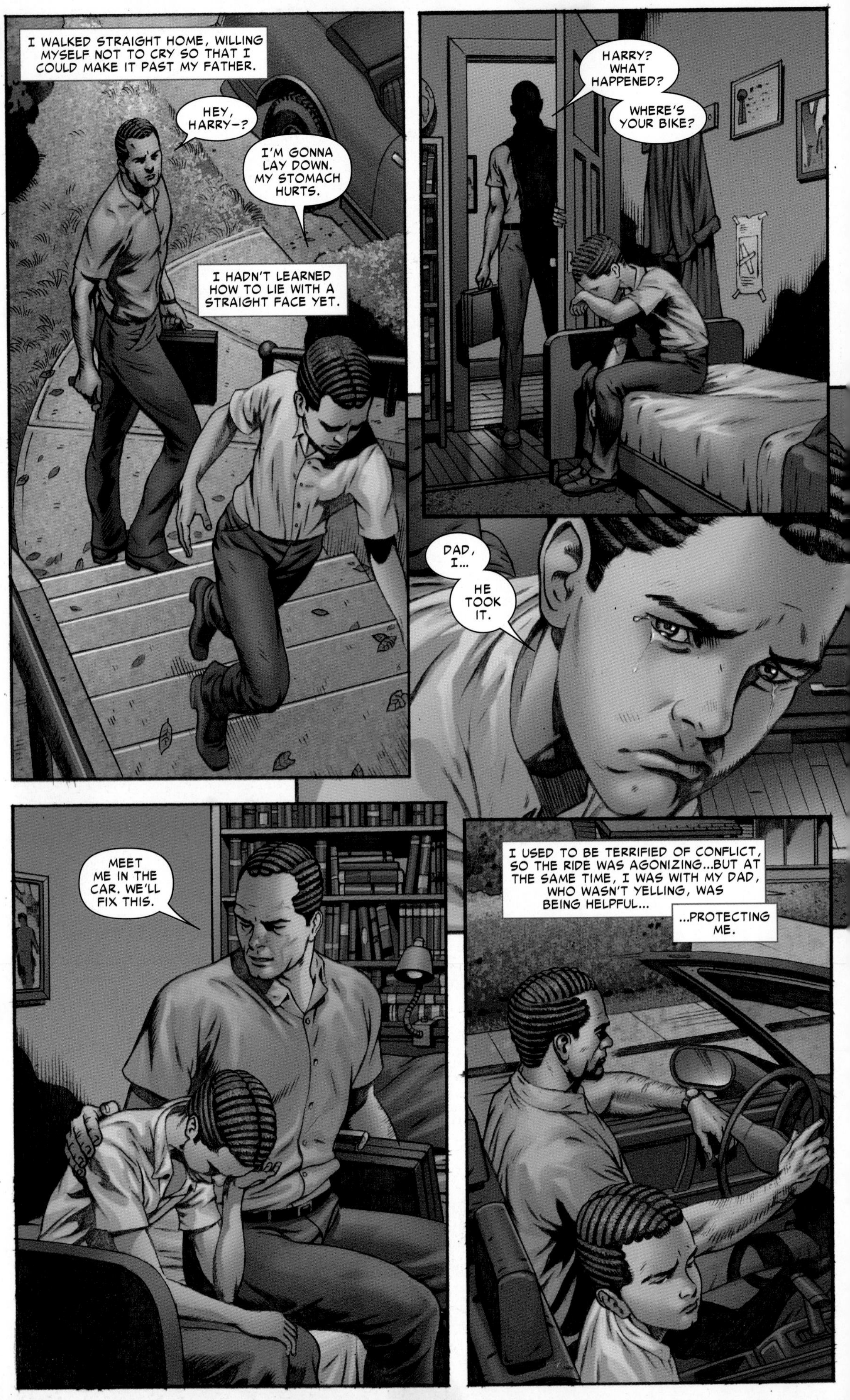

I WALKED STRAIGHT HOME, WILLING MYSELF NOT TO CRY SO THAT I COULD MAKE IT PAST MY FATHER.
HEY, HARRY–?
I'M GONNA LAY DOWN. MY STOMACH HURTS.
I HADN'T LEARNED HOW TO LIE WITH A STRAIGHT FACE YET.
HARRY? WHAT HAPPENED?
WHERE'S YOUR BIKE?
DAD, I...
HE TOOK IT.
MEET ME IN THE CAR. WE'LL FIX THIS.
I USED TO BE TERRIFIED OF CONFLICT, SO THE RIDE WAS AGONIZING...BUT AT THE SAME TIME, I WAS WITH MY DAD, WHO WASN'T YELLING, WAS BEING HELPFUL...
...PROTECTING ME.

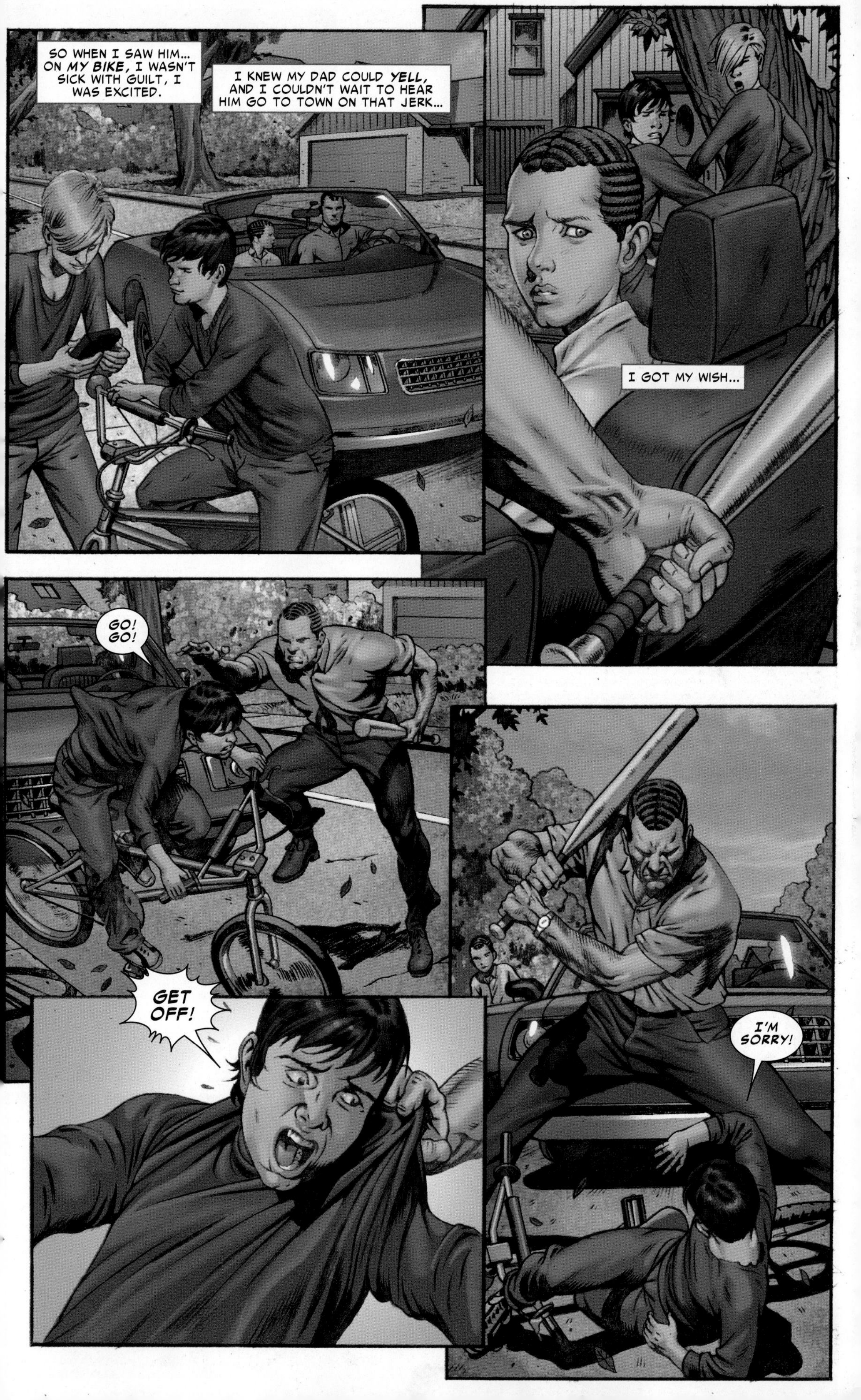

SO WHEN I SAW HIM... ON *MY BIKE*, I WASN'T SICK WITH GUILT, I WAS EXCITED.
I KNEW MY DAD COULD *YELL*, AND I COULDN'T WAIT TO HEAR HIM GO TO TOWN ON THAT JERK...
I GOT MY WISH...
GO! GO!
GET OFF!
I'M SORRY!

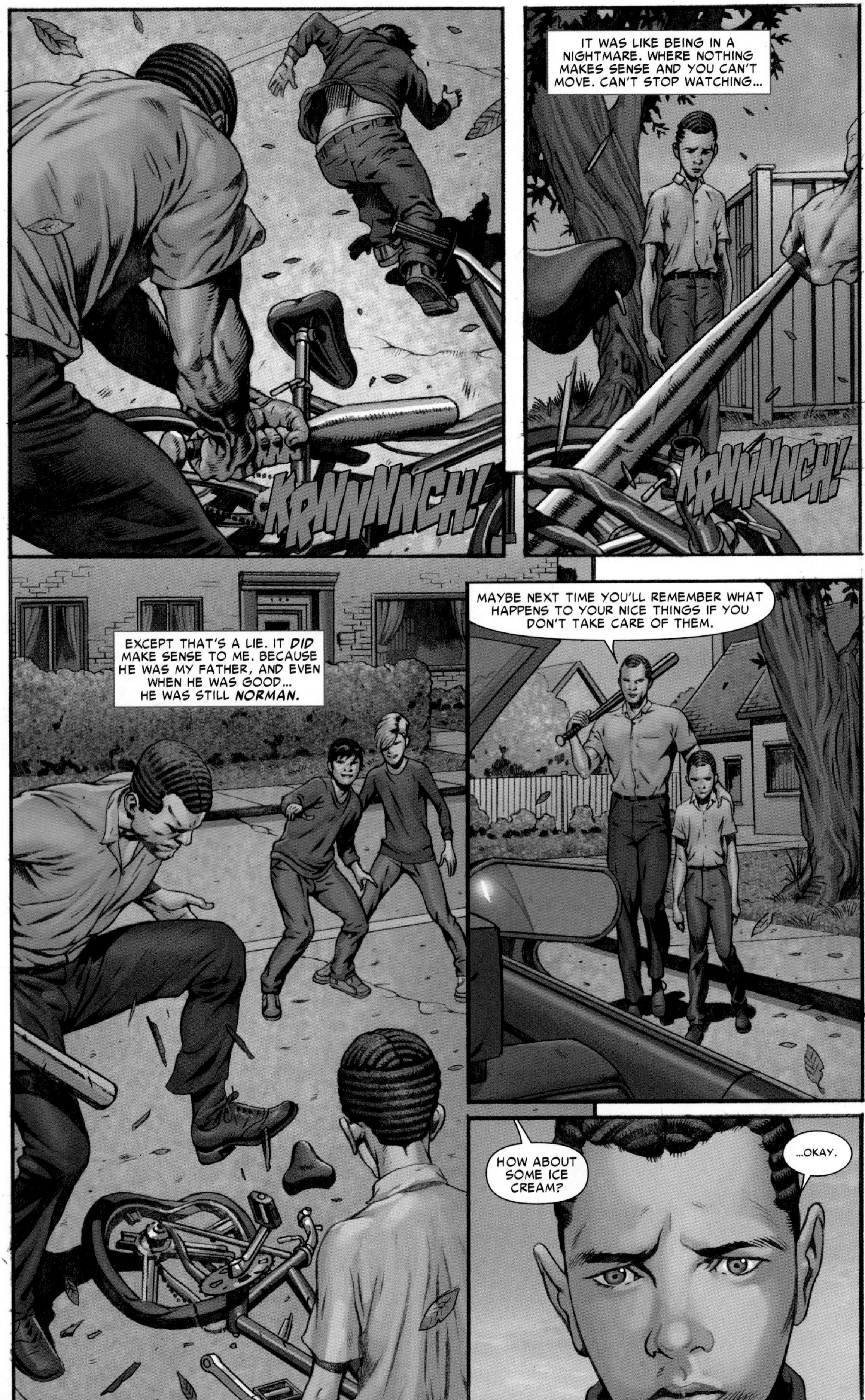
KRNNNNCH!
IT WAS LIKE BEING IN A NIGHTMARE. WHERE NOTHING MAKES SENSE AND YOU CAN'T MOVE. CAN'T STOP WATCHING...
KRNNNNCH!
EXCEPT THAT'S A LIE. IT DID MAKE SENSE TO ME. BECAUSE HE WAS MY FATHER, AND EVEN WHEN HE WAS GOOD... HE WAS STILL NORMAN.
MAYBE NEXT TIME YOU'LL REMEMBER WHAT HAPPENS TO YOUR NICE THINGS IF YOU DON'T TAKE CARE OF THEM.
HOW ABOUT SOME ICE CREAM?
...OKAY.

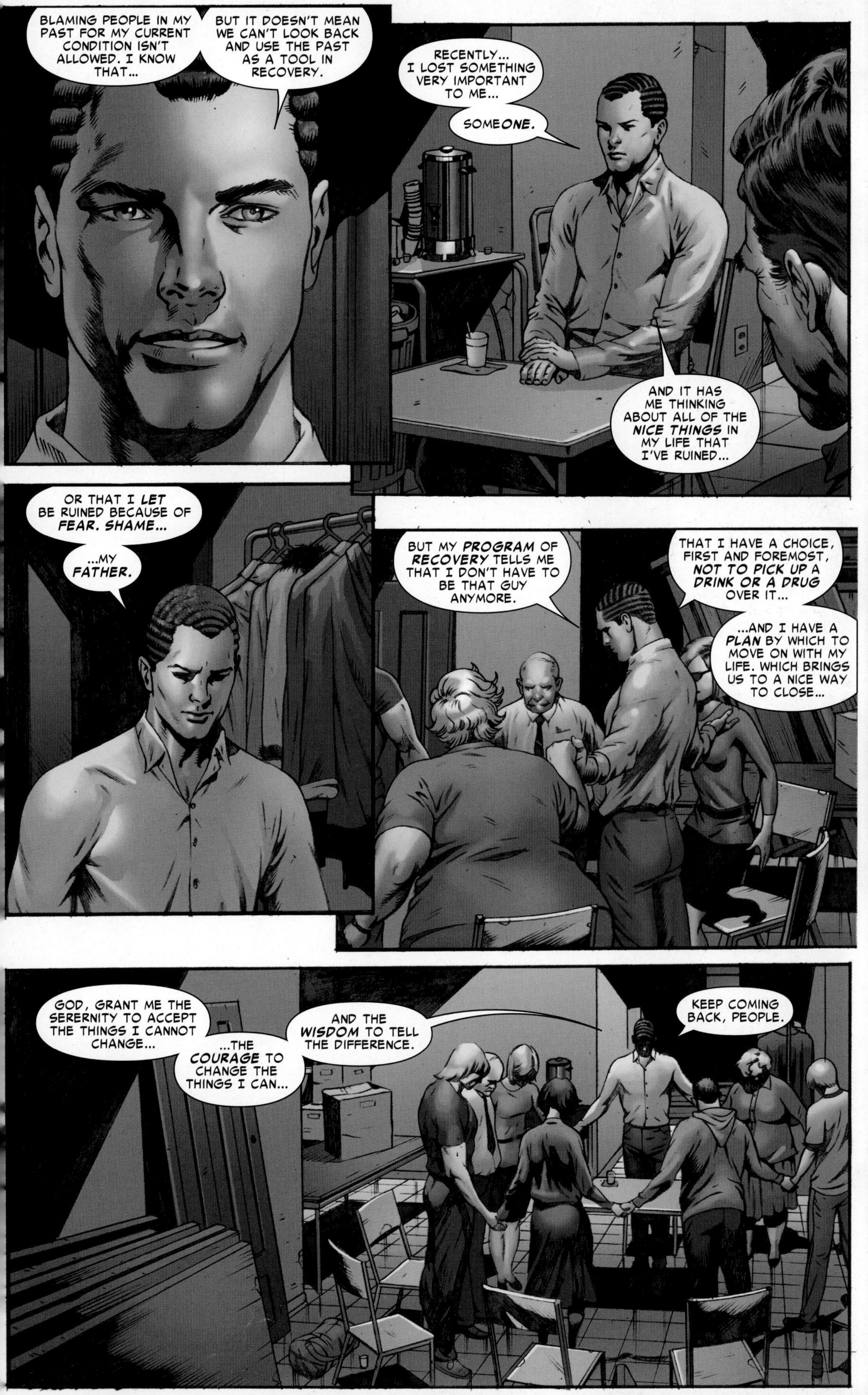
BLAMING PEOPLE IN MY PAST FOR MY CURRENT CONDITION ISN'T ALLOWED. I KNOW THAT...
BUT IT DOESN'T MEAN WE CAN'T LOOK BACK AND USE THE PAST AS A TOOL IN RECOVERY.
RECENTLY... I LOST SOMETHING VERY IMPORTANT TO ME...
SOME*ONE.*
AND IT HAS ME THINKING ABOUT ALL OF THE *NICE THINGS* IN MY LIFE THAT I'VE RUINED...
OR THAT I *LET* BE RUINED BECAUSE OF *FEAR. SHAME...*
...MY *FATHER.*
BUT MY *PROGRAM OF RECOVERY* TELLS ME THAT I DON'T HAVE TO BE THAT GUY ANYMORE.
THAT I HAVE A CHOICE, FIRST AND FOREMOST, *NOT TO PICK UP A DRINK OR A DRUG* OVER IT...
...AND I HAVE A *PLAN* BY WHICH TO MOVE ON WITH MY LIFE. WHICH BRINGS US TO A NICE WAY TO CLOSE...
GOD, GRANT ME THE SERENITY TO ACCEPT THE THINGS I CANNOT CHANGE...
...THE *COURAGE* TO CHANGE THE THINGS I CAN...
AND THE *WISDOM* TO TELL THE DIFFERENCE.
KEEP COMING BACK, PEOPLE.

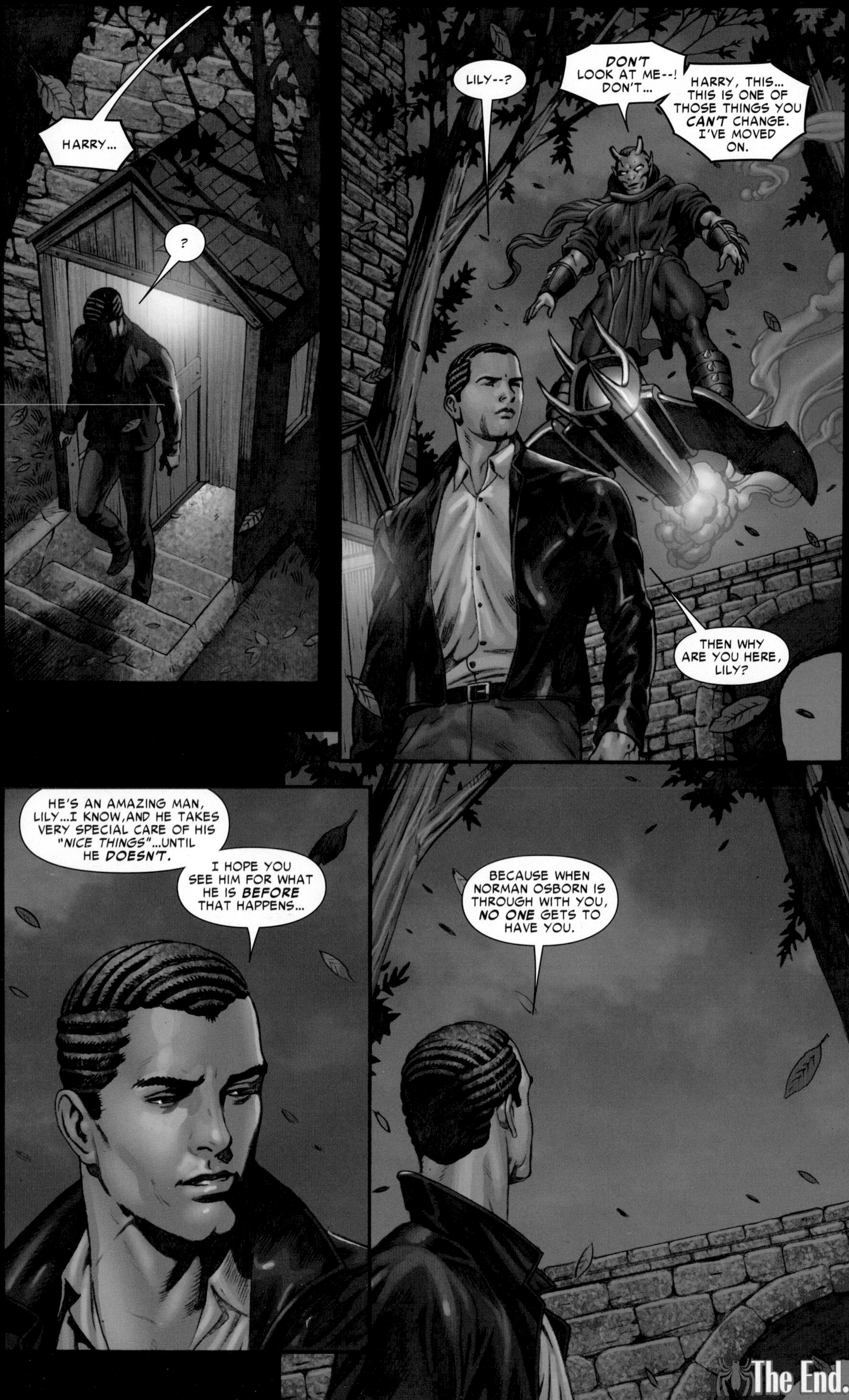

HARRY...
?
LILY--?
DON'T LOOK AT ME--! DON'T...
HARRY, THIS... THIS IS ONE OF THOSE THINGS YOU CAN'T CHANGE. I'VE MOVED ON.
THEN WHY ARE YOU HERE, LILY?
HE'S AN AMAZING MAN, LILY...I KNOW, AND HE TAKES VERY SPECIAL CARE OF HIS "NICE THINGS"...UNTIL HE DOESN'T.
I HOPE YOU SEE HIM FOR WHAT HE IS BEFORE THAT HAPPENS...
BECAUSE WHEN NORMAN OSBORN IS THROUGH WITH YOU, NO ONE GETS TO HAVE YOU.
The End.

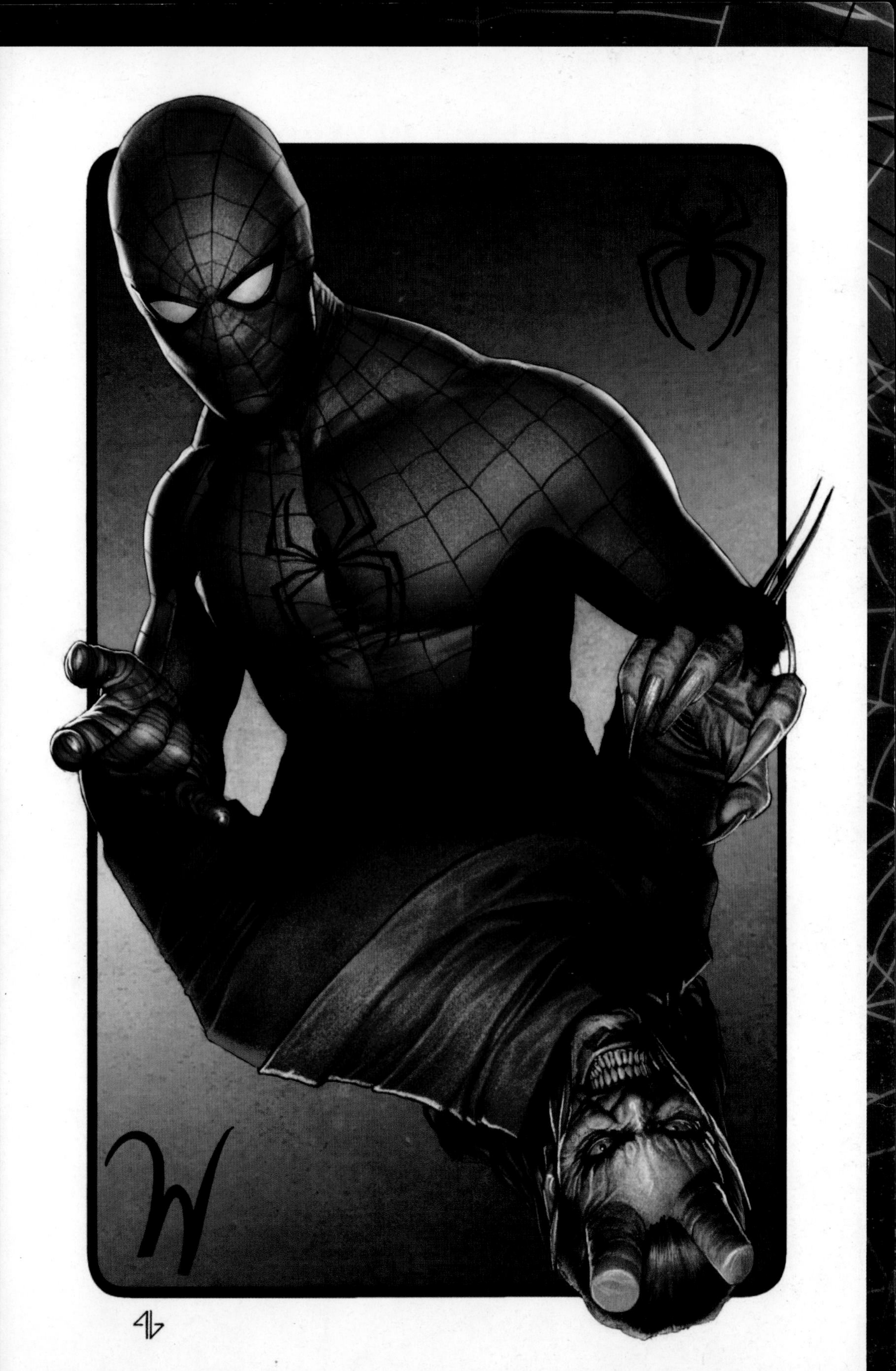

AMAZING SPIDER-MAN #595 VARIANT
BY ADI GRANOV

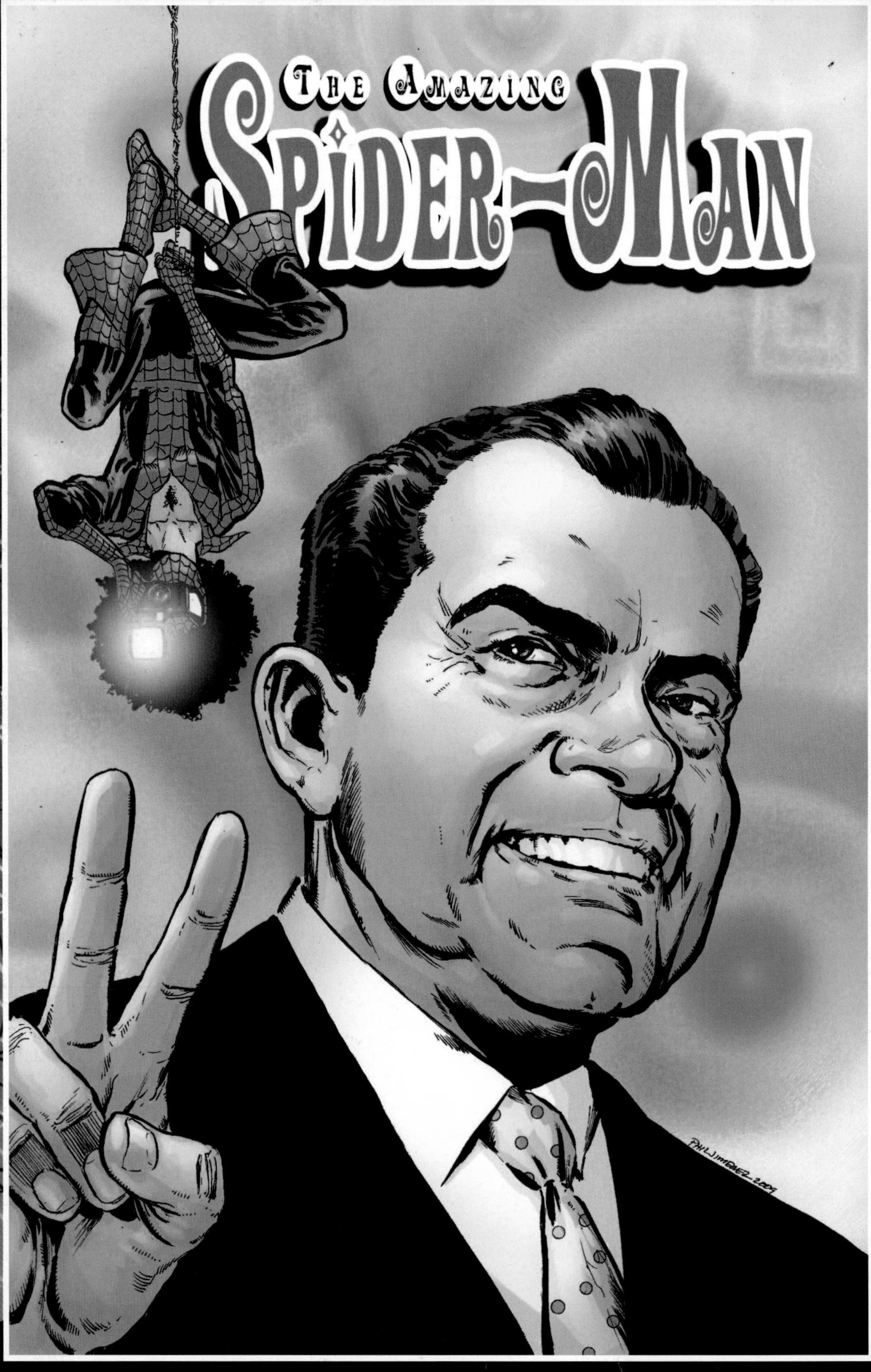
THE AMAZING
SPIDER-MAN
PHIL JIMENEZ 2009

AMAZING SPIDER-MAN #599 '70s DECADE VARIANT
BY PHIL JIMENEZ

AMERICAN SON SKETCHBOOK

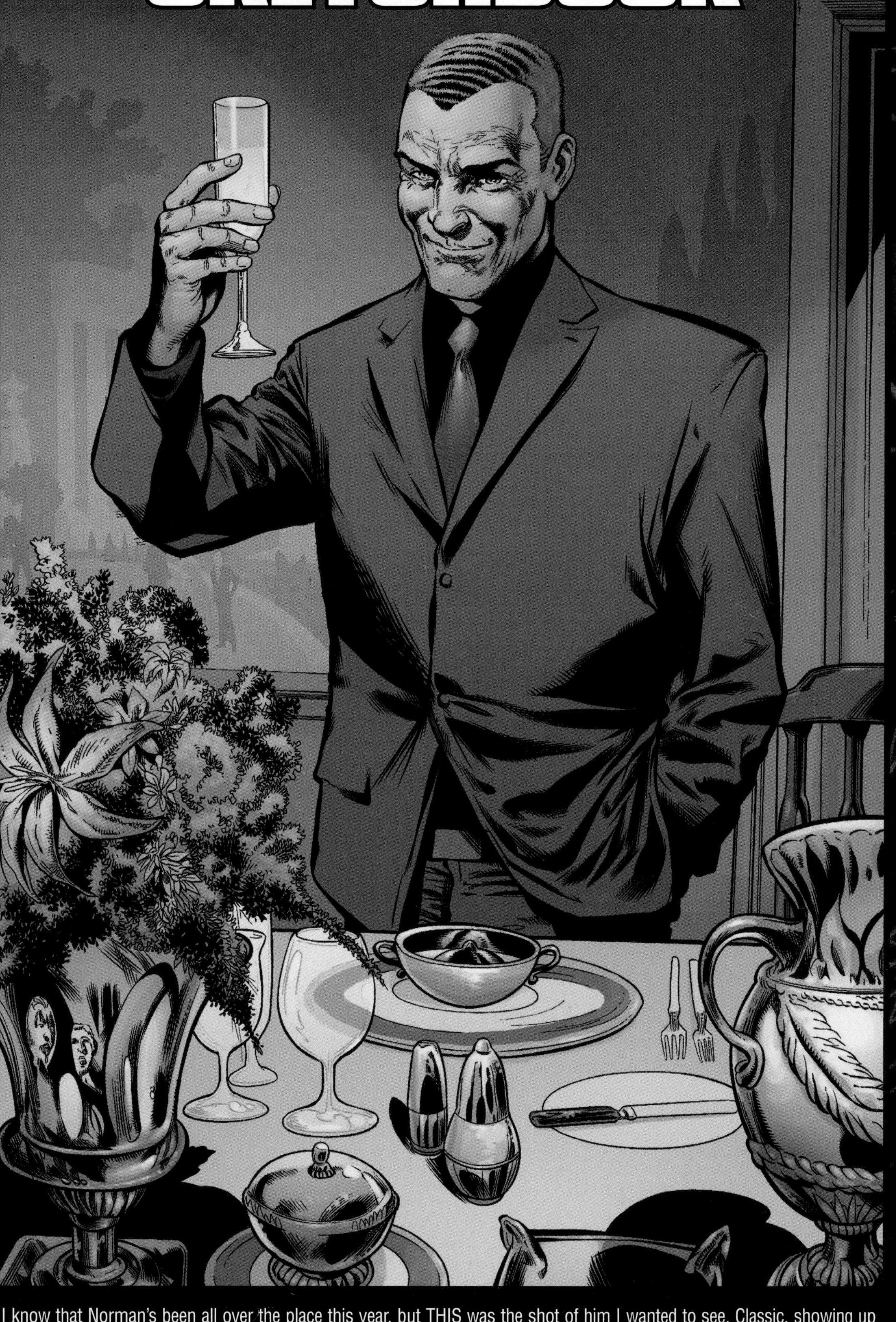

I know that Norman's been all over the place this year, but THIS was the shot of him I wanted to see. Classic, showing up where Pete positively does NOT want him to be, with that "cat and the canary" grin across his face. Originally this was one panel on a page, but thankfully Phil went for the gusto and gave it the feel (if I may geek out for a second) of Vader's reveal in Lando's dining room. The reaction shot reflected in the silver is priceless. **– Joe Kelly**

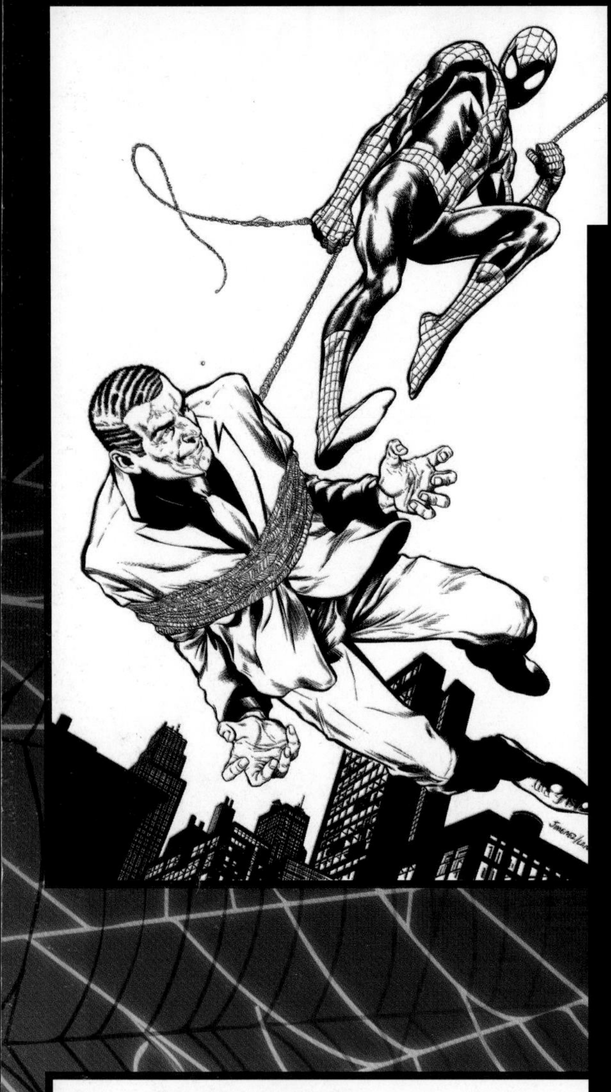

I'm waving the nostalgia flag big time on this one, but I can't help but laugh seeing Spidey swinging with a trussed up Norman. The best part about this page (other than the fact that Phil killed it!) is how it sets you up for a joke, and then you turn the page and see a Spidey as savage as we've ever seen. When Spidey gets his hands on Norman — no Dark Avengers, no New Avengers — it's years of anger and frustration behind each punch, and Phil executes it to perfection. **– Joe Kelly**

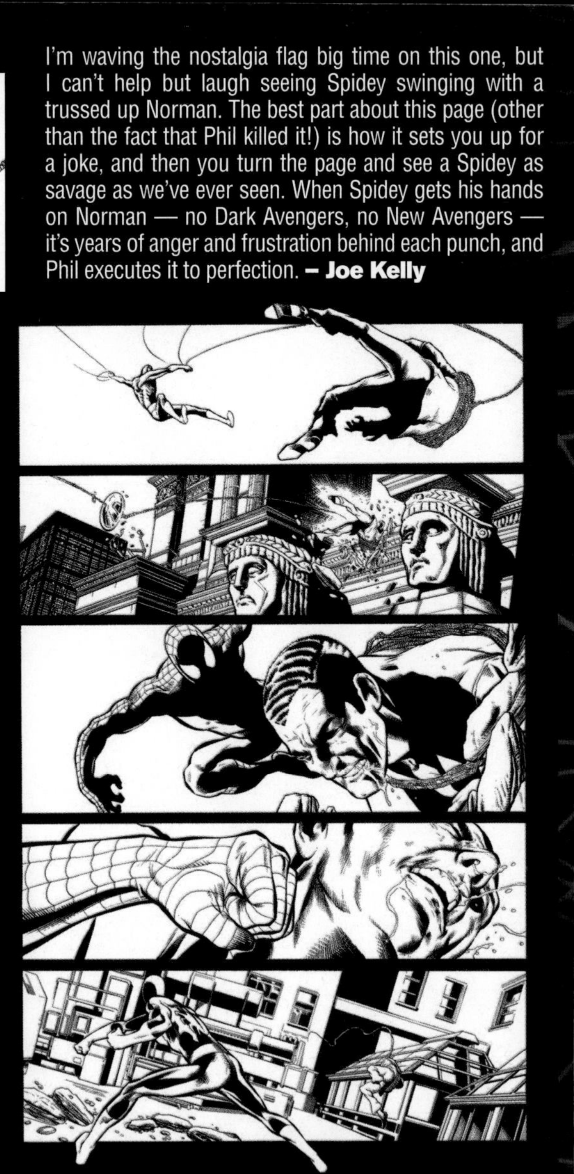

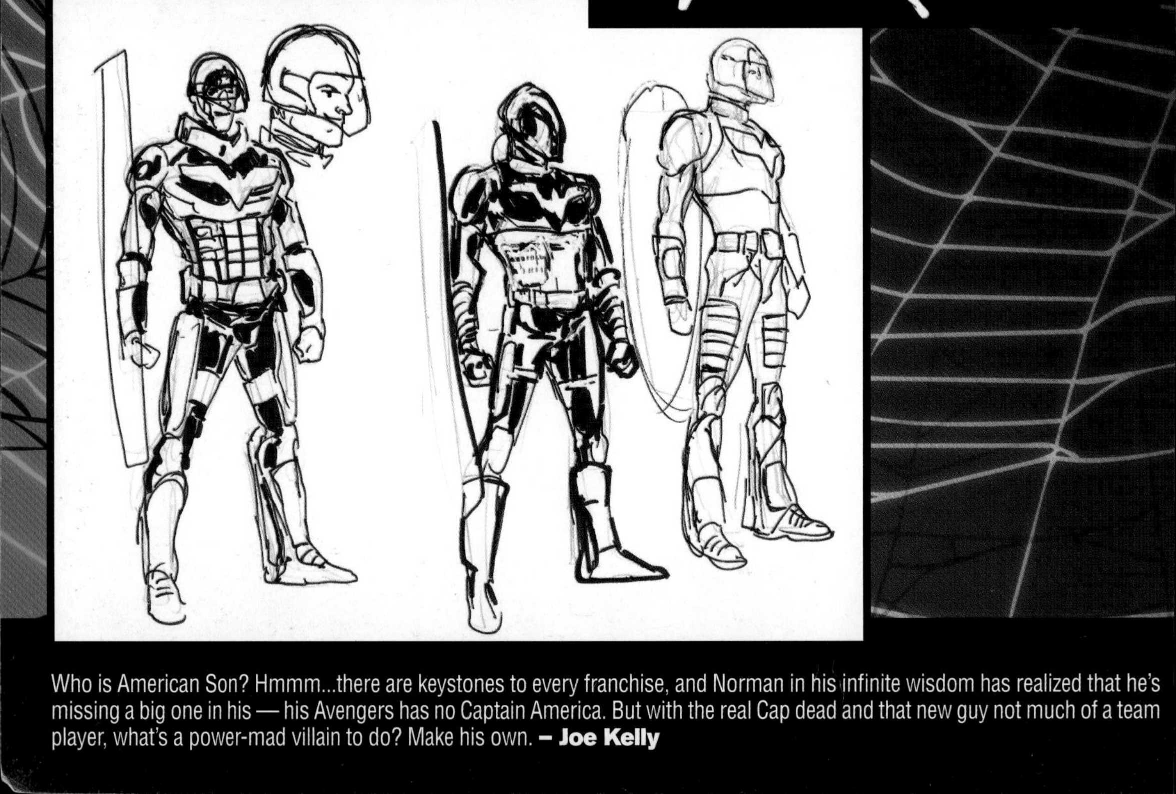

Who is American Son? Hmmm...there are keystones to every franchise, and Norman in his infinite wisdom has realized that he's missing a big one in his — his Avengers has no Captain America. But with the real Cap dead and that new guy not much of a team player, what's a power-mad villain to do? Make his own. **– Joe Kelly**

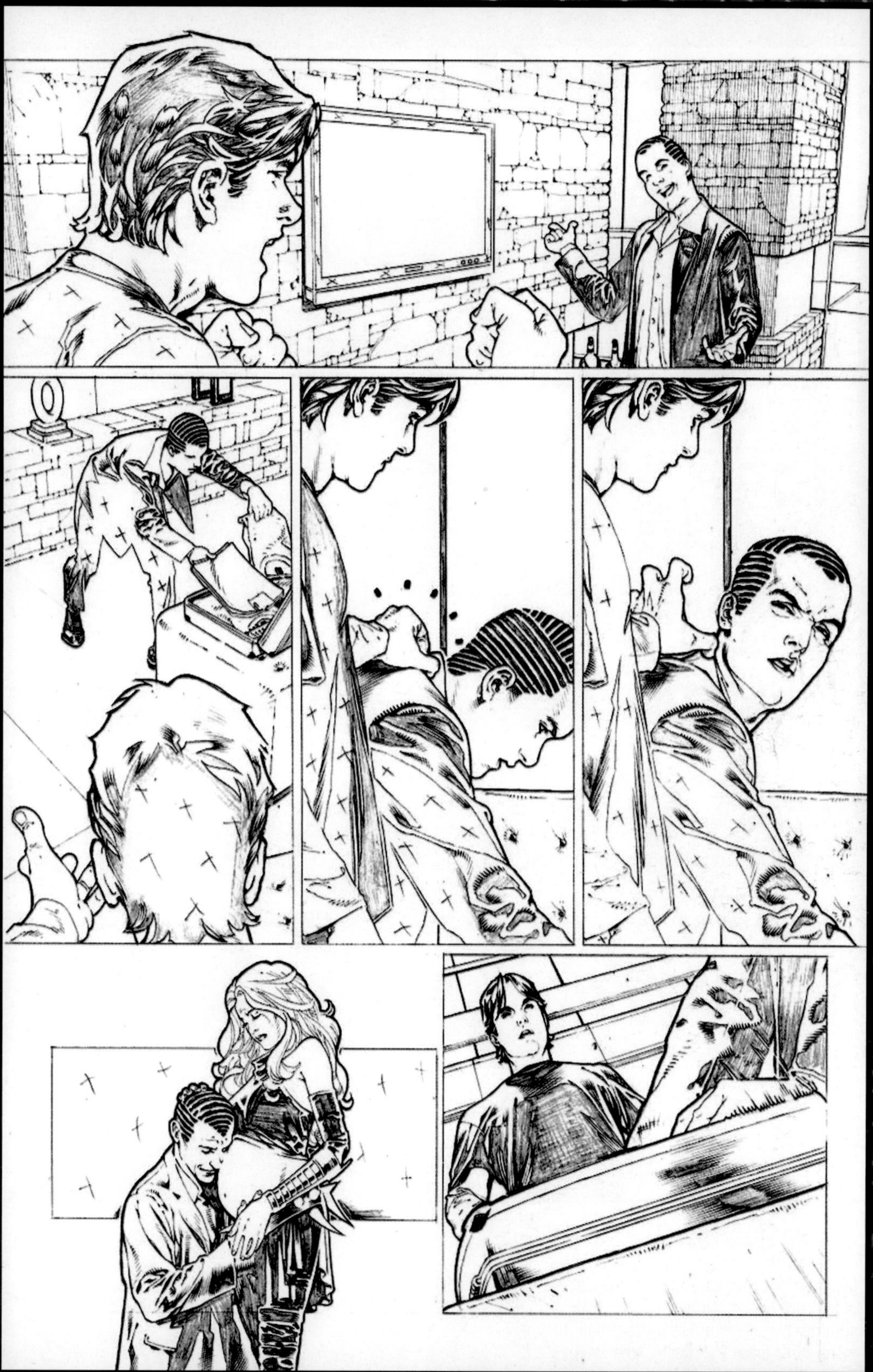

The team spent a lot of time brushing Harry off and putting him on his own two feet well before I ever showed up, and the truth is I like him as a character. The guys took him from Pete's often simpering playboy pal and reimagined him into a genuinely good guy who's buried his demons and lives on hope. That sets the tone for a strong relationship between Harry and Peter — perfect fodder for the American Son arc. Ultimately, this story is about the last temptation of Harry Osborn by his father, but also Pete's struggle to see Harry as a whole person, and not a wet mop he needs to take care of and protect. The irony is that Pete cares so much for Harry that he's blind to his friend's inner strength...and that mistake will cost them both. **– Joe Kelly**

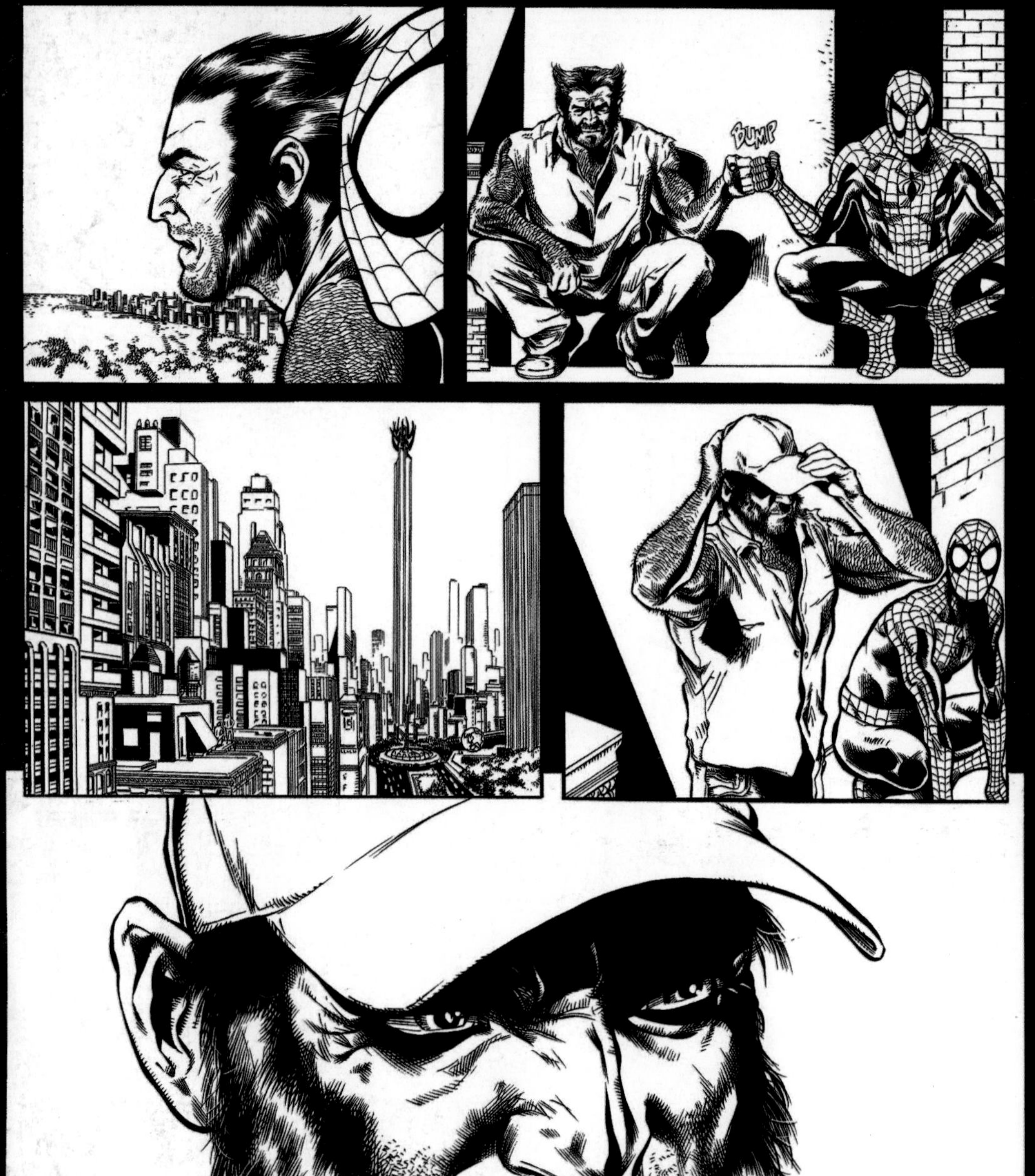
BUMP

I love that Spidey and Wolvie hang out from time to time and have a younger brother/older-psychotic-just-got-out-of-jail brother dynamic. Spidey really admires Wolverine, but he's afraid of him at the same time. The scene of the two of them plotting Norman's demise is one of my favorites in the arc. **– Joe Kelly**

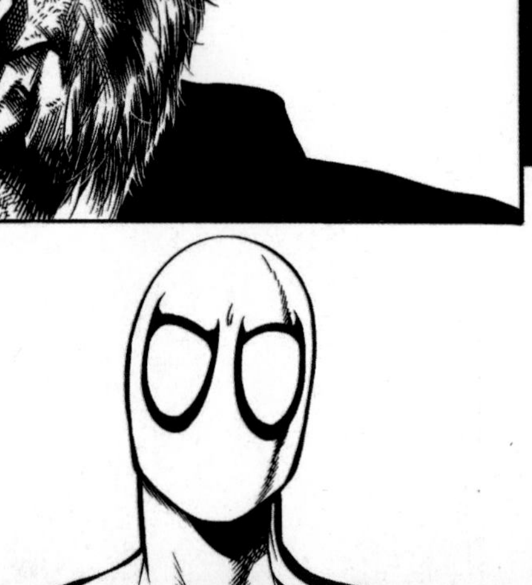

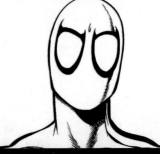

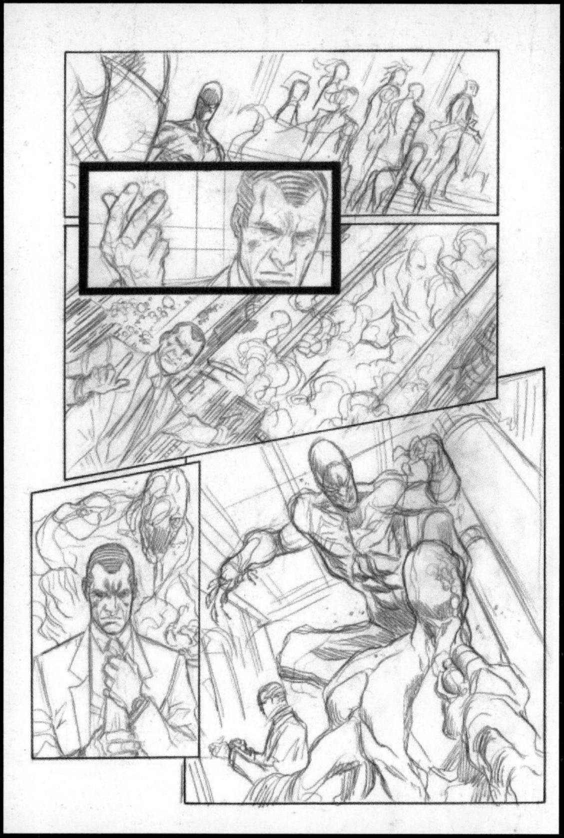

Artist Marco Checchetto steps in to take us on a Norman-guided tour through the halls of the Dark Avengers HQ and the beginnings of the American Son project. I'll warn you right now though, not everything on these pages is as it appears. **– Steve Wacker**

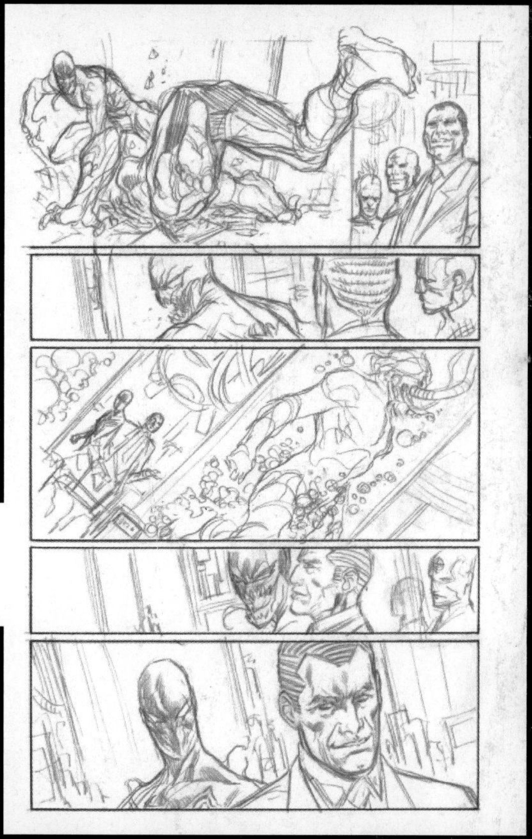

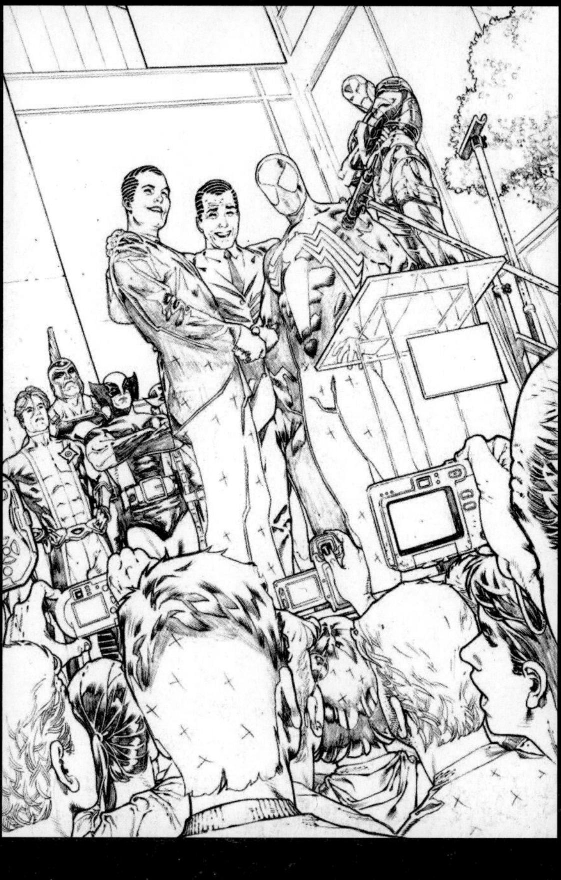

Joe keyed in on the father/son dynamic right away. And what better way for a father to show his love than to introduce him to the world as the man that will save the country. "Prince Harry" is ready to take his place up front with the king. Note Peter Parker up front. **– Steve Wacker**

Phil Jimenez tried a couple different takes on the cover until he landed on that feeling of real defeat and desperation for Spider-Man. This cover probably does the best out of all five to really give you a sense of the pressure that Peter is under as he watches his worst enemy become the country's #1 citizen. **– Steve Wacker**

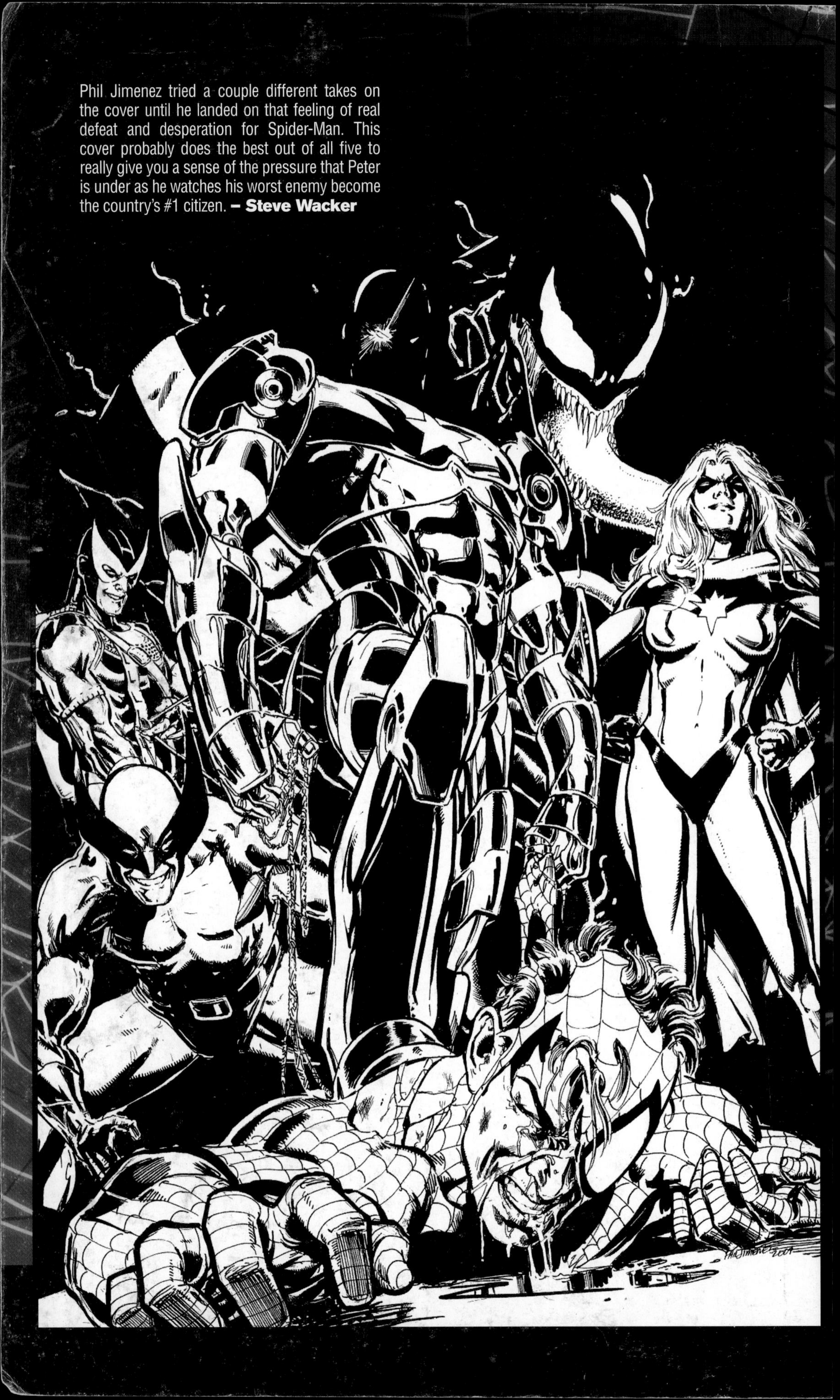